Poverty, AIDS and Hunger

Also by Malcolm J. Blackie

SYSTEMS SIMULATION IN AGRICULTURE (*with J.B. Dent*)

SUCCESSFUL SMALL FARMING

ACCELERATING AGRICULTURAL GROWTH IN SUB-SAHARAN AFRICA
(*editor, with J. Mellor and C. Delgado*)

Poverty, AIDS and Hunger

Breaking the Poverty Trap in Malawi

Anne C. Conroy, Malcolm J. Blackie, Alan Whiteside,
Justin C. Malewezi and Jeffrey D. Sachs

Preface by Bono

Foreword by Stephen Lewis
UN Special Envoy for HIV/AIDS in Africa

Afterword by Tom Arnold
Chief Executive of Concern Worldwide

All proceeds of this book go to Lilongwe Lighthouse, Malawi

First published 2006 by
PALGRAVE MACMILLAN
Houndmills, Basingstoke, Hampshire RG21 6XS and
175 Fifth Avenue, New York, N.Y. 10010
Companies and representatives throughout the world

PALGRAVE MACMILLAN is the global academic imprint of the Palgrave Macmillan division of St. Martin's Press, LLC and of Palgrave Macmillan Ltd. Macmillan® is a registered trademark in the United States, United Kingdom and other countries. Palgrave is a registered trademark in the European Union and other countries.

ISBN 13: 978–1–4039–9833–0   hardback
ISBN 10: 1–4039–9833–7   hardback

This book is printed on paper suitable for recycling and made from fully managed and sustained forest sources.

A catalogue record for this book is available from the British Library.

Library of Congress Cataloging-in-Publication Data

Poverty, AIDS and hunger : breaking the poverty trap in Malawi / Anne C. Conroy ... [et al.].
    p. cm.
Includes bibliographical references and index.
ISBN 1–4039–9833–7 (cloth)
    1. Poverty–Malawi. 2. Malawi–Economic conditions. 3. Malawi–Social conditions. 4. AIDS (Disease)–Economic aspects–Malawi. 5. AIDS (Disease)–Social aspects–Malawi. I. Conroy, Anne C.

HC935.Z9P62727 2006
362.5096897–dc22   2006044839

10   9   8   7   6   5   4   3   2   1
15 14 13 12 11 10 09 08 07 06

Transferred to Digital Printing 2007

Contents

List of Figures   xi

List of Tables   xii

Foreword by Stephen Lewis   xiii

Preface by Bono   xv

Acknowledgements   xvii

Introduction   1
Anne Conroy and Malcolm Blackie
The issues   1
Prosperity not poverty   4
Some background to the book   7
Bringing dignity to the poor   9
Bibliography   12

**Chapter 1   The History of Development and Crisis in
Malawi**   14
Anne Conroy
Introduction   14
Geographical summary   14
Historical perspective   15
   Malawi at independence and post-independence economic
   policy: 1964 to 1977   17
   Crisis and structural adjustment policies in the 1980s   18
Political developments and the emergence of multi-party
democracy in Malawi   20
   Economic performance: 1994 to 2004   21
Key challenges in Malawi today   22
Poverty and powerlessness in Malawi   26
Conclusion   30
Bibliography   31

Chapter 2   Health and Disease in Malawi   33
Anne Conroy
Health and poverty   33
Health indicators in Malawi   34

Key causes of morbidity   35
   Malaria   35
   Tuberculosis   36
   Maternal mortality   37
   Malnutrition   39
   Parasitic infections   42
   Sexually-transmitted infections and HIV/AIDS   42
Key challenges to health care in Malawi   43
   Human resources   43
   Financing   44
Conclusion   45
Bibliography   47

Chapter 3   The AIDS Crisis   49
Anne Conroy and Alan Whiteside
Introduction   49
The HIV/AIDS pandemic   49
   Modes of transmission of HIV   54
Drivers of the pandemic   54
   Gender inequality   54
   The vulnerability of young people   57
   Special risks for adolescents   58
   High risk sexual behaviour   60
   Income inequality, low levels of wealth and political
   transition   61
   Mobility   62
The demographic consequences of HIV/AIDS   63
   Increasing mortality rates   65
   Infant and under-five mortality   65
   Life expectancy   66
Conclusion   66
Bibliography   68

**Chapter 4   The Impact of the AIDS Pandemic on the
National Economy and Development**   70
Alan Whiteside and Anne Conroy
The Malawi case study: the economy   70
Macro-level impacts of AIDS   72
   AIDS and the private sector   73
   Impacts on the public sector and the development
   process   74

The impact of AIDS on the vulnerable – children and the
elderly   75
The impact of HIV/AIDS on agriculture and livelihoods   77
   The impact of HIV/AIDS on agricultural production systems
   and rural livelihoods in the central region of Malawi   79
Conclusion   81
Bibliography   83

Chapter 5   The Collapse of Agriculture   87
Malcolm Blackie and Anne Conroy
Tradition and African smallholder cropping systems   87
   No 'silver bullet'   88
Land, agricultural productivity and land policy   92
Macro-economic policy reform: a Malawi case study of
disaster   94
   Market and crop pricing reform   96
   Fertiliser subsidies   98
The collapse of agriculture reviewed   100
Bibliography   102

Chapter 6   Economic Isolation   104
Anne Conroy and Jeffrey Sachs
Poor Infrastructure equals low economic growth   104
Transport   106
   Internal   106
   External   107
Energy   109
Other key infrastructure   110
The regulatory and taxation environment   110
Responding to the need for change   112
Conclusion   114
Bibliography   117

**Chapter 7   Malawi and the Poverty Trap – A First Person
Account**   118
Anne Conroy
Introduction   118
From food insecurity to famine: the 2002 food crisis   119
   Widening access to improved agricultural technology 120
   Managing grain reserves   121
   Ignoring the warning signs   122
   Raising the alarm   124

Lessons from the 2002 famine	125
Budget disruption	125
Disruption to on-going programmes	126
Disruption to household coping mechanisms	128
Deterioration in macro-economic management and governance after 2002	130
Politics and fertiliser subsidies	131
Bibliography	136

Chapter 8 Breaking Out of the AIDS and Disease Crisis — **138**
Anne Conroy and Justin Malewezi

Introduction	138
Malawi's responses to the HIV/AIDS pandemic	139
Voluntary counselling and testing (VCT)	140
Information, education, and communication (IEC)	140
Prevention strategies	141
Reducing the spread of the virus	141
Engaging influential groups in the fight against HIV/AIDS	142
Impact mitigation	144
Community of home-based care	144
Care of orphans	144
The health sector	146
The Essential Health Care Package (EHP)	146
The Sector Wide Approach (SWAP)	147
Investment in human resources	148
Scaling up best-practices from the community level	149
The health sector response to the AIDS pandemic	150
Blood safety and waste disposal	150
Mother to child transmission	151
Treatment strategies	152
Reflections of Malawi's attempts to break out of the AIDS and health crisis	154
Bibliography	158

Chapter 9 Breaking Out of Food Insecurity — **160**
Malcolm Blackie, Anne Conroy and Jeffrey Sachs

Introduction	160
Making fertilisers profitable	160
Malawi, soil fertility, agricultural policy and famine	162
A comprehensive smallholder strategy	164
The Starter Pack	164
Complementary measures	167
A return to free inputs	168

The food crises of 2001–2002 and 2002–2003 169
   The National Food Crisis Recovery Programme 170
   Providing emergency food to the vulnerable 171
Lessons for the future 173
   The humanitarian response 173
   A Malawi Green Revolution 174
     Interventions to provide access to inputs and markets 174
Concluding comments 178
Bibliography 183

Chapter 10   Breaking Out of Economic Isolation and the Poverty Trap 185
Anne Conroy and Malcolm Blackie
Introduction 185
Education in Malawi 187
   Primary education 187
   Secondary education 188
   Tertiary education 189
   Investments in education 189
   Civic education 190
Building environmental sustainability 192
Investments in economic infrastructure 193
Addressing constraints to private sector development 195
   Government interventions in the fertiliser market: a case study of unhelpful government/private sector relations 197
Transforming trading rules 198
Conclusion 200
Bibliography 201

Chapter 11   Changing Mindsets 203
Anne Conroy and Malcolm Blackie
Introduction 203
Human rights and human development 206
Issues that have to be addressed at the national level 208
   Improving governance 208
   Donor relationships 210
   Exploiting national talents and skills 213
   Information sharing, communication and collaboration 214
   Changing mindsets 215
     Core values 215
     Actions not just words 217
Bibliography 220

Chapter 12   Ending Extreme Poverty in Malawi   222
Anne Conroy and Jeffrey Sachs
Introduction   222
What is needed   223
A perspective on what can be done   226
Some thoughts on debts   228
Concluding comments   230
Bibliography   233

Afterword by Tom Arnold   234

Index   238

List of Figures

1.1 GDP growth rates, 1995–2003   22
3.1 Sentinel survey sites, Malawi 2003   51
3.2 HIV prevalence: observed and projected   52
3.3 Age and sex distribution of AIDS cases in Malawi   53
3.4 Population projections for Malawi with and without AIDS,
    1985–2010   64
3.5 Impact of AIDS on adult mortality in Malawi, 1985–2003   64
3.6 Life expectancy with and without AIDS, 1985–2003   65
4.1 GDP (US$ bn) in Malawi, 1993–2003   72
5.1 Interaction between weeding and fertiliser use in maize   90
7.1 Starter pack/TIP contribution to total maize production,
    1998–2003   120
7.2 Local market prices for maize in the southern region   123
7.3 Yields of cassava and sweet potatoes, 1994–2002   124

List of Tables

1.1 Millennium development goals: selected indicators   23
1.2 Key macro-economic indicators: 1994–2003   26
1.3 Analysis of the 2003–2004 government budget   27
4.1 Malawi and African economies   71
4.2 Selected social and demographic indicators in Malawi and
     other countries, 2003   71
4.3 Costs of HIV/AIDS on a tea estate in Malawi, 1995–1996   74

Foreword

Malawi was a touchstone for me. It was at the Lilongwe General Hospital, stumbling through wards late one night in blighted darkness, that I recoiled with horror at the pain and suffering of the AIDS pandemic. And it was in the Malawian hinterland that I most vividly remember the impact of poverty and hunger, particularly on women, most particularly on grandmothers. I had always believed that people living with AIDS would clamour for drugs: I was wrong; they clamour for food.

The beauty of this book is the way in which heart and mind are intertwined. The analysis is fierce and unanswerable. Compassion is writ in every page.

But its special strength lies in the ability to move from the specific to the general, from the needs of Malawi to the realities of the world. Most authors separate the local from the global, as though life exists in a series of compartments. Nothing could be more realistic.

The truth ... as you will read ... is that the Millennium Development Goals will never be reached in Malawi, or anywhere else in Southern Africa, unless the levels of Official Development Assistance (ODA) rise exponentially. At the G8 Summit in Gleneagles in July of 2005, the promise was to double aid to Africa – that is to say another \$25 billion – by 2010. It's already clear that the target will not be reached through ODA; in fact, that's why there are all the schemes of so-called 'innovative financing', from a surtax on airline tickets to the International Financial Facility (IFF). They're emerging precisely to compensate for the shortfall that's already looming. In any event, the additional \$25 billion is needed right now, in 2006, not in 2010. Africa and Malawi can't wait another four years – only the graveyards benefit from delay.

The issue of debt is similarly fraught with crisis. While it is true that a chunk of the debt was written off by the G8 countries, the vast majority of African debt still hangs as a millstone around the neck of the continent and of Malawi. How well I remember Susan George's book 'A Fate Worse Than Debt' in which she argues that debt, and the interest on debt, has acted as an obscene transfer of wealth to the donor countries for a quarter century and more.

And as to trade, tied so indelibly to agricultural subsidies in the western world, there's not so much as a significant whisper of movement. In fact, after the hopeless failure of the Doha round of trade talks in Hong Kong in December of 2005 – a symposium of duplicity and betrayal – even Gordon Brown, the apostle of international development, had nothing but scorn to heap.

It's a sorry mess of a world in the face of the Millennium Development Goals (MDGs). And little countries like Malawi, whose only wish is to survive the assault of poverty and AIDS, pay a terrible price.

What makes it all so painful is how little it would take to turn things around. One of the most fascinating details of the analysis in the book lies in a footnote. According to the Millennium Project, and the data it produces, supplemented by related data from equally reliable sources, it would take, on average, $121 per capita in 2006 to meet all the MDGs and other development priorities for Malawi, rising to $189 per capita in 2015. Based on a population of twelve million, that would mean $1.5 billion is 2006, rising to $2.7 billion in 2015.

In the grand scheme of things, can there be any sums more paltry? The western world spends $1 billion a day in agricultural subsidies, and we can't afford to take a weekend off to redistribute income to Malawi that covers an entire year? The western world spends $2 billion a day on military budgets, and we can't afford to take a day off to redistribute income to Malawi that covers an entire year? To be sure, there are lots of other African countries involved, but there's lots of money involved as well, including the G8 commitment to reach 0.7 percent for foreign aid.

No matter how you make the calculations, the misery of Malawi, the present scourge of famine and AIDS, need not be.

It's a matter of incalculable dismay that we have allowed poverty to run amok. If the old testament prophets were alive today, they'd have more material for their messianic pronouncements than ever was in ancient times – more swords to beat into ploughshares; more spears to turn into pruning hooks.

That's all Malawi wants: ploughshares, pruning-hooks and life. Evidently, it's too much to ask.

Stephen Lewis
UN Special Envoy for HIV/AIDS in Africa

Preface

You can miss it on a map. On a continent of a big sky, big game, big challenges, the little country of Malawi – less than half the size of the UK, smaller than the state of Pennsylvania – is an unassuming place. But within its borders, it embodies the greatest contradictions of our time: poverty and generosity. Urgency and serenity. Despair and hope.

Despite twenty years of interest in Africa, of travel across Africa, I might have missed Malawi itself – if it hadn't been for Anne Conroy. In 2002, partly at her urging, I went to Malawi. It changed me, that trip – filled my head with visions, scenes, people I can't and won't forget. Anne, herself, I certainly couldn't forget: freckled Irish face, calm and collected as a host, but itchy and irritated when describing the wasted opportunities of Africa. That was her daily toil in her host nation. Almost immediately she seemed very familiar to me.

At the hospital in Lilongwe, taken round by another Irish Anne – this one Sister Anne Carr, and her Medical Missionaries of Mary – we met AIDS patients queuing up to die, three to a bed. Doctors and nurses were doing their best, but in the West we wouldn't even call this a 'hospital,' we'd call it a 'hospice' – a place where people come not to be cured, but to die with some small measure of comfort, of dignity.

Outside were gangs of children living on the streets, orphaned by AIDS. And it seemed that everywhere, any time of day, people were hungry. Living on the inedible ... banana skins, corn husks, grass seed, eating grass to survive – I had thought that ended with the Irish Famine of the 19th Century.

In Malawi, crisis compounds crisis, and the results are doubly cruel. Where people are too weakened by AIDS to work the fields, a food shortage can become a famine. Where people can't take medications, lacking clean water or food in their bellies, epidemics flourish. Where debt burdens stifle government action, medicine and food are in short supply. In the streets and villages of Malawi, the unholy trinity of AIDS, debt and hunger can be found – in its most full-blooded incarnation.

But Malawi, as I said, is a contradiction.

Though poverty plagues them, the people of Malawi share what they have. Grandmothers care for dozens of orphans. Nuns and priests reenact the miracle of loaves and fishes daily, stretching meager food supplies to their limits and beyond. The sisters, the community workers reach somewhere very deep – or very high – and grab onto something like hopefulness. It's hard to fathom, but it's real; we all felt it.

In this book – and in her life's work – Anne Conroy and her co-authors Malcolm Blackie, Alan Whiteside, Justin Malewezi and Jeffrey Sachs give Malawians reasons to hope and gives us all ideas for action. By forgiving the debts that, in a breach of conscience and common sense, we hold over Malawi, we can free that country to feed more people, train more nurses, build more clinics. By boosting aid, we can provide medicines that will allow Malawi's workforce to rise out of the hospital wards and return to the fields and classrooms. And by changing wealthy nations' ludicrous trade laws, we can help Malawi's farmers to feed their families, sell their products in our markets – and take their own future into their own hands.

And because we *can* do these things, we must.

After reading *Poverty, AIDS and Hunger*, you feel confident that we can look disease and extreme poverty in the eye – in Malawi, in all of Africa – and say this and mean it: *We do not have to stand for this.* We can change the world ... the world is waiting for us to do so. Because if enough people want this, and are bothered to get organized, we really can turn the supertanker of indifference around. And if we really believe in the equality of the Africans whose world it is to change, we will become their servants, none greater than Anne Conroy.

Bono

Acknowledgements

We would like to thank Concern Worldwide, the Department for International Development in Malawi, the Royal Norwegian Embassy in Malawi, the DFID Funded HIV Knowledge Programme at Imperial College London and at HEARD and the John Lloyd Foundation for their generous support to this publication. We would like to express our sincere gratitude to the following individuals within those organisations for their constructive support: Tom Arnold and Breda Gahan from Concern Worldwide, Andrea Cook, Harry Potter and Alan Whitworth from DFID Malawi, Ashbiorn Eidhammer, Michael Tawanda and Agnes Kiromera from the Royal Norwegian Embassy, Professor Charles Gilks from the DFID Funded HIV Knowledge Programme at Imperial College London and Robert Estrin and Melanie Havelin of the John M. Lloyd Foundation. The grant from DFID Malawi was administered through the Liverpool School of Tropical Medicine. We would like to thank Dr Bertie Squire, Ms Teresa Jackson and Dave Haran for their support and administration of the grant. The grants from the Royal Norwegian Embassy and John M. Lloyd Foundation were administered through Imperial College London and we would like to thank Dr Lorna Colquhoun and Ms Claire Puddephatt for handling the grants so competently.

We would also like to acknowledge our friends and colleagues working on poverty, the AIDS and health crisis and hunger in Malawi. In particular, we thank our friend and colleague Honourable Aleke Banda, former Minister of Finance, Health and Agriculture; Bishop James Tenga Tenga, Dr Elias Ngalande Banda, former Governor of the Reserve Bank of Malawi; Raspicious Dzanjalimodzi, former Secretary to the Treasury; Randson Mwadiwa, Secretary to the Treasury; Patrick Kabambe, Secretary for Agriculture, Dr Richard Pendame, former Secretary for Health; Dr Rex Mpazanje, former Director of Clinical Services in the Ministry of Health; Dr Wes Sangala, Secretary for Health; Dr Mike O'Carroll, Senior Technical Advisor in the Ministry of Health; Dr Biziwick Mwale, the Executive Director of the National AIDS Commission; Roy Hauya, the Director of Programmes in the National AIDS Commission; Dr Owen Kalua, former Executive Director of the National AIDS Commission and our colleagues working in health and population: Dr Tarek Meguid of Bottom Hospital Lilongwe, Dr Athenas Kiromera of Namitete Hospital and Dr Nyovani Madise of Southampton

University. We would like to acknowledge the contribution of the late Dr Ellard Malindi, former Secretary for Agriculture; Dr Andrew Daudi, former Secretary for Agriculture. Thanks also to Jane Harrigan, Elizabeth Cromwell, Charles Mann and Stephen Carr for their long-term commitment to Malawi.

Thanks to all our colleagues in Malawi within the Government, the faith communities, civil society and Non Governmental Organizations who address issues of poverty, AIDS and hunger with great dedication at the field level. Thanks also to the committed individuals and advocates throughout the world who work for peace, justice and human dignity. Their work is rarely recognised, but without them progress is impossible.

Thank you to the three outstanding individuals who we invited to write the preface, foreword and afterword: Bono, Stephen Lewis and Tom Arnold. They have all shown extraordinary dedication to Malawi and we are privileged to have them as our friends. Throughout history, people are inspired by writers, artists and musicians. Bono's first influence comes through music, but he is far more than a great musician. From the beginning he used his influence as a musician to support the peace process in Northern Ireland and to work against poverty, exclusion and drug abuse in Dublin. He and his wife Ali committed to Africa after Live Aid going behind the headlines to work in a refugee camp in Ethiopia. Since then, they have given their support to so many campaigns for justice and to support individuals affected by tragedy including Children in Chernobyl and many others. Bono came to Malawi in early 2002 with Jeff and Sonia Sachs, and the people of Malawi are now in his soul and the lyrics of his songs. For the last 20 years, Bono has been in the forefront of advocacy for debt cancellation, increased aid and trade justice worldwide – thank you. Stephen Lewis is remarkable in his tireless commitment to the fight against AIDS, his compassion, his outrage at indifference and his outspoken advocacy on behalf of the poor and also his humour. Prophecy is most effective when it is combined with humanity and humour. His book 'Race against Time' is phenomenal in its honesty and the accessibility of the writing – it brings the fight against AIDS to a broad audience. Stephen never backs away from telling the truth – nothing is tempered for political correctness whatever the consequences. Tom Arnold is the Executive Director of Concern Worldwide an effective Non Governmental Organization working throughout the world. Tom is a solid technocrat with an eye for detail and an insistence on professionalism but he also recognises the importance of networking across constituencies. He works with civil society, governments, the Universities, the United Nations and other global bodies, the faith communities, the media and national Governments to raise awareness and resources for development and then to spend them effectively to promote human development. He works behind the scenes quietly and persistently to use his influence constructively on behalf of the poor in Malawi and throughout the world.

Hilary Benn, the Secretary of State for International Development in the United Kingdom deserves a special mention for the dedication he has brought to that position, and the work of the Africa Commission and his leadership of the Department for International Development. Malawi was one of the first countries he visited when he was appointed as Deputy to Clare Short – he impressed us with his willingness to listen. That visit influenced policy – especially in terms of access to anti-retroviral medicine by the poor. He also listened to us when we advocated for resources to strengthen health systems and invest in human resources. It is always great to find a politician of obvious integrity, who listens and most importantly acts.

During the course of writing this book, Malawi struggled to recover from the 2002 food crisis, the contentious bid for the Third Term, the tense 2004 Election and the 2005 Food Crisis. Completing the book was a long and difficult struggle as time and events continued to influence our analyses. Our thanks to all our friends and colleagues who helped us through these challenging times.

We would also like to acknowledge our colleagues at Palgrave: Jen Nelson, Phillipa Grand, Shirley Tan – and the whole production team.

While we acknowledge the generous support of all our donor partners, the arguments advanced and views expressed in the book are those of the authors and do not represent the views of any of our donor partners.

Individual Acknowledgments

Anne Conroy

I would not have been able to complete this book without the generosity and kindness of so many people. I start with my family, my parents Jim and Mary Conroy who gave me a background of love, support and a value system rooted in Christianity and commitment justice and human dignity. My father died in 1993 – a well-loved quiet man of few words and great integrity. Dad, your influence continues to guide me. Mum is the communicator in the family; she continues to give unconditional love, friendship and support. My brother John has always supported my work in Africa and has given consistently sound counsel and love throughout my life. John's wife Pat and their sons James and Michael help me keep things in perspective and provide love and distraction when it is needed so much. My grandmother Mary MacCabe and my mother's brothers Frank and Robbie MacCabe were also very influential in my upbringing. It was indeed impossible to escape the influence of Irish Catholicism! Frank worked with disadvantaged young people in Dublin – establishing football clubs and youth clubs where none existed. My grandmother's house in Sandycove was always full of young people connected to Frank, and the extended family – not so different from Africa. Frank died far too young – financially in debt because all his investments were in people. Robbie is a doctor and priest in Kenya still working mobile medical clinics at the age of 80 – still a legend on the tennis court! Robbie was the first person to bring me to Africa in 1982 – the Turkana District in Northern Kenya. This is where I started to love Africa and its people.

I would also like to acknowledge the invaluable support of my friends in Malawi. Julia Kemp, Matt Boxhall and their children Emma and Ffion; Wina Sangala, Erik Schouten and their children Maya and Paulo, Wilma Roscoe and her children Roberto and Francesca, Martin and Nicky Ott and their daughter Sophia, Kathryn English, Adam Stapleton and their boys Fergal, Finn, Louis and Luke, are well-loved friends who were always there for me.

Fr. Joseph Mpingangira and Fr. Boniface Tamani continue to inspire me with their courage and commitment to justice and truth. I acknowledge your friendship, guidance and efforts (always sincere but not always successful) to keep me on the right path. I would also like thank Fr. Demetrius Kaderera, Sr. Anne Carr and everyone in the broader community around Maula Cathedral and Chigoneka Parish in Lilongwe. Thanks to the Kiltegan Fathers and Medical Missionary Sisters who work with the poor, the sick and the marginalised throughout Africa. You have always welcomed me into your houses. Your willingness to welcome everyone irrespective of religion, background or race is an example that we should all follow. Thank you for your hospitality, support, guidance and friendship.

I would also like to thank my co-editors on this book for working with me – an unknown and often struggling writer. Malcolm Blackie has been a friend and guide for the last 15 years. He is above all else a teacher – someone who works with young people to develop their potential. He supported and supervised my PhD (a thankless task), guided, influenced and supported all my work and has always shown great example of collaboration, cooperation and teamwork. Together with so many of Africa's young scientists, I owe him and his family a major debt of gratitude. I have had the privilege of working for and with Justin Malewezi for the last eight years – he has led every initiative and used his influence as Vice President to campaign for increased resources for health and food security. Now a Member of Parliament, he uses his influence to promote reconciliation between political opponents, and responsibility in public service. I value his guidance and friendship. Jeff Sachs and his wife Sonia have shown outstanding commitment to Malawi – supporting us in the development of the Global Fund Proposal, inspiring us with his leadership in global health issues and the fight against poverty. Jeff's passion and commitment sustain him through his incredible work and travel schedule and yet Jeff retains such clarity of analysis, vision and leadership in the fight against poverty. Thanks also to Alan Whiteside who I have known for three years as an extraordinary teacher, great analyst and writer and global advocate in the fight against HIV/AIDS.

I would also like to acknowledge my friends at home. In Cardiff, Fr. Ed O' Connell, Sheila Williams, Jennifer, Ian, Patrick and Stuart McDowell, Rosie and Dylan Lewis and family, Anne Lydia and David Halewood and their children Issy and Milli, Karen Lyons, Jeremy Black, Neill Spooner, Peter and Raheny Goode and John, Alison, Huw, and Gareth Westwood. I must mention my friend and business partner Hermann Beck and his fiancée Helen. Hermann and my brother John manage the Royal Victoria Holiday Inn in Sheffield and generate much valued income for me! In Ireland, my thanks to my colleagues and friends at Irish Aid: Brendan Rogers, Vinny O'Neill, Bronagh Carr and Ciara O'Brien. Thanks to Helen Hall and her son Adam Chintedza, Brendan Rogers and my family, Michael, Joe and Maureen Kelly, Mike, Max and family, Donald and Marianne Magrane and their family and everyone in the Sheehy, Kelly and O' Connell clan. Thanks also to other friends throughout the world including Tom Dougherty in the Democratic Republic of Congo, Elise Jensen in Tanzania and Brendan O'Brien in New York. These and other people, too many to mention have given me innumerable acts of kindness and love.

Finally, I would like to acknowledge my debt to the people of Malawi. You inspire me with your values of hope, optimism, dedication and ability to struggle against devastating odds. The people of Malawi struggle against poverty, hunger and disease. They have suffered the repeated betrayal by many of their politicians, but their belief in a better future remains. There is such generosity, the willingness to share whatever you have and the willingness to welcome a stranger. In every community, there is compassion for the sick, care for the children, laughter, the struggle to succeed and an indomitable spirit. It is this spirit that will see them through. One day, I believe, there will be justice for the people of Malawi.

Malcolm Blackie

Thanks to my special friends – my wife Mary and our children, Samuel, Reuben, and Rose. They all helped immeasurably in the difficult times, and always provided sound advice and constructive criticism on the ideas as they took shape. My parents, sadly now passed away, taught me to listen to the voices of the poor and disadvantaged of Africa. My many friends and colleagues in Africa – especially Alois Hungwe, Paul Thangata, Adipala Ekwamu, George Kanyama-Phiri, Alexander Phiri, James Banda, Stephen and Ann Carr, Paul Woomer, Ken Giller, Richard Jones, Sieglinde Snapp, Joe DeVries – will find echoes of their advice and knowledge in these pages. I hope I have used your counsel well. Anne Conroy who led this whole venture with determination and dedication to tell a story that needed to be told deserves a particular mention, as does my co-author the Honourable Justin Malewezi whose wisdom and guidance were invaluable at all stages of the work. To the two particular individuals who illustrate so clearly the deep kindness of the African tradition – John Banda who looked after me so well in Lilongwe and John Chifamba who did the same in Harare – many thanks and may your crops yield well.

Alan Whiteside

I would like to thank DFID through the Liverpool/HEARD/Imperial Knowledge Programme and all their staff. Without this funding it would have been impossible for me to work on the book since the resources were limited. The staff at HEARD, University of KwaZulu-Natal were pillars as usual. My family Ailsa Marcham, and Rowan and Douglas Whiteside put up with the stress and long hours. And of course the friends and colleagues around the world, too numerous to mention, for their unstinting support and friendship.

Justin Malewezi

With grateful thanks to my wife Felicity, daughters Msau and Tini, and sons Myambo and Quabaniso. Their support, patience, and kindness is deeply appreciated.

Jeffrey Sachs

I would like to thank my wife Sonia, my children Lisa, Adam and Hannah and my colleagues in the Millennium Project for their support.

Introduction

Anne Conroy and Malcolm Blackie

The issues

Bishop James Tenga Tenga spoke bravely and forthrightly at the 2006 Conference Malawi after Gleneagles in Edinburgh:

> It is difficult to believe in your own self worth if all the time you are told you are failing. Africans struggle every day to survive; recognise what they are doing, the obstacles in their way, and give them a hand of friendship and encouragement. Build – don't destroy – their confidence and they will repay a hundredfold. That is the aid they need.

Malawi is not a poor country – it has significant natural resources and a people who are determined and innovative. But it is a country with devastating and crippling levels of poverty. The statistics are frightening. The average Malawian dies before the age of 40; 73 out of every 1000 infants die in their first year, and a further 133 fail to reach their fifth birthday. The children who survive face a continuing struggle against disease and malnutrition. Africa is the global epicenter of malaria, an entirely preventable disease – yet the majority of outpatient treatments in Malawi are for malaria and the disease is the major killer of children under five. Diarrhoea, another entirely preventable illness, is also a killer and a major health burden.

These diseases do not only cause illness and death. They are a major cause of poverty. Agriculture in much of Africa is reliant on the rain. The tropical heat ensures that most soils are warm enough to grow crops most of the year round. What the soils lack is the moisture to sustain plant growth. With the first rains comes a flush of activity. Soil organisms spring to life and there is a burst of new fertility in the soil. Farmers who plant with the first rains not only catch this annual flush of nutrients for their crops but also gain the longest possible season for their crops to grow and mature. Every week that is missed at the start of the season reduces the final harvest substantially. Once the crop is planted, it must be cared for – the weeds, which also take advantage of the new moisture and fertility, thrive and must be controlled. Poor weeding guarantees a poor harvest.

But the rains also bring a new hatching of mosquitoes – adults and children alike fall prey to malaria. Unprotected water sources mean that diarrhoea soon becomes rampant. Sick people (and mothers caring for sick children) cannot do the heavy work of preparing the land, planting and weeding. Poor crop husbandry at the start of the season inevitably brings a disappointing harvest. Families go hungry and slide inexorably into poverty.

Malawi is also gripped by the HIV/AIDS pandemic. Some 15 percent of the adult population are infected with the virus; while close to half a million children under 14 have lost their parents to the pandemic. The AIDS pandemic exacerbates poverty. A family member becomes ill. What few resources the household has are used to buy treatment. Crops are left untended as carers attend to the needs of the sick. Food supplies dwindle and other family members have to seek cash or food elsewhere. They may work on neighbours' farms, they may seek jobs in town (but employment for the unskilled is scarce), and they may turn to crime or prostitution to keep alive. The pandemic is further fuelled by children who have to drop out of school to care for adults, to work on the farm, or to seek what sources of food they can. The next generation of AIDS victims is assembling.

Hungry people are malnourished. Too many Malawians do not get enough to eat. Half of all children under five are stunted – a fifth of them severely so. These children will never reach their growth potential, as the effects of chronic malnutrition in childhood are irreversible. Malnutrition reduces a child's ability to learn by reducing interaction and exploration. Such children are often too weak to go to school or fail to complete their studies. Poor nutrition not only makes the individual more susceptible to disease, it exacerbates the effect of the disease as well. Two-thirds of child deaths can be linked to nutritional factors. The effects of malnourishment carry on to the next generation. Children from mothers malnourished in childhood may be impaired directly by their mothers' condition, and indirectly by the increased likelihood that their mothers may die in or around childbirth.

In Malawi, most do not have enough to eat, even in normal years. When shortages occur, food prices rise sharply and hunger becomes desperate. The average Malawian consumes around 1800 calories per day, well below the number needed for a normal, healthy life (especially when faced with the backbreaking work of planting and tending crops). Two-thirds of the population consume only 1400 calories and the poorest around 1100. When food prices rise, the effect on households is devastating. The average daily per capita cash income is US$0.14, of which 60 percent is spent on food (the poor spend 80 percent). The struggle for food and survival dominates life.

It is not just Malawi's problem – Malawi just illustrates starkly the interactions between food, AIDS, and poverty on the continent.

More than 300,000 died when the most devastating earthquake of modern times sent a gigantic wave across the seas, destroying everything in its path when it hit the shore. It was an event of particularly dramatic horror – there is a Tsunami every month in Africa. But its deadly tide of disease and hunger steals silently and dramatically across the continent. It is not dramatic, and it rarely reaches the television news. Its victims die quietly, out of sight, hidden in their pitiful homes. But they perish in the same numbers. The eyes of the world may be averted from their routine suffering, but the eyes of history are upon us. In years to come, future generations will look back, and wonder how our world could have known and failed to act (Commission for Africa, 2005).

When, as in much of Malawi, most live on the edge of survival, it takes little to create a crisis. Malawi is today locked in almost routine annual food crises and deepening poverty. The situation looks increasingly desperate. We, the authors of this book, have all worked to bring about change for the better. Sadly, as we will show, we find ourselves angry and frustrated. Frustration because, as we will illustrate in the book, with entirely reasonable resources, change for the better is possible and achievable. Anger, because at both national and international levels, so much of what is provided is misdirected.

It is not just our perspective. Two influential reports published in 2005 show clearly that poverty can be overcome. The UN Millennium Commission has outlined the key interventions needed to halve poverty by 2015 and eliminate extreme poverty by 2025. The cost is affordable if the international community implements its existing commitment to allocate 0.7 percent of GDP to finance international development.

The Millennium Commission report also spelt out the key interventions and investments that are necessary to reach the Millennium Development Goals. The powerful *Commission for Africa* report emphasises that Africa is today ready to absorb an additional US$25 billion per annum to implement programmes to reduce poverty and promote growth as well as development in the world's poorest continent. The report notes, 'The contrast between the lives led by those who live in rich countries and poor people in Africa is the greatest scandal of our age.'

Prosperity not poverty

The title for this book is 'Poverty, AIDS and Hunger: Breaking out of Malawi's Poverty Trap'. It describes Malawi's plight as a storm that brings together climatic disaster, impoverishment, the AIDS pandemic, the long-standing burden of malaria and other communicable diseases. The result is very high rates of child malnutrition and adult deaths. Malawi's main industry, agriculture, is constrained by economic isolation, high transport costs, growing environmental degradation and depleted soils. Malawi's farmers are too poor to invest in fertilisers and other needed inputs to increase productivity and allow food production to keep pace with the rapidly growing population.

Yet the situation is far from hopeless. The problems that Africa faces, demonstrated clearly in Malawi, are difficult but not insurmountable. Diseases can be controlled, crop yields can be increased, and basic infrastructure can be extended to the villages in order to promote growth. These basic investments, if applied systematically, in a coherent and coordinated manner, and attuned to local needs, can enable African countries such as Malawi to break out of the poverty trap. According to Sachs (2005), with focused attention by both African countries and the international community, Africa could achieve a takeoff in rural-led growth – sparing the coming generation of Africans the misery of food insecurity and its devastating partners of malnutrition, disease and poverty.

If current policies and approaches were working as claimed, the UN Millennium Project Task Force on Hunger would not need to identify Africa as the region facing the greatest challenge in attaining the Millennium Development Goal for hunger – reducing the proportion of people who suffer from hunger by half between 1990 and 2015 (Sanchez and Swaminathan, 2005). In agriculture, for example, we know from experiences in other developing regions that increases in fertiliser use can improve short-term food production and stimulate the long-term growth of an economy. During the Green Revolution, chemical fertilisers played a critical role in increasing food production despite the expanding population in South Asia. In India, wheat production increased six-fold from the 1960s to today; rice yields more than doubled resulting in the percentage of undernourished people falling from 38 percent to 21 percent (Mukherjee, 2003).

We propose fresh, clear and radical thinking on new strategies and interventions. The Green Revolution was a child of its time – capital intensive, hierarchical, and based on the Schultz hypothesis of disruptive, rapid change as central to creating change in conservative peasant societies (Schultz, 1964). In the 'Green Revolution' countries of Asia, moderately fertile, well-drained soils account for 33 percent of cultivated land, and in sub-Saharan Africa only 19 percent (Eswaran *et al.*, 1997). In Africa, nutrient deficiencies override water shortages as the factor limiting crop productivity – such that the crop can absorb only 10 to 15 percent of total rainfall.

On marginal lands especially, and where water is unreliable, the Asian combination of improved seeds and enhanced fertility management does not provide a sufficient 'bang' for the Schultzian hypothesis to work. High transport costs make it difficult to compete in agricultural export markets, and the use of expensive fertilisers is unprofitable, except on very high-value crops – which are typically too risky for the poor to grow. Consequently the poor (above 80 percent, in the case of Malawi) become poorer, their food supplies dwindle, and national growth stalls. At the same time, the AIDS pandemic causes suffering and death in almost every family.

For the majority of Africa's population, agriculture is the most important livelihood activity and agricultural constraints are immediate and critical with far-reaching consequences. Transforming agriculture must be at least a significant part of the solution to African poverty. That transformation will come, as elsewhere, from the development, and subsequent adoption of productive and profitable new technologies.

An alternative 'Green Evolution' approach builds on an evolving partnership of scientists, farming communities and development agencies (both private and public). It encourages the efficient and swift transformation of agricultural production through harnessing the best of skills in a collaborative, 'learning by doing' manner in which all have a sense of ownership and pride. Existing structures are improved and enhanced to build change through an evolutionary, rather than a revolutionary approach. This is cost-effective, brings the best of developing countries and international expertise together in a problem-solving format, and can be rapidly scaled up to reach the poor quickly and effectively.

The 'Green Evolution', in common with evolution in nature, is efficient in selecting the best and encourages partnership and collaboration. This creates broad-based opportunities for the poor to benefit directly from effective access to improved seeds, fertilisers and other critical inputs that are the foundations for growth in agricultural productivity. Unlike the hierarchical and prescriptive nature of the 'big bang' revolution, an evolutionary strategy uses multiple channels and players, and allows for choices to emerge and be tested – and the best to be adopted. It fits comfortably into the increasingly practiced participatory framework for development that facilitates the empowerment of the poor and disadvantaged. Such a strategy, based on solid scientific foundations directed by farmers' needs and determined by the commercial, social and ecological environments of the continent, can provide gains, not only for richer off producers, but also for the poor and excluded (Blackie, 2005).

Using examples from Malawi, we will show that this approach is not just theory – it works. The 1998 nationally-led Maize Productivity Task Force came up with a cost-effective and resilient plan to break the food crisis cycle in Malawi. We will show how this, even in its imperfect form, actually performed to a remarkably high standard of accuracy and effectiveness. But, because it did not fit with the commonly accepted (and failing) policies promoted by the most powerful development agencies, the programme was derailed. We will show how, during the subsequent 2002 famine, a major international response was mobilised, resources were provided and there was a unique spirit of collaboration and partnership as all worked together to deliver humanitarian assistance to the most vulnerable communities. The generosity of the international community, combined with dedication and hard work on the part of government officials, donors, civil society and Non Governmental Organisations working at the community level allowed lives to be saved and a process of recovery to begin.

We will argue that this approach encourages both local expertise and contributions at all levels, as well as providing a platform for integrated and informed international support. Change can be fast and far-reaching, but costs are affordable. It will create the needed broad based development and sense of ownership that is needed to break out of the poverty trap which ensnares so many of the poor and disadvantaged of

Africa. A strong African voice is built in throughout the endeavour. Most importantly, it provides an environment in which the full dimensions of the poverty trap – hunger, disease, and poverty – can be tackled in a comprehensive and synergistic manner. Those in the field and policy makers need to actively and creatively start integrating their capabilities to bring about a swift end to the suffering of the poor. The examples provided in the final chapters of this book provide evidence that this is both achievable and effective. What is lacking is the leadership and vision to make it happen.

Some background to the book

The focus on hunger, poverty and the AIDS and health crisis reflect the core challenges that the five co-editors of this book have worked on for most of their professional lives. Anne Conroy and Malcolm Blackie have long shared a common interest in addressing chronic hunger through improving food productivity. Malcolm Blackie was responsible for the Rockefeller Foundation Agriculture Programme in southern Africa for 12 years, working from an office in Lilongwe. His work in Malawi, Zimbabwe and Mozambique focused on improving maize productivity – the staple food for the majority of smallholders. Anne Conroy was a volunteer Evaluation Officer in Lilongwe Agricultural Development Division in Malawi. Her early research with poor smallholders highlighted the fact that farmers needed access to improved seed and fertilisers to meet subsistence requirements and promote food security. Subsequently she has worked as an advisor to senior Malawian policy makers and donor agencies.

It was this latter phase of Anne's career that exposed her to the linkages between food security, health and the AIDS crisis. As she explored this complex problem, she worked with the other three co-authors of this book – Alan Whiteside, Justin Malewezi, and Jeffrey Sachs. Alan Whiteside is the leading analyst of the economic impact of AIDS in Africa and has focused on multi-sectoral drivers and the economic impact of the AIDS pandemic. In his teaching, research and writing he has explored the causes and consequences of the epidemic in Africa, Asia and Eastern Europe. He first worked on AIDS as an issue for migrants (including Malawians) in 1987.

As Vice President of Malawi in the Muluzi administration, Justin Malewezi was Chairman of the Cabinet Committee on Health and HIV/AIDS with Anne Conroy as his advisor. The focus of the Cabinet Committee in the middle to late 1990s was to support efforts to raise awareness of how AIDS would devastate the economy. The Committee collaborated with the Malawi National AIDS Commission to develop a multi-sectoral and comprehensive response to HIV/AIDS prevention and care of HIV/AIDS victims. Malawi's National Strategic Framework for HIV Prevention and Care (National AIDS Commission, 1999) reflected the widespread perception that treatment was unaffordable in resource-poor African countries. As a result, it did not place sufficient emphasis on the care and treatment of AIDS victims.

The XIII International AIDS Conference in Durban in July 2000 drew international attention to the needs of the millions of Africans suffering from AIDS without any hope of treatment. Justin Malewezi recognised that this was unacceptable. He immediately convened a technical working group to integrate prevention with care and treatment. The technical working group included scientists from the Ministry of Health, National AIDS Commission, the Medical College, the Office of the Vice President, representatives of HIV/AIDS victims and civil society. It benefited from the support of international civil society and international scientists. The technical working group developed a proposal to provide a comprehensive management of opportunistic infections, to strengthen the overall health sector and to invest in human resources in order to expand access to anti-retroviral therapy.

This approach was highly controversial. Several influential development agencies believed that to focus on treatment would divert attention from prevention. The approach was seen in some circles as, at best, irresponsible. Jeffrey Sachs invited the Malawi team to Harvard University in June 2001 just before the United Nations General Assembly on HIV/AIDS for detailed discussions. He shared his work with the Macro-Economic Commission on Health and the UN Millennium Commission. He and Bono visited Malawi in early 2002. They were shocked by the extent of poverty, hunger and malnutrition in the villages and the conditions in the hospitals. They and their partners at the national and international levels work tirelessly to keep the focus on Africa. Jeffrey Sachs returned to Malawi in July 2005 to support the Malawi Government in the 'Comprehensive Programme to Address Hunger' and to promote planning around the Millennium Development Goals.

We also received invaluable support and guidance from Professor Charles Gilks formerly of Liverpool School of Tropical Medicine and now at Imperial College and the 3*5 Initiative at the World Health Organisation. With funding from the DFID funded HIV Knowledge Programme, Charles Gilks financed the Malawi team to visit the leading specialists in Britain and the World Health Organisation in order to improve the technical content of our proposal. The combination of external support from international scientists and national commitment at all levels resulted in Malawi's successful application to the Global Fund. Malawi was awarded US$196 million in August 2002 that enabled it to strengthen programmes in prevention including the expansion of programmes for voluntary counselling and testing and the prevention of mother to child transmission of the virus. The programme also included resources to expand the management and treatment of opportunistic infections and provision of anti-retroviral therapy for 25,000 people. With the reduction in drug prices and the launch of the World Health Organisation 3*5 Initiative, Malawi now plans to expand anti-retroviral therapy to 80,000 people by the end of 2006.

Hilary Benn, at that time the Deputy Secretary of State for International Development visited Malawi in late 2001. He saw how the Lilongwe Lighthouse provided anti-retroviral treatment to people living with HIV/AIDS enabling them to return to health and employment and to care for their children. Once he was appointed Secretary of State for International Development we continued the dialogue. We stressed that investments in health systems and human resources were the prerequisites to providing comprehensive health care and greater access to treatment for HIV/AIDS. Hilary Benn was willing to listen and to act to increase DFID's support for treatment and investment in health systems infrastructure and human resources development. A significant programme to support human resources in Malawi's health sector was launched in January 2005. Hillary Benn's and his fellow commissioners' deep commitment to promote justice for the people of Africa is evident in the *Commission for Africa* Report.

Bringing dignity to the poor

Throughout the book we continue to stress the need to place human rights at the centre of development policy. This is based on justice and the dignity and equality of human beings. The concept of equality is very important. Bono points out in his foreword to Jeff Sachs' 2005 book:

Fifteen thousand Africans dying each and every day of preventable, treatable diseases – AIDS, TB and malaria – for lack of drugs that we take for granted. This statistic alone makes a fool of the idea that many of us hold on to tightly: the idea of equality. What is happening in Africa cast doubts on our concerns, and questions our commitment to the whole concept. Because if we are honest, there's no way that we would ever conclude that such a disaster would ever be allowed to happen anywhere else. Certainly not in North America, in Europe or Japan. An entire continent bursting into flames? Deep down, if we really accept that their lives – African lives are equal to ours, we would all be doing more to put the fire out. It's an uncomfortable truth.

The *Commission for Africa* also reminds us of the equality and dignity of all human beings

> To convey the enormity of that injustice we speak in millions – and yet we have to remember that behind each statistic lies a child who is precious and loved. Every day that child and thousands like her will struggle for breath – and for life – and tragically and painfully lose that fight.

For those of us who live in Africa, we do not have to be reminded. The people who die are members of our families, our friends, our colleagues and our children. We try to support them as they suffer and struggle to regain their health. We are at their bedsides to see the pain and incomprehension in their eyes, and the fear and grief of their families as they try to comfort them. We are there when they lose the battle for life. We attend their funerals. We commit their bodies to the ground and their souls to God. We try to comfort each other, their parents and try to support and educate their children. We grieve time and time again – the pain is unrelenting. At times our anger becomes outrage because their deaths, and the deaths of thousands of our fellow human beings, could and should be prevented.

In this current devastating hunger crisis we see how poverty affects people's lives and how people affected by the crisis recognise the relationship between poverty and powerlessness.

> Poverty indeed turns a man into nothing. A poor man is never listened to. He has nowhere to go to complain for no one will take action on his story. This is the case because the people in the system know each other and they protect each other too. It feels bad to have a heavy heart and to have nowhere to go to express your concerns. (Joseph Graciano, Bangwe Township in Blantyre 2006).[1]

Poverty and hunger also force people into impossible choices. 'You would see a little girl child that is supposed to be in school leave school to do housework to raise money that is needed by the family. This is not something that parents were pleased to do, but they felt forced to sacrifice their children in this manner for the sake of survival.' (Peter Madeya, Dedza District 2006).

Decision makers in the international community and indeed in the national authorities are far removed from the reality of grinding poverty and the sense of despair and frustration when people fail to feed their families or recover from a food crisis. Today in Malawi, hungry people are surviving on grass seed because food aid requirements were under-estimated and under-resourced. Old people are labouring from five in the morning until the mid-day sun on neighbouring farms to earn some money to buy a single pumpkin to share with a whole family in their single meal for the day. As poverty becomes more entrenched, the scope for exploitation increases. We have met people who have worked for over 10 days without any wages in their hope for food.

Tragically, hunger also fuels poverty and the AIDS pandemic. Primary school enrolment falls as children go to sleep hungry. Parents are forced to withdraw their children from school to save the cost of school fees. The majority of the poor have not recovered from the food crisis of 2002. They sold everything – bicycles, livestock, cooking utensils and even their own clothes. When this is not enough and the harvest is still distant, they may be forced to sell their bodies. 'With the present hunger, women who have children and whose families cannot get any food go to the extent of selling their bodies to vendors who in turn give them maize.' (Peter Sofolian 2006 – same in the above verbal quote cited in the Conroy *et al.* report for World Disasters Report, Nsanje District). This is a tragedy and an outrage. It is the result of the failure by many in the international community to meet their commitments with regards to official development assistance. The promise to the world's poor has been broken.

In addition to undermining education and fuelling the AIDS pandemic, poverty and hunger erode faith in politicians – and set back prospects for the transition to democracy in Malawi and elsewhere in Africa. Until African governments can ensure their citizens' right to food, they will struggle to gain the support of the people. Most African politicians recognise the centrality of ensuring national and household-level food security, but are often ill-served by the international community who underplay the significance of food security. It is the farmers of the rich countries of the West who are deemed worthy of subsidies, not the poverty-stricken farm households in Africa. Subsidies are derided as unsustainable – but huge sums are spent annually on even more unsustainable (and often inequitable) feeding programmes to keep the poor alive. There is a better way – which we will discuss as a central theme of this book.

Hungry people are angry people. 'Our politicians are focusing on trivial issues and never pay attention to the issues that really affect the people. This hunger was known long before and all of us knew that it would be very, very serious. But no proper mechanisms were put in place. We were promised fertiliser coupons but we did not get them – we feel betrayed.' (Martin Naluso (2006) same verbal quote in the Conroy *et al.* (2006) paper for World Disasters Report, Blantyre District).

This book is a very personal journey for all of us and the struggle to express ourselves clearly took us through tough arguments and difficult times. We wrote it for the people of Malawi. Our hope is that we do justice to the issues of poverty, hunger and health that the poor face every day in their struggle to live lives of dignity.

Note

1. See Anne Conroy, Malcolm Blackie, Austin Ngwira and Boniface Tamani 'Malawi the Neglected Emergency' in World Disasters Report 2006 forthcoming. NB: the quotes from Joseph Graciano and Peter Madeya are verbal quotes in the Conroy, Blackie, Ngwira and Tamani report for The World Disasters Report – they are not separate papers. We are grateful to the International Federation of the Red Cross for financing fieldwork in affected communities in February 2006.

Bibliography

Blackie M. (2005) 'The possible dream – food security and prosperity in Africa', Keynote address, 7th Annual African Crop Science Society Conference, Entebbe, Uganda, 6–10 December, 2005.

Conroy A. Blackie M., Ngwira A. and Tamani B. (2006) 'Malawi: the Neglected Emergency' in World Disasters Report forthcoming.

Eswaran H., Almaraz R., Reich P. and Zdruli P. (1997) 'Soil quality and soil productivity in Africa', *J. Sustainable Agric. 10*: 75–94.

Malawi Government (2005) 'Malawi Millennium Development Goals: Progress Report for the UN Summit 2005', Lilongwe, Malawi.

Mukherje S.K. (2003) 'Fertilisers in Developing Countries: Opportunities and Challenges', 15th Francis New Memorial Lecture.

National AIDS Commission (1999) 'National Strategic Framework for HIV Prevention and Care', Lilongwe, Malawi.

Sachs J. (2005) *The End of Poverty: How we can make it happen in our lifetime*, Penguin UK.

Sanchez P.A. and Swaminathan M.S. (2005) 'Hunger in Africa: the link between unhealthy people and unhealthy', *Lancet, 365*: 442–44.

Schultz T. (1964) *Transforming Traditional Agriculture*, New Haven: Yale University Press.

The Commission for Africa (2005) 'Our Common Interest: Report of the Commission for Africa', London [http://www.commissionforafricaorg/English/11–03–05_cr_report.pdf]

United Nations Millennium Commission Project (2005) 'Investing in Development: A Practical Plan to Meet the Millennium Development Goals', Report to the UN Secretary-General. London: Earthscan.

1

The History of Development and Crisis in Malawi

Anne Conroy

Introduction

This chapter provides the context for understanding the evolution of development and crisis in Malawi. It begins with summarising Malawi's geography, together with a brief historical overview of pre-independence Malawi. It outlines Malawi's difficulties and challenges after independence and documents the emergence of one-party rule and subsequent dictatorship under Malawi's first President, Dr Hastings Kamuzu Banda. The factors underlying economic growth in the early years of independence, and the causes of the economic crisis at the end of the 1970s, are examined. This economic crisis led to the introduction of structural adjustment policies which failed to achieve their objective of a broad-based and sustained economic growth. As poverty became even more pervasive, combined with changes in the geopolitical situation, the first challenges to one-party rule appeared in the early 1990s and subsequently gathered momentum, leading to the Malawi's first multi-party elections in May 1994. The chapter concludes by reviewing Malawi's economic performance from 1994 to 2004, the structure of the economy, and the key challenges in relation to the nature and extent of poverty in Malawi today.

Geographical summary

Malawi is a small land-locked country in southern Africa. It has a land area of 11,484 square kilometres and a population of around 12 million. It has one of the highest population densities in sub-Saharan Africa[1] with only 0.23 hectares of land per person living in the rural areas – compared to 0.86 in neighbouring Zambia and 0.40 in sub-Saharan

Africa as a whole (World Bank, 2003). Malawi is bordered by Tanzania to the east and north, by Zambia to the west and by Mozambique to the south and east. The name 'Malawi' literally means 'flames'. It has its roots in traditions which link the people to the land, the life of the spirits and the seasons through the use of fire, both ritual and practical (Reich Verlag, 1984).

Malawi is a beautiful country dominated by the Rift Valley. Approximately one-fifth of the country consists of Lake Malawi which extends down two-thirds of the country and is the most southern of the African Rift Valley Lakes. It is 580 km long and is the third largest lake in Africa. Lake Malawi drains into the Shire River to the south; the Shire River joins the Zambezi, and ultimately the Indian Ocean through Mozambique. Administratively, Malawi is divided into three major regions. The northern region is the least densely populated. It includes steep escarpments, rivers, the Nyika Plateau, forest plantations and good quality agricultural land. The central region is dominated by the high interior Central African Plateau and has some of the highest potential farm land, the new capital city of Lilongwe, and the tobacco auction floors (critical for the sale of one of Malawi's major exports). The southern region is the most densely populated and diverse region. It includes the former colonial capital, Zomba, and Malawi's major commercial city, Blantyre. The southern region has the Shire Highlands to the east, Zomba Plateau and Mount Mulanje (the highest mountain in central Africa rising from the tea plantations of Thyolo and Mulanje). The low-lying Shire River basin forms the southern tip of the country.

Historical perspective

Like most countries in Africa, Malawi has suffered brutally at the hands of outsiders. In the nineteenth century, the country that is now Malawi was a major trading route for the slave trade. Thousands of people were rounded up from villages in the interior and transported to ports on Lake Malawi, and then on to the slave markets of Zanzibar. The British Government established the Protectorate of Nyasaland in 1893 in response to David Livingstone's concerns about the slave trade which persisted along the east coast of Africa well after the demise of the Atlantic trade. The aim was ostensibly to protect the people from slavery but it also served to support Britain's strategic interests in southern Africa.

The southern African British territories (which include today's Malawi, Zambia and Zimbabwe) were acquired just as enthusiasm for colonial expansion in Britain was waning. Overseas territories were increasingly seen as a drain on the UK taxpayer and, therefore, were expected 'to pay their own way'. The Protectorate opened the way for alienation of land by outsiders, and the imposition of taxation on the indigenous population. The colonial authorities even forced conscription of the 'natives' into the British Army to fight the First World War. Malawians, understandably, were unenthusiastic about many of these changes. The socio-economic situation worsened in 1912 when there was a famine and the British increased taxation. The first challenge to colonial rule was the Chilembwe Uprising of 1915. This was suppressed and the leaders killed; but the seeds of national consciousness and the desire for independence were already sown.

The colonial economy in Malawi was divided into three sub-economies: the plantations (concentrated in the south), peasant cash cropping (throughout the remainder of the country), and the labour reserve economy. The colonial administrators encouraged the growth of the plantation sector in an attempt to make the economy self-sustaining. Plantation growers were accorded preferential treatment, including the exclusive right to grow the most lucrative export crops. A typical plantation consisted of a large tract of land, only a small portion of which was cultivated at any one time. Labour came, at least in part, from tenants living on the plantation. The predominant form of tenancy was *thangata* which was a quasi-feudal arrangement under which small farmers had to supply labour to the plantation in order to use the land. Peasant farming was encouraged as a source of food for the plantations, missions and administrative centres. The labour reserve economy involved migration to the mines of Southern Rhodesia (now Zimbabwe) and South Africa (Christiansen and Kydd, 1987).

As the century progressed, the British Government sought to extract itself from its colonial possessions. In southern Africa, in a half-hearted attempt to placate the irreconcilable demands of British settlers (who wanted to retain settler control of the economy) and those of the indigenous populations (who had a very different vision), the colonial authorities imposed a federation between Nyasaland and Britain's other colonies of Southern and Northern Rhodesia (now Zimbabwe and Zambia). The people of Nyasaland opposed the Federation through organised passive resistance and non-cooperation with British colonial rule. Eventually the Nyasaland African Congress (NAC) emerged to lead the fight for independence. Dr Hastings Kamuzu Banda, an older, educated and conservative man, was invited by the Congress to return from

Ghana and lead the fight against the Federation. The Federation was dissolved in 1963 and Malawi became an independent nation in 1964.

Malawi at independence and post-independence economic policy: 1964 to 1977

At independence in 1964, Malawi's population was estimated at 3,787,000[2] (Pryor, 1988). Malawi was impoverished and mainly illiterate, fertility rates were very high and there was rapid population growth. Only a tiny proportion of the population had access to formal education. Nevertheless, the young leaders of the independence movement, the Nyasaland African Congress, were dynamic, far-sighted and brilliant. They had a clear understanding of development priorities and the dangers of dictatorship. It is tragic that they ceded the Presidency to the most senior amongst them – Dr Hastings Kamuzu Banda. He rapidly became an authoritarian, suppressed all opposition, and established a one-party state. The Constitution was changed in 1971 to make Dr Banda Life President.

At independence, the Malawian economy was based around the established colonial agricultural model. The estate subsector produced 40 percent of Malawi's merchandise exports (mainly tea and tobacco) – a smallholder subsector was based mainly around subsistence, but providing a marketed food surplus, and a labour reserve supplied estate labour and migrant labour to the neighbouring countries. The country was predominantly agricultural (agriculture accounted for 55 percent of GDP and 90 percent of national employment). The country lacked mineral resources, capital, skilled labour and possessed a limited small domestic market (Harrigan, 2001). In recognition of these constraints, the post-independence strategy focused on an export-orientated, agro-based, and labour intensive expansion path with import-substituting industrialisation playing only a secondary role.

Between independence and the late 1970s, this development strategy generated rapid rates of economic growth.[3] The estate sector (farming leasehold land) was the engine of growth, exporting tobacco, tea and sugar. The smallholder subsector (farming customary land) focused on food production – especially maize for national food self-sufficiency. Growth rates averaged 5.5 percent per annum from 1964 to 1977. The estate subsector grew at an average of 17 percent per annum, while the smallholder subsector grew at an average rate of 3 percent per annum (Harrigan, 2003).

The bias in favour of estates at the expense of smallholders took many forms: customary land was annexed from the smallholder subsector;

smallholders were legally prevented from growing important high-value crops (burley tobacco, tea and sugar were reserved for the estate sub-sector); smallholder producers of export crops were paid less than the export parity price by the state marketing board (ADMARC, the Agri-cultural Development and Marketing Corporation), with most of the resulting profits channelled into the development of the estate subsector. The smallholder sector was relied upon to provide a marketable surplus of the staple food, maize, to feed estate and urban workers (Kydd and Christiansen, 1982). The effect of the policy of land alienation was dev-astating. The transfer of land from, and increasing land pressure within, the smallholder sector contributed to the continual fragmentation of plots. Today, as a result, many smallholders' land holdings are too small to support the families that live on them and some rural households are effectively landless. To gain access to land, some smallholders cultivate land that is not suitable for farming (such as erosion-prone steep slopes).

Unsurprisingly, growth was not sustained. A series of exogenous shocks at the end of the 1970s (a 35 percent collapse in the terms of trade,[4] catastrophic drought in 1979–80, and a civil war in Mozambique that disrupted the external transport routes) exposed fundamental weaknesses in the economy and showed that the post-independence estate-led strategy was no longer viable. Exports were highly concen-trated around the single crop of tobacco, leaving the economy vulner-able to shocks. The estate subsector was very import-dependent, while the smallholder subsector was marginalised and impoverished. GDP growth barely kept pace with population increases. Food and foreign exchange became increasingly scarce (Harrigan, 2003). The Banda regime chose to neglect distributional issues and ignore the growing evidence of increasing poverty. Public investment was concentrated in the productive sectors, and the complementary social sectors, especially education and health, were starved of resources.

Crisis and structural adjustment policies in the 1980s

The 1980s saw a reorientation of agricultural policy in Malawi, largely under the auspices of the World Bank and the IMF structural adjust-ment and stabilisation programmes. Three structural adjustment loans focused on removing distortions in the smallholder subsector and increasing smallholders' contribution to export earnings. Prices for smallholder export crops were raised, while the relative price of maize was reduced. This led to significant crop substitution between hybrid maize and groundnuts – but smallholder households were still pre-cluded from growing the most lucrative export crop (burley tobacco).

At the same time, subsidies on smallholder fertiliser and maize seed were phased out. The Malawi Government feared these policies would undermine food security. Sadly, this proved true when market liberalisation measures resulted in a food crisis in 1987 and the Government was forced to import 140,000 metric tonnes of maize.

By the end of the 1980s, poverty had increased and food security was very precarious. It was clear that the structural adjustment loans were not having the desired impact. Economic growth was just over 1 percent in 1986 and it was less than 1 percent in 1987. The World Bank shifted their focus from general structural adjustment credits towards specific sector-based loans that were intended to remove structural obstacles to increased production. It was increasingly apparent that non-price factors were the critical constraints (Harrigan, 2001).

The World Bank approved the Industrial and Trade Policy adjustment credit in 1988. The programme consisted of a two-pronged strategy involving macro-economic stabilisation and structural reform. The World Bank accepted that, in the interests of growth, 'a higher proportion of grants and concessional loans' would be needed to bridge the balance of payments gap, and to support import growth and gross investment. The adjustment credit was intended to change the market structure of the industrial sector by increasing competition, and promoting trade liberalisation. It was complemented by a flexible exchange rate management, reforms to foreign exchange allocation, a gradual reduction in fiscal deficit and a removal of price controls (Harrigan, 2001).

In the agricultural sector, the Agricultural Sector Adjustment Credit (ASAC) presented to the World Bank Board in 1990 provided a total of US$170 million for reforms in the agricultural sector. The credit was designed to address key structural constraints – including the shortage of land in the smallholder subsector caused partly by the post-independence policy of transferring land from the smallholder to the estate subsector.[5] The World Bank agricultural credit provided for the removal of restrictions on smallholder burley tobacco production, and the piloting of better targeting fertiliser subsidies and credit to the poor.

ASAC was constructive: it accepted moves by the government to realign producer prices back towards hybrid maize. As we will discuss in Chapter 5, the credit, together with the release of two appropriate flint hybrid varieties[6] led to an increased adoption of hybrid seed and fertiliser, and the start of what could have been a climb out of poverty. The sector credit was closely integrated with macro-policies and poverty issues and could have formed the basis for a more constructive

World Bank investment portfolio in Malawi. But events intervened. A major drought in 1992 precipitated another food crisis. The opposition to one-party rule grew as the economy stagnated, and the ferocious discipline which had checked dissent in Malawi crumbled. The farm level credit scheme to help the poor gain access to improved seed and fertiliser collapsed, and Malawi entered what became a series of food crises and famines.

Political developments and the emergence of multi-party democracy in Malawi

The Cold War had a powerful effect on Malawi's development. Despite a truly appalling human rights record (which included oppression of human rights and the widespread use of torture), Malawi was long accorded favourable treatment by powerful friends in the West. Dr Banda was staunchly anti-communist and also maintained cordial diplomatic relations with the apartheid regime in South Africa. When the Cold War ended in the 1990s, Malawi lost its strategic importance.

As a result of the changes in global politics, Malawi's dreadful human rights record was no longer ignored. Malawian politicians were forced to recognise the increasingly vocal clamour throughout the African continent for more democracy. The Malawian people were disaffected, due to human rights abuses and also the institutional denial of crippling poverty. The Catholic Bishops opened up a new struggle for freedom with a powerful Lenten Letter in 1992 that spoke for the millions of voiceless people deprived of their human rights.

The Letter was hardly revolutionary;

> We are aware of a growing gap between the rich and the poor with regard to expectations, living standards and development. We appeal for a more just and equal distribution of the nation's wealth. (Episcopal Conference of Malawi, 1992).

But by laying out the major issues starkly and clearly in a way that had not been possible for decades, their simple rhetoric had a major catalytic effect, mobilising civil society, the students, and ultimately the majority of the population. Sixty-four percent of the population backed the introduction of multi-party democracy in a referendum in June 1993 and Malawi held the first multi-party elections in May 1994.

Economic performance: 1994 to 2004

President Bakili Muluzi of the United Democratic Front (UDF) won the election in 1994 with 47 percent of the Presidential Vote. Dr Kamuzu Banda's party, the Malawi Congress Party (MCP), became the main Opposition, while the Alliance for Democracy (Aford) spent the next 10 years in and out of alliances with the ruling party and the opposition.

In 1994, the Government took over a highly unstable economy, a fiscal deficit of –16.2 percent, a large current account imbalance and inflation of 34.6 percent (Office of the Vice President, 1999). The economy was still recovering from the drought of 1992. Political unrest, security problems and macro-economic volatility reduced investments. The Government budget was out of control (following election-related spending); public and private savings were negative. Poverty, as always, remained deep-rooted and pervasive. The small-holder agricultural credit system had collapsed, maize profitability (and thus production) was falling, and the estate subsector was in decline. Industries faced intense competition from imports, and infrastructure was dilapidated. However, peace in Mozambique, democratic transition in South Africa and in Malawi itself, and the introduction of a new Constitution in 1995, allowed the new Government to rethink economic policy under a new strategy of poverty alleviation.

During the first 2 years, the UDF Government made important progress with macro-economic stabilisation, economic growth and structural reforms. Key elements of the reform agenda included privat-isation of parastatals, investment and export promotion, the creation of a stable macro-economic environment of low inflation and interest rates, and investment in key infrastructure and utilities (particularly telecommunications and power).

Burley tobacco production was liberalised to allow smallholder farmers to sell their crops on the Auction Floors – opening this valu-able cash crop to some of the smallholders. The introduction of Free Primary Education, and increased allocation of resources to education and health, confirmed the new Government's commitment to human development and poverty alleviation. The Government also started to address the AIDS pandemic seriously. Government policies aimed to improve efficiency, redistribute wealth, and create employment, and increase investment and technical change. The private sector was seen as an engine of growth.

The initial signs were good. Economic growth rates averaged 4.6 percent per annum between 1995 and 1998, (but then fell back to

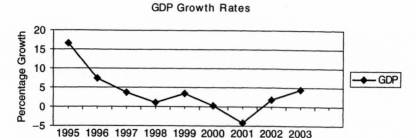

Figure 1.1 GDP growth rates, 1995–2003
Source: 1995–1997 World Bank – Country Economic Memorandum 2003, 1998–2003
Reserve Bank of Malawi *Monthly Economic Review*, October 2003.

a disappointing 1.4 percent between 1998 and 2001). Growth in 2001
and 2002 became negative due to food crises. Growth was 1.7 percent
of GDP in 2003 and the Economist Intelligence Unit projected
growth at 2.6 percent in 2004 and 2.3 percent in 2005. However,
these growth rates are insufficient to have an appreciable impact on
poverty.

Key challenges in Malawi today

Malawi's position on the human development index[7] is 165 out of
177 countries. Most of those countries lower on the human development index than Malawi have suffered from recent conflicts or famine.[8]
Life expectancy is low and declining – from an average of 41 years in
1975 to 37.8 today. There is now an almost a 60 percent probability of
not living to 40 years. The infant mortality rate is 189 per 1000 and the
under-five mortality rate is 114 per 1000 – confirming the tragedy that
one in five children will not survive to their fifth birthday. The reported
maternal mortality rate is 1100 per 100,000 live births while the adjusted
maternal mortality rate is 1800 per 100,000 (World Health Organisation,
2005). Only Sierra Leone performs worse than Malawi on this critical
indicator of human development.

Seventy-six percent of Malawi's population live on less than two
dollars a day and 42 percent of the population live on less than one
dollar a day. According to national data, 64 percent of the population
live below the poverty line. Per capita income is estimated at US$177
in 2002. Malawi's per capita income has grown only by 0.2 percent
per annum over the last 30 years despite attempts by successive

Table 1.1   Millennium development goals: selected indicators

	1990	1995	2001	2002
Adult literacy rate (percentage of people ages 15+)	51.8	55.9	61.0	61.8
Youth literacy rate (percentage of people ages 15–24)	63.2	67.3	71.8	72.5
Ratio of girls to boys in primary and secondary education	63.2	67.3	71.8	72.5
Under 5 mortality rate (per 1000)	241.0	216.0	188.0	182.0
Prevalence of HIV (percent of women ages 15–24)	....	....	14.9	....
Access to an improved water source (percent of population)	49.0	....	57.0	....
Fixed line and mobile telephones (per 1000 people)	3.1	3.6	10.6	....
Life expectancy at birth (years)	44.6	41.9	38.2	37.5

Source: http://www.developmentgoals.org/

governments and donors to improve the lives of the poor. Income inequality remains very high with the richest 20 percent consuming 56.1 percent of total consumption and the poorest 20 percent consuming only 4.9 percent. The Gini index[9] is 50.3 which is one of the highest in the Southern African Development Community (SADC) Region. Inequality appears to be increasing as the poor become even more marginalised. Malawi's economy is highly indebted with an external debt of US$3.23 billion. The economy is heavily aid-dependent (but development assistance is falling) while foreign direct investment (FDI) accounted for only 0.1 percent of GDP in 2002 (EIU, 2004). Total external aid was US$377 million in 2002 representing US$31.8 per capita, down from US$446.8 million in 1999 (EIU, 2004). Aid as a proportion of GDP has declined from 26.8 percent in 1990 to 19.8 percent in 2002 (UNDP, 2004).

Malawi is largely a rural economy. Nearly 85 percent of the population lives in the rural areas and only 10 percent of the population is engaged in formal sector employment. Agriculture accounts for 33 percent of the country's GDP.[10] The continuous cropping of the same land has led to a decline in soil fertility, environmental degradation and stagnation in agricultural productivity. At least 55 percent of the rural population are food insecure even in years of above average harvests.

Agriculture contributes more than 90 percent of foreign exchange earnings – mainly from tobacco which accounts for more than 60 percent (with tea, sugar and cotton accounting for the balance). Prospects for export diversification remain limited and external transport costs are very high. In fact, export concentration has increased over recent years, making the economy very vulnerable to exogenous shocks such as collapsing commodity prices and the vagaries of climate such as drought and localised floods. The economy is also highly dependent on imported fuel and inputs for both the agricultural and small manufacturing sector, increasing the economy's vulnerability to exogenous factors which are outside national policy makers' control (Harrigan, 2001).

Agriculture in Malawi is highly dualistic. Eighty-four percent of agricultural production comes from approximately 2 million smallholder households who cultivate using one hectare of land. Maize is the principal food crop, with cassava, sweet potatoes and drought-resistant grains as secondary food crops. Only one-third of smallholders cultivate any cash crops; burley tobacco is the major cash crop, with cotton, paprika and groundnuts as secondary cash crops. Approximately 30,000 large-scale farmers (known locally as estates) cultivate 1.1 million hectares of land and produce about one-third of burley tobacco, flue-cured tobacco, coffee, sugar cane and tea.

The fisheries sector directly employs about 57,854 fishers and indirectly employs about 300,000 people who are involved in fish processing, fish marketing, boat building and engine repair. Furthermore, around 1.6 million people in lakeshore communities (about 10 percent of the Malawian population) are supported by the fishing industry. The fisheries sector contributes around 4 percent to GDP and total fish catches were around 46,000 metric tonnes in 2003 (Malawi Ministry of Economic Planning and Development, 2005).

Manufacturing has been in steady but relentless decline for the past decade to the extent that a crisis point has been reached (Ministry of Economic Planning and Development, 2003). The country's industries consist mainly of agricultural processing, textiles and the production of clothing and footwear, and building and construction materials. Manufacturing accounts for roughly 85 percent of industrial activity and one-quarter of industrial output is exported. There has been little new investment and considerable disinvestment due to the difficult conditions for businesses and manufacturers.

Key constraints to private sector development include poor macro-economic conditions and instability, weaknesses in the legal and regulatory environment, weaknesses in the infrastructure that supports the economy, and poor dialogue and cooperation between the public and private sectors. Malawi is largely uncompetitive in the regional market, with unsatisfactory transport infrastructure – including poor access to ports, limited air links and rail capacity, and poor roads. Utilities, including electricity, water and communications are unreliable and expensive. Insecurity and theft deters investment and trade. The HIV/AIDS pandemic has a major impact on private sector development through losses of skilled technical and managerial staff.

Gross fixed investment has fallen from about 14 percent of GDP in the early 1990s to only 10 percent of GDP in 2001. Private investment has been only around 2–3 percent of GDP; the rest is public investment directed towards health, education and rural roads and is mainly financed through external aid. Domestic savings at 4 percent are very low compared with 16.6 percent average for sub-Saharan Africa as a whole. Most of the domestic savings are private, with government savings either low or negative (World Bank, 2003).

Malawi has received support from the international financial institutions to finance structural reform programmes. Although Malawi borrows on concessional terms, the debt stock has increased more rapidly than exports or GDP, jeopardising Malawi's credit-worthiness. At the end of 2001, total external debts amounted to US$3.23 billion compared with US$1.6 billion in 1990. Although Malawi has reduced its bilateral debt through Paris and the London Club rescheduling, this did not have a significant impact on the country's overall debt stock (mainly owed to multi-lateral creditors). The various debt ratios are still above critical levels. Malawi's debt burden drains foreign exchange, diverts budgetary expenditure from priority social sectors, and widens the budget and balance-of-payments financing gap. Malawi was not one of the 18 countries that received total debt cancellation in 2005. It may be eligible for debt cancellation in 2006 if it continues to strengthen macro-economic management and reaches the decision point for Highly Indebted Poor Country (HIPC).

In addition to external debt, Malawi has a very high rate of domestic debt as the Malawi government has consistently spent more than revenues and grants. The government had to resort to borrowing from the domestic market to finance the fiscal deficit. Public finances went out of control from 2001 to 2004. This reflected the deterioration in commitment to fiscal discipline during recent election campaigns, and the

Table 1.2   Key macro-economic indicators: 1994–2003

	1994	1995	1996	1997	1998	1999	2000	2001	2002	2003
GDP annual growth rate (1994 factor cost) (%)		13.8	10.0	6.6	1.1	3.5	0.2	–4.1	1.8	4.4 (Nov)
Average annual inflation (%)	34.7	83.1	37.7	9.1	29.8	44.8	29.6	22.9	14.8	10.7
Interest rates (lending) (%)	31.0	47.3	45.3	28.3	37.7	53.6	53.6	45.0	45.0	45.0
Average exchange rate (MWK to US$)	8.7	15.3	15.3	16.4	31.1	46	80	67.3	87.3	109

Source: www.nso.malawi.net

cost of external borrowing to finance maize imports and maize subsidies during the 2002 Food Crisis. As a result, domestic debts increased from MK9.5 billion at the end of 2001 to MK54.5 billion early in 2004. Interest on domestic debts accounted for almost 10 percent of the national budget (Whitworth, 2004). The new government also inherited almost MK10 billion in arrears to the private sector. While the new government has strengthened fiscal discipline and stayed within budget during the 2004–2005 financial year (Malawi Ministry of Finance, 2005), it was only able to retire MK2.5 billion of domestic debt and MK2 billion from that owed to the private sector.

Poverty and powerlessness in Malawi

Malawi needs to average 6 percent average annual GDP growth rates in order to make any impact on poverty. These rates were only achieved in the early years of multi-party democracy. The economy presently suffers from high inflation (mainly driven by high levels of government borrowing), very high interest rates (deterring private sector investment), and exchange rate depreciation (making essential imported items such as fuel and fertilisers very expensive). In addition, the investments in education, health and agriculture needed to address the underlying causes of poverty are held back by other calls on the budget.

The total Government budget has averaged US$527 million per annum between 1998/99 and 2003/04. In 2004, total expenditure was US$706 million for a population of approximately 12 million. This works out to a meagre US$58.8 per capita. An analysis of actual expenditure in the 2003/04 Government Budget shows how difficult it is to find funds to pay for services needed by the growing population. Of the total expenditure of US$706.1 million the public sector wage bill accounted for US$111.2 million or 15.7 percent of total expenditure. Interest payments on external debts accounted for US$25.3 million or 3.6 percent of expenditure. Interest payments on domestic debts accounted for US$156.4 million or 22.1 percent of the budget. Pensions, gratuities and transfers to the Malawi Revenue Authority accounted for US$38.8 million or 3.9 percent of expenditure. Protected poverty expenditure – other recurrent transactions (PPE-ORT) representing pro-poor expenditure in core areas of poverty reduction (health, agriculture, education and water and sanitation) accounts for only US$47 million or 6.7 percent of the overall budget. The total discretionary budget is US$378.8 million or 53.6 percent of the overall budget. This represents US$31.56 per capita for the provision of all services.

Such a tiny sum is clearly inadequate to provide any reasonable services. This is why it is so difficult to increase the quality of health or education services, to finance essential investments in agriculture and food security, or to maintain essential infrastructure and state functions (defence, the police, the judiciary, the legislature and watchdog institutions). This is the poverty trap in which Malawi finds itself entangled.

Table 1.3   Analysis of the 2003–2004 government budget

	USD Millions	% of GDP	% of expenditure
Total Revenue or Grants	591.3	36.0	
Total Expenditure	706.1	43.0	
Donor Funded Expenditure	155.5	9.5	
Total Domestic Expenditure	550.6	33.6	
Interest Domestic	156.4	9.5	22.1
Interest Foreign	25.3	1.5	3.6
PPE ORT	47.0	2.9	6.7
Wages Total	111.2	6.8	15.7
Pension & Gratuities	18.1	1.1	2.6
Transfers to MRA	20.7	2.9	1.3
Maize Operations	0	0	0.0
Non discretionary Exp	378.8	23.1	53.6
Discretionary expenditure	164.1	10.5	23.2
Overall Fiscal Balance	–114.8	–7.0	
Domestic Debt Stock	491.8	30	
Normal GDP	1,641	100	

Source: Analysis of Government Budget Documents and Whitworth (2004)

The lack of resources translates down to the personal level. As the Millennium Commission (2005) notes 'when individuals and whole economies lack the most basic infrastructure, health services and education they remain trapped in poverty.' Poverty in Malawi is widespread, deep and severe. The majority of the population fail to receive basic nutritional requirements. What little income Malawians have is largely spent on food just to survive.[11] In a country where per capita income is US\$177 and where there has been virtually no growth in per capita incomes for the past 30 years, the poor in Malawi truly represent the poorest of the poor.

However, stark numbers on income and income inequality fail to capture the reality of lives lived in desperate, grinding poverty. They do not show the houses where families sleep on the floor, the houses which lack even the most basic amenities of chairs and cooking pots, the households where an old and tired grandmother struggles to care for eight orphans or the homes where the father lies dying of AIDS without medical treatment. There are the mothers who struggle to care for their dying husbands, till the soil and feed the family. Worse still, there are the households where a 12-year old child tries to care for her younger brothers and sisters alone. Children are sick from diarrhoea, pneumonia and malaria, and permanently stunted by persistent malnutrition. There are funerals every day in every community.

Communities living in villages or slums in Africa understand poverty. In Malawi 'well-being' is defined as security of livelihood (agriculture, fisheries or employment) and access to the basic necessities of life, shelter, food, security and health care. Such households have regular and reliable sources of income so that they can withstand crises such as famine and disease. They have some peace of mind and are not living in a state of perpetual anxiety (World Bank, 1999). The burden of ill-health falls most heavily on the poor as these households have no food. In rural areas the key concern is how to produce sufficient quantities of food and to make some income from selling crops or from off-farm employment. By contrast, 'ill-being' is defined as 'no peace of mind and no money to pay for transport or medical care'. Poor communities identify lack of food security, limited employment opportunities, rising food prices, lack of access to basic amenities (including clean water) and disease as the key causes of poverty.

In urban areas, the key factor is access to secure employment. Without strong economic growth, formal and informal sector employment will not keep pace with population growth. With retrenchment in government, public sector employment shrinks. Poor access to family planning services and an increase in rural-urban migration exacerbates the problem of over-population in urban areas. As people become unemployed, they build up unsustainable levels of debt because of responsibilities to the extended family. At worst, when rental arrears build up and people are about to be forced out of the slum dwellings that are their homes, young men may turn to crime, and women to transactional sex, as the only viable survival strategy. But such a strategy all too often proves fatal as men are subjected to the justice of the streets and women can contract HIV.

Poverty in rural areas is possibly more picturesque but no less severe. Land pressure and environmental challenges become more acute every year. Households are forced to cultivate more marginal land exacerbating environmental degradation. Soil fertility declines and the vast majority of smallholder farmers are unable to afford fertilisers. Perpetual hunger is cited as a major problem. Children are often withdrawn from school during the 'hunger season' which is normally the three months prior to harvest. Poverty also fuels early marriage by girls as a survival mechanism. Again, as poverty increases, women are forced into transactional sex in order to feed the family. Theft and insecurity is a growing problem in rural areas and this also undermines investment and growth.

Issues of gender inequality and domestic violence are major concerns of the poor. 'Women will continue to he major victims because culture marginalizes them' (World Bank, 1999). Gender inequality fuels the AIDS pandemic because women are unable either to refuse sex or to negotiate safe sex. Women are very vulnerable because they are most likely to be illiterate and, as a consequence, have limited access to employment or credit. Violence against women within the household takes many forms – including being over-worked, beaten, verbally abused, being kicked out of the home, or forced to have sex. Gender-based violence has increased over the last 10 years and women who are the victims of domestic violence or rape within marriage have little recourse to the law.

In Malawi, as elsewhere in the world, the poorer the household, the less able it is to recover from a crisis. The most serious crisis is the death of the breadwinner. Even where the deceased has left some property or investments, these rarely last long as the family will often have to sell these to survive or pay debts incurred due to ill-health or funeral expenses. This problem is often compounded by 'property grabbing' where relatives of the deceased take all the property, leaving the widow and children destitute. Children are likely to be withdrawn from school, compromising their future chances of breaking out of poverty.

Conclusion

This grim tale documents how a poor, beautiful country was exploited by the slave trade and then colonised by the British. The best land was extracted for the colonial plantation economy while smallholders focused on subsistence production. The first President Dr Hastings Kamuzu Banda became increasingly authoritarian and suppressed all opposition to one-party rule. The post-independence agricultural strategy continued to favour the estate subsector at the expense of the smallholder subsector leading to an unsustainable growth strategy. Following an economic crisis at the end of the 1970s, economic policy was dominated by the World Bank and International Monetary Fund during the 1980s. Structural adjustment policies also failed to generate sustained economic growth or address underlying constraints to the attainment of food security. As the population became more impoverished and the geopolitical situation changed, Malawi made a peaceful transition to multi-party democracy in 1994. The new Government focused on private sector growth and liberalisation. It also prioritised the social sectors, introducing free primary education, increasing the health budget and developing institutions to promote democratic consolidation. The strategy initially led to growth, but this was undermined by recurrent food crises. In addition, the attempt to amend the Constitution to allow a third presidential term fuelled political instability and undermined macro-economic stability. Despite the efforts to transform the economy, food security became increasingly precarious and there has not been any significant economic diversification. A new Government was elected in 2004. In spite of its attempts to strengthen macro-economic management and address corruption, it still lacks the resources to increase the quality of services and is increasingly indebted. Malawi is still shackled with an external debt of US$3.23 billion which eats into the very small sums that are needed to develop the country. The combination of all these factors results in widespread, deep and pervasive poverty.

Notes

1. Other African countries with comparable population densities do not experience the monomodal rainfall pattern which further constrains Malawi's agricultural potential.
2. Population growth was rapid, averaging around 3 percent per annum. Twenty years after independence, the population had almost doubled to 6.8 million (Pryor, 1988). The present population of Malawi is estimated at 12 million. Malawi continues to have one of the highest fertility rates in the World – estimated at six children per woman (National Statistical Office DHS, 2005).

3. The decision of Southern Rhodesia (now Zimbabwe) to declare illegal independence from Britain provided a boost to this policy. Malawi entered the critical tobacco export market (now officially closed to Rhodesia due to UN trade sanctions) with a major competitor operating at a considerable disadvantage.

4. Tobacco and tea prices plummeted and oil-based imports like fuel and fertiliser increased in price.

5. By the end of the 1980s, some 700,000 hectares of land had been transferred from the customary (smallholder) sector to the leasehold (estate) subsector. The principal beneficiaries of this land transfer were members of the political elite, party functionaries and richer smallholders. The land transferred to the estate subsector was not used efficiently and a significant part of the land remained underutilised due in part to low land rents (Cross, 2002).

6. Flint, or 'hard' maize stores better and processes better under smallholder conditions. Most improved varieties of maize available were of the soft, dent type which was better suited to the harvesting and storage methods employed by estates (and derived from materials developed for large-scale farmers in Zimbabwe).

7. The Human Development Index focuses on three measurable dimensions of human development: a healthy life, education and a decent standard of living. Thus it combines measures of life expectancy, school enrolment, literacy and income.

8. The countries that perform worse than Malawi on the Human Development Index (HDI) include Angola, Chad, the Democratic Republic of Congo, the Central African Republic, Ethiopia, Mozambique, Guinea-Bissau, Burundi, Mali, Burkina Faso, Niger and Sierra Leone.

9. The Gini index measures inequality over the entire distribution of income or consumption. A value of 0 represents perfect equality and a value of 100 represents perfect inequality.

10. Manufacturing accounts for 12 percent and the distribution sector 22 percent. Furthermore, the distribution sector is mainly trading or retailing activities, most of which are based in or linked to the rural economy (World Bank, 2003).

11. Overall levels of income are exceptionally low with average daily per capita incomes of US$0.14. Ultra-poor households have daily per capita incomes of US$0.04 and poor households' per capita incomes of US$0.05. The MDG target of US$1.00 per capita per day would be wealth indeed.

Bibliography

Christiansen R. and Kydd J. (1987) 'Malawi's Agricultural Export Strategy and Implications for Income Distribution', United States Department of Agriculture, Economic Research Service.

Cross S. (2002) 'Customary Land Tenure, Taxes and Services Delivery in Rural Malawi: A Review of Institutional Features of Rural Livelihoods', Centre for Development Studies, University of East Anglia.

Economist Intelligence Unit (EIU) (2004) 'Malawi: Country Report'.

Episcopal Conference of Malawi (1992) 'Living our Faith: A Pastoral Letter of the Catholic Bishops of Malawi', Balaka: Montfort Press.

Harrigan J. (2001) 'From Dictatorship to Democracy: Economic Policy in Malawi 1964–2000', Hampshire, England: Ashgate Press.

Harrigan J. (2003) 'U Turns and Full Circles: Two Decades of Agricultural Reform in Malawi: 1964 to 2000', *World Development* 31 (5), 847–63.

Harrigan, J., (2005) 'Donor Policies on Food Security and Starter Pack'. In Levy S. (ed.) 'Starter Packs: A Strategy to Fight Hunger in Developing and Transitional Countries', CAB International, Wallingford.

Kydd J. and Christiansen R. (1982) 'Structural Change in Malawi since Independence: Consequences of a Development Strategy based on Large Scale Agriculture', World Development, 10 (5), 355–75.

Malawi Government, Ministry of Finance (2005) 'Budget Statement', Lilongwe, Malawi.

Malawi Government, Ministry of Economic Planning and Development and National Action Group (2003) 'A Growth Strategy for Malawi: Part One, Overview and Macro-Economic Environment Strategy', Lilongwe, Malawi.

Malawi Ministry of Economic Planning and Development (2005) 'Economic Report 2005', Government Printer, Lilongwe, Malawi.

Malawi Government, Office of the Vice President (1999) 'Sectoral Report on Macro-Economic Policy', Lilongwe, Malawi.

Office of the Vice President (1999) 'Policy Analysis Initiative: Sectoral Report on Macro Economic Policy', Lilongwe, Malawi.

Pryor F. (1988) 'Income Distribution and Economic Development in Malawi: Some Historical Statistics', World Bank Discussion Papers, No. 36, Washington, DC.

Reich Verlag H. (1984) 'Malawi: The Warm Heart of Africa', Munich, Germany.

Whitworth A. (2004) 'Malawi's Fiscal Crisis: A Donor Perspective', Department for International Development, Lilongwe, Malawi.

World Health Organization (2005) 'World Health Report 2005: Make Every Mother and Child Count', World Health Organization, Geneva.

UNDP (2004) 'Human Development Report: Cultural Liberty in Today's Diverse World', United Nations, New York.

United Nations Millennium Development Project (2005) 'Investing in Development: A Practical Plan to Achieve the Millennium Development Goals', Millennium Project, New York.

World Bank (1999) 'Consultations with the Poor', World Bank Office, Lilongwe, Malawi.

World Bank (2003) 'Malawi Country Economic Memorandum: Policies for Accelerating Growth', Report No. 25293 MAI, World Bank, Washington DC.

2
Health and Disease in Malawi

Anne Conroy

Health and poverty

Freedom including 'the liberty of political participation or the opportunity to receive basic education or health care are constituent components of development' (Sen, 1999). The anguish of disease and premature death makes disease control a central preoccupation in all societies, and has motivated the inclusion of health among the basic human rights enshrined in international law (Attaran, 2001). Good health is widely acknowledged to be a critical factor in poverty reduction and economic development. The WHO Commission on Macro-Economics and Health argued that societies with a heavy burden of disease tend to experience a multiplicity of severe impediments to economic progress. Conversely, several of the great 'take-offs' in economic history were supported by important breakthroughs in public health, disease control and improved nutritional intake. Disease reduces the annual incomes of society, the lifetime incomes of individuals and prospects for economic growth. A concerted attack against diseases, therefore, directly serves to reduce poverty (World Health Organization, 2001).

The Millennium Development Goals (MDGs), agreed by the world's heads of government at the Millennium summit in 2000, focus on poverty reduction. The health-related goals underscore the linkage between overall poverty alleviation and investments in health. MDG Health targets include:

- A reduction in child mortality by two-thirds of the 1990 level by 2015,
- A reduction in maternal mortality by three-quarters of the 1990 level by 2015, and
- An end in the rise of HIV/AIDS and other major prevalent diseases by 2015 at the latest.

Addressing the AIDS pandemic is not only crucial for poverty alleviation, it is also central to achieving international security. The World
Health Organization (2001) argues that 'the evidence is stark: disease
breeds instability in poor countries which rebounds on the wealthy
countries as well'. A high infant mortality rate was recently found to be
one of the main predictors of subsequent state collapse through coups,
civil wars, and other unconstitutional changes in regime (State Failure
Task Force, 1999). Intelligence studies have stressed the strategic
significance of controlling worldwide infectious diseases including
AIDS (National Intelligence Council, 2000). While global pledges to
address the AIDS and health crisis are made repeatedly at international
conferences, the battle will be won or lost at the ground level. We,
therefore, return to Malawi to see how these good intentions play out
in reality.

Health indicators in Malawi

The major causes of mortality and morbidity in Malawi are mainly
preventable; with malaria accounting for 40 percent of all outpatient
visits in Malawi, 40 percent of hospitalisation for the under-fives and
18 percent of inpatient deaths. Anemia, most of which is attributed to
malaria, is estimated to be responsible for about 53 percent of all
under-five hospitalisation and 23 percent of all hospital deaths in children under five. Diarrhoeal diseases (including cholera) and acute respiratory infections contribute significantly to outpatient visits.

Life expectancy in Malawi has declined to less that 40 years, largely
due to the generalised AIDS pandemic where over 14 percent of the
adult population (aged between 15 and 49) are HIV-positive (National
AIDS Commission, 2004). HIV-related conditions account for over
40 percent of all inpatient admissions. Sexually transmitted infections
are also of growing public health concern. Despite the concerted efforts
of the Ministry of Health and its partners, tuberculosis (once thought
to be on the decline) has increased five-fold in the past few years
(Ministry of Health, 2004). The major challenge to the tuberculosis
control programme is the AIDS pandemic which continues to fuel the
number of TB cases and contributes to high mortality among TB
patients.

On the positive side, despite the very high disease burden, infant
and childhood mortality rates are declining. The infant mortality rate
has declined from 104 per 1000 in 1990–1994 to 76 per thousand in
2000–2004. The under-five mortality rate has also declined from

190 per 1000 to 133 per 1000 over the same period (National Statistical Office, 2005). Fertility rates have declined modestly – from 7.6 in 1984 to 6.7 in 1992 and to 6.3 in 2000. The fertility rate is now estimated at 6.0 (implying that a Malawian woman would have six children in her lifetime). The total fertility rate is higher for rural (6.4) than urban areas (4.2). Fertility is also higher among women in the younger age groups (National Statistical Office, 2005). More adults are using contraceptives. The contraceptive prevalence rate is now 33 percent among married women – an increase from 7 percent in 1992.

Key causes of morbidity

Malaria

Malaria in Africa is particularly intractable. Africa's malaria mosquitoes almost exclusively feed on humans, enhancing human-to-human transmission. When this factor is combined with high year-round temperatures, and sufficient precipitation to allow mosquito breeding throughout much of the year, it is not surprising that Africa is the global epicentre of malaria. The situation has worsened markedly in the past decade, with the spread of resistant strains of malaria, and the breakdown of public health systems in the face of unrelenting poverty, the HIV/AIDS pandemic and civil conflict (Sachs, 2005). It is estimated that there are six million episodes of adult malaria per annum and 9.7 million episodes of malaria amongst children. Malaria is responsible for almost 40 percent of deaths in children aged less than two years of age (Ministry of Health, 2002).

Malaria contributes directly to poverty. With the start of the season's rains, farmers have to plant their crops on time. Every week's delay in planting means a significantly smaller harvest. But the rains also bring a new hatching of mosquitoes – adults and children alike fall prey to malaria. Sick people (and mothers caring for sick children) cannot do the heavy work of preparing the land, planting, and weeding. Poor crop husbandry at the start of the season causes a poor harvest at the end of the season. Families go hungry and slide inexorably into poverty.

The impact of malaria is further complicated by the escalating HIV pandemic. Pregnant women who are HIV-positive have a higher density of peripheral and placental parasitaemia. In addition to its vast health impact, malaria also exacts a high economic cost – directly in terms of prevention and treatment of the disease, and indirectly due to the potential loss of income for work days lost. The total cost of malaria to the average Malawian household is estimated to be US$35 per annum or 22 percent of household income. For every low-income household (and these comprise 40 percent of all Malawian households), the annual cost of malaria is nearly US$20 or 32 percent of household income (Ministry of Health and Population, 2002).

Malawi's health services are reeling under the heavy burden of malaria. The Malawi Government has embraced the Roll Back Malaria initiative launched in 1998 to address the global problem of malaria. It is fully committed to achieve the programme's overall goal and is on track to meet the Abuja target of 60 percent bed net coverage by the end of 2005. Under the malaria programme, over 3 million bed nets have been distributed from health facilities over the last three years. Today, it is estimated that 55 percent of under-fives and 50 percent of pregnant women are sleeping under insecticide-treated nets. A successful re-treatment campaign has resulted in 61 percent of used nets retreated in 2003 and 73 percent of used nets retreated in 2004. There has also been reasonable progress in providing chemoprophylaxis during pregnancy. Coverage is over 60 percent even among very poor women (DFID, 2005a). The progress in providing insecticide-treated nets and treatment during pregnancy has undoubtedly contributed to the decline in infant and under-five mortality reported above.

Tuberculosis

Malawi has one of the highest incidences of tuberculosis (TB) in sub-Saharan Africa, in line with the high HIV prevalence. The number of TB cases per 100,000 of population has increased from 95 in 1987 to 211 in 1999. The tuberculosis case notification increased from 7581 in 1987 to 24,936 in 1999. The AIDS pandemic is driving the increase in cases of tuberculosis. Seventy-seven percent of TB patients are HIV-positive. Since 2000, the number of reported cases of tuberculosis has increased at a lower rate than in the 1990s. In 2000, 24,846 cases registered for treatment, and this grew gradually to a case notification of 28,234 in 2003 (DFID, 2005b). Tuberculosis is a debilitating and potentially fatal disease. The management of tuberculosis requires a prolonged 8-month course of treatment using expensive drugs. These are delivered free through the National Tuberculosis Control Programme. Having started treatment, there is a risk that a patient will fail to complete the full course. Failure to comply can lead to a recurrence of the disease in the patient, transmission to family members and emergence of drug resistance.

The National TB Programme (NTP) has maintained good cure rates; with 70 percent of patients cured despite high mortality rates due to

HIV/AIDS (19 percent) (DFID, 2005b). Malawi was one of the first countries in the world to introduce the Directly Observed Treatment Supervised (DOTS) Programme and this programme now covers 100 percent of Government health facilities, as well as many private sector health facilities. There has been an uninterrupted supply of drugs and reagents for several years and more effective treatment regimes have been introduced. Laboratory diagnosis has been decentralised, the needy treated, and staff and the public have been educated in tuberculosis. The areas worst affected by TB are prisons, overcrowded urban areas, and boarding schools where the DOTS Programme needs further development. It will also be important to emphasise earlier identification of TB cases (especially among the poorest members of the community), the integration of services for TB and HIV, and the prevention of multi-drug resistant TB. But although TB diagnosis and treatment is provided free at the point of delivery, TB patients still face economic and social barriers in accessing healthcare. Early detection of TB cases remains a challenge for the NTP.

Maternal mortality

For both mother and baby, childbirth can be the most dangerous moment in life. Complications of childbirth claim an estimated 529,000 maternal deaths worldwide every year. A maternal death is a death from a pregnancy-related complication occurring throughout pregnancy, labour, childbirth and the post-partum period up to the 42nd day after birth (World Health Organization, 2005). Such deaths can occur suddenly and unpredictably. The tragedy is that almost all of these deaths (80 percent) are preventable and avoidable. While many other health indicators have improved in the developing world over the last decades, maternal mortality and morbidity continue to take a high toll. Of the 136 million women that give birth every year, some 20 million experience pregnancy-related illness (World Health Organization, 2005).

The global maternal mortality rate (MMR) is 400 maternal deaths for every 100,000 live births. Where nothing is done to avert maternal death, 'natural' mortality is around 1000–1500 per 100,000 live births[1] (World Health Organization, 2005). The 2005 MMR for Malawi as published by the World Health Organization (2005) is a staggering 1800 per 100,000 births – up from 620 in 1996 (Meguid *et al.*, 2005). By comparison, the MMR rates for Tanzania is 1500, 750 in Zambia and 1000 in Mozambique. Countries with similar MMR rates as Malawi are those recently affected by conflicts such as Afghanistan (1900), Angola (1700), and Sierra Leone (2000) (World Health Organization, 2005). The direct causes of maternal mortality include haemorrhage (33 percent), sepsis (33 percent), obstructed labour and ruptured uterus (20 percent), eclampsia (12 percent), and ectopic pregnancy (2 percent) (Ministry of Health, 2005). Indirect causes include underlying diseases such as HIV/AIDS, malaria and anaemia.

The key reason for the high rate of maternal mortality in Malawi is the lack of access to basic emergency obstetric services.[2] While Malawi has invested in *comprehensive* emergency obstetric care services (double the WHO recommendation), it has only 2 percent of the recommended number of *basic* emergency obstetric care services (Ministry of Health, 2005). Consequently, only 18 percent of women in Malawi have access to basic emergency obstetric services compared with the World Health Organization recommendation of 100 percent. Maternal deaths in Malawi are the result of wrong diagnosis (11 percent of deaths), delay in starting treatment (19 percent of deaths), wrong treatment (16 percent), and lack of blood for blood transfusion (WHO, 2005). WHO (2005) cites three factors, all linked to the deterioration of the health workforce:

- A sharp proportional increase in the number of deaths due to HIV/AIDS.
- Fewer mothers giving birth in health facilities.
- Deterioration in the quality of care within health facilities.

The critical lack of skilled medical staff at the front-line health centres undermines the Malawi Government's ability to provide the most basic emergency obstetric care. The Ministry of Health assessed 166 health facilities (62 in the Christian Health Association of Malawi and 104 in the Ministry of Health) (Ministry of Health, 2005). In the Ministry of Health facilities, the vacancy rate for specialist doctors was 82 percent, for nursing officers 77.4 percent, for nursing sisters 87.8 percent, for less trained nurses 42 percent, for laboratory technicians 60 percent, and for environmental and health officers 70 to 80 percent. In the Christian Health Association of Malawi (CHAM), vacancies are particularly high for medical officers and medical assistants (40 percent), combined nursing cadres (53 percent) and pharmacy and laboratory technicians around 90 percent. The Ministry of Health (2005) notes that:

At these rates of shortages, the Malawian health service is virtually paralysed.

There are also severe resource constraints throughout the health system. Only 62 percent of the health centres and 40 percent of the hospitals had adequate numbers of beds. Only 50 percent of health centres had adequate stocks of antibiotics, 26 percent of health centres had oxytocic drugs (required to prevent bleeding) and only 58 percent of hospitals had anti-convulsant drugs to prevent pre-eclampsia. Only 9 percent of health centres and 35 percent of hospitals had prenatal analgesics in their delivery room and 27 percent in their operating theatres. Basic equipment was present in most health facilities, but 39 percent of hospitals did not have vacuum extractors. Even where the required equipment was present, it was insufficient for the caseload.

In addition to human resource constraints and the shortage of essential equipment and supplies, the Ministry of Health (2005) noted weak community participation and involvement, inadequate coordination mechanisms among partners and stakeholders, harmful social and cultural beliefs and practices, poor monitoring, supervision and evaluation, and low-quality maternal health care services.

Malawi's obstetricians ask:

> How can we still have a good night's sleep after a day in any health facility in Malawi? How can we live with the knowledge that our women are dying an entirely preventable death in 2005 at a scale that has not been seen in Europe since medieval times? ... Technologically we have advanced and measured up with the more developed countries. We have cell phones, TV screens, the latest brands of cars, refrigerators, computers and all that, right here in Malawi, but when it comes to preventing mothers from dying unnecessarily, we are in the dark ages (Meguid *et al.*, 2005).

Malnutrition

The main causes of under-five mortality are infectious diseases; including malaria, respiratory infections, diarrhoea, measles and neo-natal death. Severe and moderate malnutrition is a contributory factor in more than 50 percent of child deaths. Malawi's nutritional indicators are exceptionally poor. There has been virtually no improvement in Malawi's nutritional indicators for the past three decades. Forty-eight percent of children under five are stunted, with 22 percent of children severely stunted (National Statistical Office, 2005). Six percent of children are wasted, and 1 percent severely wasted. Wasting is most common during the period of 6–23 months of age (National Economic Council, 2000). This suggests that children are most vulnerable during the weaning period and that complementary feeding practices during weaning are inadequate. Furthermore, 25 percent of children under five are underweight, which reflects stunting, wasting or both. Peak levels of low weight for age occur during the second year. Boys and girls are at equal risk of being underweight. The 1992 and 2000 Demographic and Health Surveys (DHSs) show that malnutrition is worst in the rural areas. The 2000 DHS reveals that 51.2 percent of children are stunted[3] and 27.3 percent of children underweight in the rural areas compared with 25.4 percent stunted and 12.8 percent underweight in urban areas (Mtimuni, 2004).These patterns are a direct consequence of widespread, household food insecurity. The children affected will never achieve their potential as the effects of chronic malnutrition in childhood are irreversible.

Gillespie and Haddad (2003) note that malnutrition undermines the achievement of the major Millennium Development Goals by eroding human capital, reducing resilience to shocks, and constraining productivity. Malnutrition which is manifest in growth failure, cognitive underdevelopment, immune impairment and hence morbidity and death, is caused by inadequate dietary intake, ill-health or both. Often these two factors interact in a negative synergy to precipitate or worsen malnutrition in an individual. Malnutrition reduces a child's ability to learn by reducing interaction and exploration. Such children are often too weak to go to school or may drop out earlier. Malnutrition is directly or indirectly associated with 60 percent of all child mortality and is the main contributor to the burden of disease in the developing world (Ezzati *et al.*, 2002).

Malnutrition is a process with consequences that may extend, not only into later life, but also into future generations. The process of being malnourished often starts in utero and may last, particularly for girls and women throughout the life cycle (Gillespie and Haddad, 2003). The effects of malnourishment on a foetus (particularly for a girl) can be seen throughout the life cycle and into future generations. A stunted young girl is likely to become a stunted adolescent and later a stunted woman increasing the chances that her own children will be stunted. Malnutrition compromises maternal health and is associated with most of the major risk factors for maternal mortality – including small pelvis and obstructed labour (Gillespie and Haddad, 2003).

Malnutrition and infection are intertwined in a vicious cycle as malnutrition lowers the body's ability to resist infection and leads to longer, more severe and more frequent bouts of illness. Infections cause appetite loss, malabsorption, metabolic and behavioural changes that affect feeding practices thus depleting body nutrient stores. Children who are severely underweight may be up to eight times more likely to die within the following year compared to children of normal weight for age. Moderate underweight increases mortality risk by a factor of five times while mild underweight doubles it. Low birth weight babies (less than 2.5 kilograms) are at a significantly higher risk of dying than infants of average weight (Gillespie and Haddad, 2003).

Malnutrition is severe in Malawi because the great majority of the population cannot afford to eat enough even in normal years. The situation worsens during recurrent food crises that serve to undermine public health and prospects for poverty alleviation. Data on food consumption shows that the majority of the population consumes fewer calories than is required for normal, healthy development. Nationally, Malawians consume 1818 calories per day. Poor households (65 percent of the population) consume on average 1428 calories per day. Households in the ultra-poor category consume only 1165 calories per day – even in normal years (National Economic Council, 2000).

In calorie terms, the Malawian diet is dominated by cereals (74 percent) with pulses and nuts accounting for 7.8 percent, roots and tubers 5.4 percent and sugar products 5.3 percent. Animal and dairy produce account for 1.7 percent of calories while fish contributes 1.5 percent. The poorer the household, the more the diet is dominated by cereals. In ultra-poor households, cereals account for 82 percent of calories consumed. Urban diets are less dominated by cereals with sugar and oil products accounting for almost 20 percent (National Economic Council, 2000).

Income figures are staggeringly low. Average daily per capita cash incomes are US$0.14. When expenditures are analysed, 61.5 percent of incomes are spent on food, 7.5 percent on utilities and housing, and 6.6 percent on clothes and the balance on services including health. Ultra-poor households spend 78 percent of their income on food, the poor 76 percent and non-poor households 55 percent (National Economic Council, 2000). The struggle for food and survival dominates life in Malawi. The vast majority of the population fails to meet their most basic subsistence requirements. There is no surplus for investment and growth. Until the majority of the population is lifted above subsistence requirements there can be no sustained growth in the economy.

Parasitic infections

Malnourished people are particularly susceptible to parasites. Parasitic infections interfere with nutrient uptake, making existing nutrient problems worse. Besides undermining nutrition, parasites play another important role in promoting infectious diseases. The immune system is continually activated and unable to ward off new infections – which may contribute to increased HIV transmission in Africa.

Schistosomaisis is one of the most significant parasitic infections in Malawi. It is a painful, debilitating, chronic parasitic disease which is commonly transmitted in water used for bathing. Schistosomaisis has a prevalence of approximately 50 percent of the population in Malawi. In some districts along the Lakeshore, the prevalence among school age children is as high as 80 percent.

Sexually-transmitted infections and HIV/AIDS

It is, unsurprisingly, difficult to get quantitative information about the extent of sexually transmitted infections (STIs). However, several recent studies suggest that the presence of untreated STIs is likely fuelling the HIV pandemic. For example, a study involving male workers at the Ntchalo sugar plantation demonstrated that the most significant risk factor for HIV infection in both the 1994 and 1998 cohorts was a reactive syphilis test (Kumwenda *et al.*, 2001).

Researchers for the Universities of Malawi, John Hopkins and Rutgers used a cross-sectional study to examine the association between bacterial vaginosis (BV) and HIV infection among women attending antenatal clinics. They found that BV was significantly associated with antenatal HIV seroconversion and post-natal seroconversion. There was a significant trend of increased risk of HIV seroconversion with increasing severity of vaginal disturbance among both antenatal and post-natal women (Sutcliffe *et al.*, 1998).

The management and treatment of STIs is a core strategy for reducing transmission of HIV. The probability of transmitting HIV from a single act of intercourse increases by up to five times in the presence of a STI (Office of the Vice President, 1999). Not only are the kinds of STIs in Africa more likely to be co-factors for HIV infection, they are more likely to go undetected and untreated – increasing the likelihood of transmission of an ulcerative STI and HIV. In women, some of the symptoms of an untreated STI may be mistaken for symptoms of pregnancy, or for the discomfort associated with a parasitic infection.

Malawians face problems in terms of access to drugs and syndromic[4] management of STIs. Drugs may not be available at health centres. Young people may not get access to sexual and reproductive health services. The Reproductive Health Unit of the Ministry is responsible for the management and treatment of STIs, which need to be integrated at all levels of the health services: central referral hospital, district hospital and health facility. However, progress in meeting this goal is slow, largely because adequate resources (both human and financial) are unavailable. The stigma associated with STIs prevents men in particular from disclosing the presence of an STI to their partners or sexual network. Women may have an STI without experiencing symptoms – which then delays diagnosis and treatment. Young people often lack knowledge about STIs and are reluctant to present at health centres – possibly for fear of disapproval or because they feel that they are unable to go to the health centre on their own initiative. The silence and discrimination that surround STIs continue to be a major driver of the pandemic. The presence of untreated STIs, combined with the lack of access to health services and drugs, especially for the poor, fuels the HIV pandemic in Malawi and throughout Africa.

The HIV pandemic is a major problem, not only for its economic and development consequences, but also for its impact on the health sector. The National AIDS Commission (2004) has estimated that 900,000 Malawians are infected with HIV and 170,000 people are currently in need of anti-retroviral therapy. Less than 20 percent are currently receiving treatment funded by the Global Fund. The health sector is already overwhelmed by the AIDS pandemic as close to 50 percent of people receiving treatment in hospital are HIV-positive. The annual number of cases of tuberculosis is three times higher than it would be in the absence of the AIDS pandemic. About 500,000 pregnant women need good antenatal care, including HIV counseling and testing. About 80,000 mothers need anti-retroviral therapy to prevent vertical transmission of the virus.

Key challenges to health care in Malawi

Human resources

Malawi's health staff statistics are devastating. For example, in a population of 12 million, Malawi has only 156 physicians working in the public health sector (the Ministry of Health) and the Christian Health Association of Malawi (CHAM).[5] Most highly-trained medical staff are located in urban centres and central hospitals in the regional capitals of Blantyre, Lilongwe and Mzuzu. Of the 26 districts in the country, ten have no Ministry of Health doctor and four districts are without any doctors (Ministry of Health, 2004c).

The government policy is to provide an Essential Health Care Package (EHP)[6] to address the major health challenges. These challenges include high child mortality and morbidity, high maternal morbidity and associated mortality, and the high burden of diseases (malnutrition, vaccine preventable illnesses, malaria, tuberculosis, diarrhoea, acute respiratory infections, sexually transmitted infections, HIV/AIDS), injuries and trauma. Assuming that the health services infrastructure and human resources are available, the cost of implementing the EHP is a minimum of US$22 per capita (Ministry of Economic Planning and Development, 2004).

But human resources are severely limited. The Ministry of Health and Population (2004a) noted that 'the current situation with regard to human resources in the health sector is the most critical constraint to the delivery of health services and the health sector response to HIV/AIDS in Malawi.' The Ministry also noted that the situation with regard to human resources in the health sector had been variously described as critical, close to collapse, collapsed and heading towards a melt-down.

Malawi has attempted to address the shortage of doctors by training clinical and medical officers who effectively work as doctors and are responsible for diagnosis and treatment of the most common conditions. But many posts remain to be filled. For example, consider the situation with respect to nurses. The (less than ideal) budgeted total establishment for nurses in the public sector is 6084. Of these, only 2178 positions were filled in 2004. Qualified nurses in Malawi migrate for better pay, working conditions and training opportunities elsewhere. Of the 30 nurses that completed training in 2000 and 2001, only two entered government service. Between 1999 and 2001, 278 registered nurses migrated overseas while government trained only 258 new nurses (Aitken and Kemp, 2003). In 2002 and 2003, a total of 211 registered nurses left Malawi, with 173 leaving for the United Kingdom (Ministry of Health and Population, 2004b).

While most of the population of Malawi live in the rural areas, over 80 percent of skilled health staff operate in urban areas. Only 9 percent of current health facilities are ready to implement the EHP and many rural health centres are manned by Health Surveillance Assistants with ten weeks of training (Ministry of Health, 2004b).

Financing

National health accounts show spending on health at US$12.4 per capita. The government of Malawi financed 25 percent of health expenditure, donors accounted for 30 percent and private financing sources 45 percent (19 percent from employers contributions and 26 percent from household out of pocket expenditure (Ministry of Health, 2004b)). Although health services are provided free in public health facilities, the shortage of drugs often forces people into the private sector or CHAM in order to obtain drugs. Poor people cannot afford to pay user fees for health, and may also be excluded from health services due to high transport and other associated costs.

Although the Ministry of Health estimates that the cost of delivering the EHP is US$22 per capita, and the Macro-Economic Commission on Health estimates the cost of providing basic health care at US$34 per capita (World Health Organization, 2001), Malawi's budget can provide only US$6 to US$ 8 per capita. Although health expenditure has been relatively stable at approximately 11 percent of total expenditure (excluding interest payments) from 2001 to 2003, the amount available for health is grossly inadequate to meet needs.

The Mission designing the Sector Wide Approach (SWAP)[7] for the health sector estimated that there is a funding gap of US$156 million per annum even to implement the most rudimentary of Essential Health Care Packages. Despite the funding increases programmed both under the SWAP and for training further human resources, it is unlikely that the funding gap will be met in the short term.

Conclusion

The stark statistics of the poor health system in Malawi fail to capture the reality. Although infant and child mortality rates are falling steadily, 133 children out of every thousand still die before their fifth birthday. Malaria kills children with terrifying speed and there are funerals of children every day in every community in Malawi. Adults die or are permanently impaired by cerebral malaria, and most Malawians have several episodes of malaria every year, which is extraordinarily debilitating.

Children fail to meet their physical and intellectual potential due to chronic and severe malnutrition. Malnutrition interacts with ill-health making them far more susceptible to infections which in turn exacerbate malnutrition. There is a major burden of parasitic infections – especially schistosomaisis which may affect 50 percent of children. This is a very debilitating and painful disease, which if left untreated leads to severe complications.

Malawi's maternal mortality rate is one of the highest in the world. Only Sierra Leone and Afghanistan perform worse than Malawi on this critical indicator of human development. The high incidence of maternal mortality from preventable causes reflects the absence of basic emergency obstetric care services throughout the health system and the critical human resources constraint.

Sexually transmitted infections fuel the AIDS pandemic and pose a major public health concern. The AIDS pandemic itself threatens to overwhelm health services with 170,000 people needing immediate anti-retroviral therapy, and 80,000 mothers needing drugs to prevent vertical transmission of the virus. The AIDS pandemic has increased the number of cases of tuberculosis by a factor of three.

Malawi's health services are reeling under the burden of preventable diseases, while there is also a high incidence of trauma due to car crashes requiring emergency assistance. There is a critical human resource constraint in the health sector especially at the peripheral level. There are high rates of attrition for health workers as they seek 'greener pastures' to the extent that it is very difficult to retain qualified staff. Finally, there is a major resources constraint. International estimates suggest that providing comprehensive health care requires investments of at least US$35 to US$40 per capita. The Malawi Government estimates that the Essential Health Care Package would cost US$22 per capita, but the budget for the Ministry of Health provides less than US$10 per capita. Unless human resource and financial constraints are addressed urgently and comprehensively, it will be impossible to improve the health status of Malawians.

Notes

1. MMRs in Africa are 830 per 100,000 births which tells a very sad story.
2. Basic emergency obstetric care includes the following services that are required to save lives of women with complications of pregnancy: parenteral antibiotics, parenteral oxytocic drugs (needed to prevent bleeding) parenteral anticonvulsants, manual removal of the placenta, removal of retained products (e.g. manual vacuum aspiration in the case of a normal delivery or abortion) and assisted vaginal delivery (e.g. vacuum extraction or the use of forceps). Comprehensive emergency obstetric care includes the six services listed above but also includes surgery (e.g. caesarean section) and blood transfusion.
3. This is greater than 25 times the proportion of stunting expected in a healthy well-nourished population.
4. The syndromic approach to STI management is based on signs and symptoms assessed through clinical examination rather than laboratory testing. The seven symptoms of the presence of STIs are genital ulcer disease, urethral discharge due to infection with gonococci and/or Chlamydia, genital urinary symptoms in women, lower abdominal pain in women, acute scrotal swelling, enlarged lymph nodes and balinitis. Since laboratory facil-

ities are not a prerequisite to treatment, the clinical algorithms can be used by prescribers at all levels of the health facilities. This implies that patients can be treated at their first visit, rather than returning at a later date for laboratory tests. This reduces the time they are infectious to others (Ministry of Health, 2001).

5. These two institutions provide 85 percent of health services in Malawi (Ministry of Health, 2004)

6. The design and implementation of the Essential Health Care Package (EHP) is a core strategy for improving the overall health status of all Malawians. The objectives of the EHP are to ensure universal coverage of health services and to provide cost-effective interventions that can control the main causes of the disease burden in Malawi. The EHP focuses on those conditions and service gaps that disproportionately affect the health of the poor and disadvantaged populations. It will be delivered free of charge at the point of service in line with the Poverty Reduction Strategy. It brings together interventions that can be delivered throughout the health service using the same multi-skilled health workers.

7. The SWAP is a movement away from the project approach to a sector-wide approach. It is an attempt to deliver the same quality of care to all districts in Malawi. It is also an attempt to move away from 'vertical programmes' that address a single disease or single issue (tuberculosis or safe motherhood for example). Vertical programmes have dedicated systems, specialised personnel and procurement processes that are separate from the rest of the health sector. Vertical programmes may be an effective way of addressing specific issues, but given overall financial and human resource constraints, there is an urgent need to integrate services to address all causes of mortality and morbidity. The SWAP is intended to improve effectiveness and accountability and to mobilise additional resources by reducing fragmentation and duplication resulting from a multitude of separate externally funded activities. The SWAP focuses on technical services, institutional development, human resources, health financing, financial management and procurement systems.

Bibliography

Aitken J.M. and Kemp J. (2003) 'HIV/AIDS, Equity and Health Sector Personnel in Southern Africa', EQUINET Discussion Paper Number 12, Harare, Zimbabwe.

Attaran A. (2001) 'Health as a Human Right' Commission of Macro-Economics and Health, Policy Memorandum Number 3.

Department for International Development (2005a) 'Malaria Briefing', Lilongwe, Malawi.

Department for International Development (2005b) 'Tuberculosis Briefing', Lilongwe, Malawi.

Ezzati M., Lopes A., Rogers A., Vender Hoorn S., Murray C. and the Comparative Risk Assessment Collaborating Group (2002) 'Selected major risk factors and the global and regional burden of disease', *The Lancet*, 360 (9343), 1–14.

Gillespie S., and Haddad L. (2003) 'The relationship between nutrition and the Millennium Development Goals: A strategic review of the scope for DFID's influencing role', International Food Policy Research Institute, Washington DC.

Kumwenda N.I., Tata T.E. and Hoover D. (2001) 'HIV-1 incidence among male workers at a sugar estate in rural Malawi', JAIDS Jun 1, (2) 202–8.

Malawi Government, National Economic Council (2000) 'Poverty Analysis of the Malawi Integrated Survey', Lilongwe, Malawi.

Mtimuni B., (2004) 'Situational Analysis of Food Insecurity and Malnutrition in Malawi', Background Paper commissioned by the Ministry of Agriculture for the preparation of the National Food Security and Nutrition Policy.

Malawi Ministry of Economic Planning and Development (2004) 'Economic Report', Lilongwe, Malawi.

Malawi Ministry of Health (2001) 'Malawi National Reproductive Health Service Delivery Guidelines', USAID and JHPIEGO Corporation, Lilongwe, Malawi.

Malawi Ministry of Health and Population and National AIDS Commission 'Draft Submission to the Global Fund for AIDS, Tuberculosis and Malaria', Lilongwe, Malawi.

Malawi Ministry of Health and Population (2004a) 'Human Resources in the Health Sector: Issues and Challenges', Lilongwe, Malawi.

Malawi Ministry of Health and Population (2004b) 'Joint Programme of Work', Lilongwe, Malawi.

Malawi Ministry of Health (2005) 'Assessment of Emergency Obstetric Care Services in Malawi', Unpublished Draft, Lilongwe, Malawi.

Meguid T., Mshelia S., Chiudzu G., Kafulafula G. and Masache E. (2005) 'The Obstinate Maternal Mortality Ration for Malawi: An Insult Beyond the Obstetrician? An Urgent Opinion', Unpublished paper.

Ministry of Health and Population (2002) 'Application to the Global Fund for AIDS, Tuberculosis and Malaria – Round One Application'.

National AIDS Commission (2004) 'HIV and AIDS in Malawi: 2003 Estimates and Implications', Lilongwe, Malawi.

National Intelligence Council (2000) 'The Global Infectious Diseases Threat and Its Implications for the United States', Washington DC, January 2000.

National Statistical Office (2005) 'Preliminary Results of the 2004 Demographic and Health Survey', Unpublished paper, Zomba, Malawi.

Office of the Vice President (1999) 'Policy Analysis Initiative, Sectoral Report on Population and HIV/AIDS', Lilongwe, Malawi.

Sachs J.D. (2005) 'Achieving the Millennium Development Goals – the case of malaria' in *New England Journal of Medicine* 352 (2) January 13th 2005.

Sen A. (1999) 'Development as Freedom', New York: Alfred A. Knopf.

State Failure Task Force (1999) 'State Failure Task Force Report: Phase II Findings', in the Environmental Change and Security Project Report of the Woodrow Wilson Centre, Issue 5, Summer 49–72.

Sutcliffe S., Tata T.E. and Kumwenda N.I. (1998) 'Bacterial vaginitis and disturbance of vaginal flora: association with increased acquisition of HIV', AIDS Sept. 10; 12 (13) 1699–706.

World Health Organization (2001) 'Macro Economics and Health, Investing in Health for Economic Development', Geneva.

World Health Organization (2005) 'The World Health Report 2005: Make Every Mother and Child Count', WHO, Geneva.

3
The AIDS Crisis

Anne Conroy and Alan Whiteside

Introduction

In this chapter, we examine the HIV/AIDS pandemic and its drivers in Malawi. As we have already seen, even without the AIDS pandemic, Malawi has dreadful health indicators – high rates of infant and child mortality, a doubling in maternal mortality and a crippling burden of infectious diseases. We will look at the data on the HIV/AIDS pandemic, and interactions between the disease, poverty and the health crisis.

The key drivers of the AIDS pandemic are assessed – these include gender inequality, the vulnerability of young people, special risks for adolescents, high-risk sexual behaviour, income inequality, low levels of wealth and political transition and mobility. Over 14 percent of the adult population of Malawi is infected by the AIDS virus. The National AIDS Commission (2004) estimates that as many as 110,000 new infections occur each year. Most of the key drivers of the pandemic are linked to poverty and gender inequality. Women and girls have limited opportunities to negotiate safe sex. High-risk sexual behaviour (including multiple sexual partners and the limited use of condoms) is fuelled by a widespread sense of despair for the future. When women are forced into transactional sex in order to meet basic needs, poverty and AIDS reinforce each other. In the last part of the chapter we will consider the demographic consequences of the AIDS pandemic in Malawi including the impact on population, increasing mortality rates, the impact on infant and under-five mortality and life expectancy.

The HIV/AIDS pandemic

Malawi established a reliable system of collecting HIV sentinel surveillance data through the Ministry of Health and Population. The first

49

HIV data were collected at Queen Elizabeth Hospital in Blantyre in 1985. The first survey was conducted in 1987 at a limited number of sites. Between 1989 and 1999 there were annual surveys, and since then they have been carried out every second year (the most recent data are from the 2003 survey). In 1994, a system of 19 sentinel sites was established. Sites were selected to represent the urban, semi-urban and rural areas, as well as the northern, central and southern areas (UNAIDS/WHO, 2005). The sites of the 2003 survey are shown on the map in Figure 3.1.

The main source of HIV/AIDS data came from surveys of antenatal clinic attendees. To establish what was happening with the epidemic, epidemiologists needed a broadly representative sample of the general population that could be drawn on at regular intervals. Antenatal clinic attendees provided a good sample because they are sexually-active adults and blood is routinely taken from these women. Antenatal HIV surveys are done on an anonymous, unlinked basis. It is now possible to test for HIV using saliva, and this will allow Demographic and Health surveys to get a more representative population sample.

There are biases in antenatal surveys. Younger women are over-represented as they are more sexually active and likely to fall pregnant. HIV-positive women will be under-represented, as HIV infection reduces fertility. Nonetheless, once the raw data are available, it is possible to estimate the percentage of all women, men and adults who are infected, as well as the percentage of children who will be born HIV-positive. This has been done by a technical working group organised by the Malawi National AIDS Commission (National AIDS Commission, 2003).

The sentinel surveillance data collected in 2003 indicates that HIV prevalence among adults aged 15–49 years in Malawi is 14.4 percent (with a range of 12 percent to 17 percent) (National AIDS Commission 2004). Prevalence is higher in urban areas (23 percent with a range of 19 to 28 percent) than rural areas (12.4 percent with a range of 10 to 15 percent) (National AIDS Commission, 2004). HIV prevalence is also twice as high in the southern region (approximately 20 percent) than in the northern and central regions (approximately 10 percent). In most sentinel sites, prevalence rates are stabilising – reflecting a growing number of deaths rather than a decline in new infections. Lilongwe city in the central region is the only site where prevalence rates have declined consistently since 1997 (from 25 percent in 1997 to just over 17 percent in 2003). By contrast, prevalence rates in Nsanje district increased from just over 15 percent in 1996 to almost 35 percent in 2003.

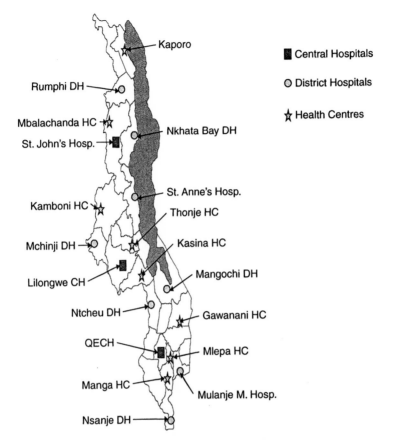

Figure 3.1 Sentinel survey sites, Malawi 2003
Source: National AIDS Commission (2003a).

While there is significant variation within regions, rural sites have consistently lower prevalence than urban or semi-urban sites, or those along key trading routes. In Southern Malawi, prevalence rates in the rural sites of Gawanani, Mianga and Milepa are all less than 15 percent. The semi-urban and predominantly Muslim site of Mangochi has a prevalence rate of 15 percent. Prevalence rates in the city of Blantyre are almost 30 percent while Nsanje is over 35 percent. In the central region, the rural sites of Kamboni, Thonje and Kasina have prevalence rates of less than 10 percent. Prevalence rates are around 20 percent in Lilongwe (an urban site), and in Ntcheu, Mchinji, and Nkhotakota – which are semi-urban or trading sites. In the north, the lowest prevalence rate is

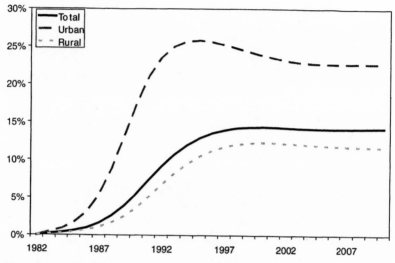

Figure 3.2   HIV prevalence: observed and projected
Source: National AIDS Commission (2003b).

the rural and remote site of Mbalachanda (7 percent). St. Johns (representing Mzuzu City and Nkhata Bay districts) has a prevalence rate of around 20 percent while the rural Rumphi and Karonga districts have prevalence rates of 15 percent.

Figure 3.2 shows that, while prevalence peaked in the mid-1990s, it has remained constant since. But this provides little grounds for comfort. Those dying are being replaced with newly infected individuals and no significant decline in overall prevalence is forecast. Malawi faces a serious HIV/AIDS epidemic. While there may be some debate about the exact numbers, there are many people infected, prevalence remains high, and there is as yet no sign of a downturn. Knowing that AIDS cases lag behind the HIV curve, we can safely predict that the number of people falling ill and dying will rise and the number of orphans will grow. The impact of the disease has yet to be fully felt.

The best estimate is that the total HIV-infected population of Malawi is 900,000, with a range of 750,000 to 1,080,000. Geographically the most infections are in the south (475,000 adults aged 15–49), followed by the central region (216,000 adults), and the north (75,000 adults) (National AIDS Commission, 2004). About three-quarters of all AIDS cases are found among adults between the ages of 20 and 40. As this is the most economically productive segment of the population, deaths in this age group are an economic burden with significant family consequences since many are raising young children (National AIDS Commission, 2004). There are an estimated 760,000 (with a range of 630,000 to 910,000) infected adults in the age group 15–49, 60,000 infected adults aged over 50 (with a range of 50,000 to 60,000) and 80,000 infected children aged 0–14 years old (with a range of 60,000 to 90,000). The data suggest that there are 240,000 infected adults in the urban areas and 530,000 infected adults in the rural areas (National AIDS Commission, 2004).

Although the total number of reported AIDS cases according to sex[1] is about equal (53.4 percent of women and 46.6 percent of men) the distribution by age and sex is quite different. 75 percent of AIDS cases among females occur in the 0–34 age groups. There are four times as many females as males in the vulnerable 14–19 age group. There are about one-third more females than males in the 20–29 age group. The pattern then reverses with more males than females reported to have AIDS in the 35 and above age group. More than 46 percent of male cases are in the over 35 age bracket. Some of the differences may be due to a pattern of transmission from older men to younger women. Women are also more physiologically vulnerable to HIV infection in the younger age groups (National AIDS Commission, 2004).

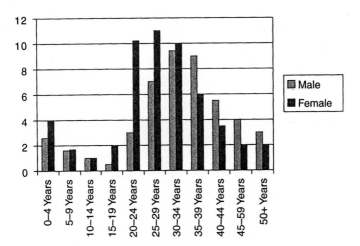

Figure 3.3   Age and sex distribution of AIDS cases in Malawi
Source: Source National AIDS Commission 2004.

Modes of transmission of HIV

The National AIDS Commission estimates that the majority of infections (about 88 percent) are transmitted through heterosexual contact. Although the probability of transmitting HIV in a single act of intercourse can be quite low, a number of factors increase the risk of infection dramatically. The two most important are the presence of a sexually transmitted infection (STI) and having unprotected sex with 'non-regular' partners. A significant number of adults have more than one sexual partner. Programmes designed to slow the rate of the pandemic should focus on reducing transmission through sexual contact, including promoting abstinence, fidelity and condom use (National AIDS Commission, 2003).

Approximately 10 percent of all new infections in Southern Africa are due to peri-natal transmission. Malawi follows the Southern African norm in this regard. Unless measures are implemented to prevent mother-to-child transmission, about 25 to 40 percent of babies born to HIV-positive mothers will themselves be infected.

Infected blood or unsafe medical practices can also transfer HIV between individuals. In Malawi, there is effective blood screening before transfusion so this mode of transmission is reported to account for a very small percentage of transmission. While the re-use of needles and syringes can also transmit HIV infection, this is thought to be negligible (National AIDS Commission, 2004).

There are no data or estimates on transmission due to homosexual contact or intravenous drug use. There is little information on the extent of homosexuality within Malawi. Key informants suggest that homosexuality is limited to situations where men are forced together such as prisons, mines and in some secondary schools. Transmission due to intravenous drug use is thought to be negligible.

Drivers of the pandemic

Gender inequality

Gender inequality is probably the major factor influencing the spread of HIV/AIDS, not only in Malawi but also worldwide. Social and behavioural factors which move women into high-risk situations include insecure employment, restricted access to assets and savings, poor education, and limited power to negotiate for safe sex. A female aged between 15 and 19 is six times more likely to contract HIV than a man in the same age group (National AIDS Commission, 2004).

Young women are at risk both for biological and social reasons. The female genital tract has a larger surface area than that of the male, increasing the likelihood for a woman to be infected during sexual intercourse. Chronic anemia and immaturity in the vaginal tract of young women (both symptoms of poverty and malnutrition) increase the probability of HIV infection. Sexual violence, to which many women are exposed, further increases risk. The weakening of marriage as an institution exposes married women to HIV infections as husbands acquire other sexual partners. Many women do not have marriage certificates or wills to protect their rights to property, and have great difficulty in securing their rights in legal and social systems. This makes it more difficult to negotiate for safe sex through the use of a condom or to refuse to have sex.

In the words of Stephen Lewis:

> Unequal power in sexual relations leads to double standards that have alarming implications for both men and women's ability to prevent sexual transmission of HIV. HIV/AIDS has brought into brutal relief the predatory sexual behaviour of men and the terrible consequences of inter-generational sex and vulnerability of women. (Lewis, 2002)

Women's vulnerability to HIV is exacerbated by poverty. Young women, orphaned by the HIV/AIDS pandemic and deprived of their opportunity to complete their education, may find themselves heads of households. This makes them vulnerable to sexual exploitation or may force them into prostitution as their only viable survival strategy. Sex is the currency by which women and girls may pay for food and shelter. In times of crisis and conflict, women are more likely to turn to prostitution. Rates of sexually transmitted infections and teenage pregnancies increased significantly during the food crisis (see Chapter 7: Honing in on the Poverty Trap).

Some aspects of Malawian culture also increase women's vulnerability to HIV infection. These include *chokolo* and *fisi*. *Chokolo* refers to the practice of 'wife inheritance' – a widow marrying her dead husband's brother. *Fisi* is the Che Chewa word for hyena and is the name given to a man who has sex with young girls after they have gone through an initiation ceremony. Both practices contribute to HIV transmission. There is growing recognition at the highest policy level that aspects of culture that increase susceptibility to HIV/AIDS must be changed and many traditional leaders have modified customs that facilitate transmission of HIV.

In addition to being more at risk of HIV infection, women are also disproportionately affected by HIV. Women bear the burden of AIDS care and girls tend to be the first to be withdrawn from school as AIDS exacerbates poverty at the household and community levels. Poverty also limits people's access to reproductive health services, prevention and treatment. Cuts in social expenditure lead to increased pressure on women and girls to take on the role of a social safety net through caring for sick relatives as other wage earners become sick and die.

The United Nations Task Force on Women, Girls and HIV/AIDS in southern Africa found that:

- Gender inequality fuels HIV infection and makes women powerless to protect themselves in the face of men whose physical and social power outweigh theirs.
- Gender inequality impacts on the way that AIDS is experienced so that women living with HIV/AIDS not only deal with being sick and ostracised; they often have to care for sick partners and continue to provide domestic labour.
- HIV and AIDS are further entrenching and worsening the imbalances between the sexes as women and girls are losing hard fought gains in education and employment (UNICEF, 2004).

The report draws attention to the central reality that women do not have the choice of saying 'No' to sexual intercourse. Where girls and women do not have the right to refuse sex, the prevailing mantra of abstinence, fidelity and use of condoms is meaningless. This hard-hitting report points out the policy paralysis in dealing with the powerful influence of gender inequality on the AIDS pandemic, noting that:

> The protection of the rights of women and girls in sub-Saharan Africa is the key to turning around the continent's AIDS crisis, and yet, relative to the scale of the problem, it is virtually ignored as a policy tool and certainly not viewed as a central element in national AIDS programmes. The abuses are many and varied – the human rights abuses have existed for a long time – but with AIDS, they are lethal on a massive scale.

Gender inequality is arguably the most significant driver of the AIDS pandemic in Malawi. It is inextricably linked to poverty. Women have less access to education, employment and credit and are extremely vulnerable when their husbands die or if their marriages split up. Until women are given more opportunities to live independently of men (if this is their choice) or the power to negotiate their sexual relationships as equal partners with men, the spread of HIV in Malawi will not be halted.

The vulnerability of young people

Children and adolescents are also very vulnerable to HIV transmission. The Demographic and Health Survey report that the median age of first intercourse is 16.9 years for women and 18.3 years for men (National Statistical Office, 2001). This implies that 50 percent of young women have sex before the age of 16.9 and half of young men have sex before the age of 18.

Care International in Malawi has conducted detailed research on HIV/AIDS in primary schools in Malawi. It gives valuable insights into young peoples' attitudes to sex, sexual behaviour and especially, into the problem of sexual abuse that exists in primary schools (Shah, 2004). Over two-thirds of children would like to have more information on sex, and on sexual and reproductive health. Shah (2004) reports the major reason that girls are involved in sexual relations is the expectation of material returns (gifts in kind or cash). Teachers offer better marks or improved chances of passing examinations. Girls also have sexual relations in the hope that the relationship will lead to marriage. This creates an incentive to get pregnant as soon as possible so that the father of the child will be forced to marry the girl. The major reasons for boys to get involved in sexual relations are peer pressure.

Shah (2004) highlighted specific risk factors for girls in school:

- Male teachers actively solicit sexual relations with their female students and have multiple sexual relationships within the school environment.
- Children are expected to have school uniforms (or at least look smart and clean). This encourages some (especially girls) into transactional sex in order to buy these necessities.

Schools have started to include life skills and sex education in the curriculum but there are problems with the teaching methodology. Sex education tends to be delivered in a lecture style with little or no room for discussion and queries for additional information (Shah, 2004). Both boys and girls prefer to have these sessions taught by teachers of their own gender in a single sex session, rather than in mixed groups as is the normal practice. Many pupils believe that asking questions about sex, sexual or reproductive health, STIs or HIV indicates that an individual is already sexually active.

In Malawian culture, it is not considered appropriate for parents to give their own children information about sex or sexual and reproductive health. While young people (aged 15–25) account for approximately 50 percent of new infections, very few children appear to understand how to prevent the transmission of HIV/AIDS. Less than 50 percent of school age children cited unsafe sex (not using condoms) as a way of transmitting HIV. Forty-nine percent of all children cited multiple sexual partners and around one-third cited 'sharing needles'. Ten percent of children did not know. Sixty-nine percent of children in school cited abstaining from sex to prevent HIV transmission. Shah (2004) notes that:

> In general, only a marginally higher proportion of girls and boys in school had information on HIV/AIDS than those who don't go to school. There remains a large gap in information and knowledge. This further verifies the finding that students do not find their lessons on HIV/AIDS at school very informative.

Practical knowledge about condom use is poor. Children **'seem to know about condoms, but they don't know about condoms'** (Shah, 2004). They may know that condoms can prevent transmission of HIV but have no idea about how to use one. Some believe that condoms are porous and the virus can pass through tiny holes in the latex. Others claim that condoms actually spread HIV. Condom use is unpopular, and they are difficult to acquire. Young people are embarrassed to request for them in shops and have limited access to free condoms in health centres.

Special risks for adolescents

Adolescence is the period of transition from childhood to adulthood and is one of the most vulnerable periods for HIV transmission, especially for girls. In Malawi, adolescence is typically defined to span the ages 10 to 19. The 1998 census showed that adolescents comprise 23 percent of the total population of Malawi, and the majority live in rural areas. The population of adolescents is estimated to have increased from 1.86 million in 1987 to 3.01 million in 2002 (National Statistical Office and ORC Macro, 2001).

The period of adolescence is characterised by physical and emotional changes, the search for identity, and greater maturity in reasoning. As adolescents go through these changes, they tend to experiment with sexual intercourse and may adopt risky behaviours, making them vulnerable to HIV and other sexually transmitted infections. HIV/AIDS-prevalence data show that adolescents and adults aged between 15 and 24 have the highest rates of new infections with adolescent girls far more likely to be infected than adolescent boys (UNAIDS, 2000).

The prevailing cultural and socioeconomic context affects patterns of adolescent sexual and reproductive behaviour. Young people are influenced by opinion leaders including village headmen, traditional initiators (*anankungwi* or *nkhoswe*), traditional birth attendants, preachers at churches and mosques, local political leaders, and teachers. Some cultural practices, such as initiation ceremonies, early sex, early marriage and funeral cleaning rights have a strong role in shaping the behaviour of youths (Munthali *et al.*, 2003). While Malawian culture does not encourage boys and girls to mix freely, initiation rites often encourage young people to start sex early. As a result boys and girls have poor socialisation skills regarding sexuality and other issues. The culture also encourages girls to view men as superior, and teaches girls that their role is to submit and to please men.

Males initiate sex in 92 percent of relationships and girls often feel powerless to refuse sex or to negotiate for safer sex (Zulu, 1996). The sexual behaviour of girls is often monitored closely by their elders, while young men are left alone to explore relationships. While traditional culture emphasises the importance of abstinence before marriage and fidelity within marriage, the present situation is full of contradictions. There is also much misinformation and confusion. Peer groups and the media encourage multiple sexual relationships, while the faith communities promote abstinence and discourage condom use.

Malawians marry young, with young women marrying at an average of 18.2 years of age and men at 22.7. The relatively early age for marriage of girls indicates that many are marrying before they are physically and psychologically ready for pregnancy. Marrying at such a young age also limits their ability to negotiate with their older husbands. Poor young people are vulnerable, disempowered and cannot protect themselves against unwanted pregnancies, sexually transmitted infections and HIV/AIDS (Hickey, 1999).

Sexual abuse is any form of sexual relations where consent is not given freely in an equal relationship. It leads to feelings of guilt, unworthiness, self-disgust, and undermines self-confidence and trust in the members of the opposite sex. Poverty increases the opportunities for sexual abuse. Children and women may suffer sexual abuse due to the threat of violence, psychological coercion or unequal power relationships. Sexual abuse, especially of children and teenage girls fuels the spread of sexually transmitted infections and HIV. It also leads to unwanted pregnancies, unsafe abortions and maternal deaths. Sexual abuse (and its multiple tragic consequences) may force vulnerable young people into the commercial sex industry. Even where the worst physical outcomes of sexual abuse are avoided, it still undermines confidence and self-respect.

Adolescents are also very vulnerable to sexual abuse. Most sexually active female adolescents report their first sex with men older than themselves. Fifty-six percent of female adolescents experienced forced sex and 66 percent reported that they accepted money or gifts in exchange for sex (Pathfinder International, 1998). Sexual abuse also forces young women into unsafe abortions. Abortion is against the law in Malawi, yet it is a significant medical and social problem. Hospital records show that many women, particularly young girls resort to dangerous and unorthodox abortions that put their health and lives in danger (Munthali *et al.*, 2004).

High risk sexual behaviour

The dangers of high-risk sexual behaviour can, to an extent, be modified through behaviour change and by the use of condoms to help minimise the chances of transmission between adults. But the challenges to widespread adoption of such practices are considerable in a very poor and conservative society where there is great reluctance to talk about sex openly, and where men have a greater influence over sexual relations and on the decision whether or not to use condoms. This implies that behaviour change strategies must be targeted at men.

Condom use is low, despite the reported general knowledge of their effectiveness in preventing transmission of HIV/AIDS. According to the Malawi Demographic and Health Survey (2000), only 5 percent of women and 14 percent of men who had sex in the past year reported use of a condom during their last sexual intercourse (with any partner). Among both men and women, condom use is higher with non-cohabiting partners than with spouses or cohabiting partners. Twenty-nine percent of women and 39 percent of men used a condom during the last sex act with non-cohabiting partners, compared with 3 percent of women and 6 percent of men with spouses/cohabiting partners. The overall supply position for condoms, especially female condoms, needs to be improved.

Total male condom supply availability was estimated at 19 million annually in 2003 (National AIDS Commission *et al.*, 2003). This is inadequate in a country where the sexually active population is probably between five and six million.

Younger respondents tended to report a higher use of condoms than older ones. Urban women and men are more likely to use condoms than their rural counterparts, and use of condoms is also associated with higher levels of educational attainment. For example, just 9 percent of women without formal education used a condom at the last episode of sex with non-cohabiting partners compared with 50 percent of women who attended secondary school (Ministry of Health: Demographic and Health Survey, 2000).

Levels of condom use are also relatively low when men pay for sex. Only 35 percent of men reported using a condom during the last episode of paid sex. Data on HIV infection among sex workers in Lilongwe showed that in 1994 some 70 percent were HIV-positive. This highlights the importance of strengthening programmes targeted at sex workers. It also shows that there is an urgent need to update information about levels of infection and condom use among commercial sex workers throughout Malawi.

There are many factors militating against condom use. It is almost impossible for most women to insist that their partners use condoms, as they are disadvantaged in sexual negotiation. If a young woman asks her boyfriend to use a condom, she is often accused of being sexually promiscuous. Even when condoms are used at the start of a sexual relationship, couples usually stop using them once the relationship becomes established. Wives cannot insist on condom use even when they fear that their husband is in an extra-marital relationship. Nor can they refuse to have sex with their husbands as many men find the concept of rape within marriage incomprehensible. The inability of unmarried or married women to insist on the use of condoms contributes significantly to HIV transmission. In addition, many believe that condoms should not be used 'within the family' as this is viewed as a confirmation that one of the partners is involved in an extra-marital relationship.

Income inequality, low levels of wealth and political transition

Malawi has a high degree of income inequality, poverty is widespread, and social cohesion low.[2] Barnett and Whiteside (2002) have noted that countries exhibiting these traits tend to have high rates of HIV prevalence. An epidemic may take time to gather momentum in countries with low levels of social cohesion and low wealth. But once it does, the increase will be exponential and the infection rate will remain high as the country does not have the resources to deal with the problem. The implication is that HIV-infection rates will remain high in Malawi without effective policies to improve governance, enhance social cohesion, and promote more equity in the distribution of wealth.

Malawi data confirm the relationship between income inequality and higher rates of HIV prevalence. Income inequality and HIV-prevalence rates are higher in urban areas. The gini coefficient[3] is 0.52 and the HIV-prevalence rate is 23 percent in urban areas.[4] This compares with a HIV-prevalence rate of 12.4 percent in rural areas where income inequality is not as high (gini coefficient of 0.37). Similarly, the highest rate of HIV prevalence is in the densely populated South (20 percent) which has the highest rates of income inequality and poverty in Malawi. In urban areas traditional structures have typically broken down, leading to a marked decline in social cohesion.

In addition, since the early 1990s, Malawi has undergone a period of rapid transition from a closely regulated and centrally controlled society to a more conventionally democratic and free market economy. This change has been very difficult for many Malawians who struggle to find their way in the new society where many of the social norms appear to have altered sharply. The new freedoms associated with democracy have been associated with an increase in income inequality, poverty and crime. There is also an increase in gender-based violence as young women challenge the traditional authority of older men. The recent food crisis, combined with political uncertainty, has caused a further breakdown in social cohesion.

Mobility

Poverty leads to high levels of human migration both within Malawi and to other countries. In the past, a significant number of Malawian men migrated to the South African mines. While employment opportunities in the South African mines have ended, many men still seek work away from home – but within Malawi. Men leave the rural areas to work in tobacco processing at the Auction Floors in Kanengo (Lilongwe) and in Blantyre. This separates men from their families for months on end. It also places them in close proximity to high risk sexual networks that often include sex workers who have high rates of HIV prevalence. Whilst men are away, their wives may have to supplement their incomes with non-traditional sexual partners. This was a major problem during the recent food crisis (see Chapter 7: Honing in on the Poverty Trap).

A study of male workers on the Nchalo sugar plantation in the Shire Valley (where men work as cane cutters from March to November leaving their families in rural areas) found that men's rate of HIV acquisition followed a gradient based on distance from the Nchalo Trading Centre, where most recreational activities and commercial sex occur. Both HIV and syphilis prevalence were highest in communities closest to the trading centres, and lowest in communities furthest from the trading centres (Kumwenda *et al.*, 2001).

Throughout the late 1980s, Malawi was host to one million Mozambique refugees. At present, there is considerable cross-border trade on the Mozambique border. Malawian men and women are increasingly mobile as they pursue trading activities. Female cross-border traders are believed to be especially vulnerable to HIV infection. Other key mobile groups in Malawi include truck drivers, sex workers, fishermen/women and the military. Natural disasters including cholera, floods and famine also prompt increased mobility and regrouping of family units – which may entail exposure to new sexual networks.

Children orphaned by HIV/AIDS may have to migrate and may find themselves in new communities without family support or friends. These orphans will have suffered enormously even before the deaths of their parents; many would have been taken out of school to act as primary carers for their dying parents. They may be vulnerable and isolated in their new environments as they have to make new social contacts, and attend new schools. They may turn to high risk sexual behavior as a coping mechanism and are also vulnerable to sexual abuse.

The demographic consequences of HIV/AIDS

The National AIDS Commission has produced population projections up to the year 2010. These projections assume a stable or very modest decline in the HIV rate, and a modest reduction in fertility to about 5.4 births per woman by 2010. The projections presented in Figure 3.4 show that if there were no deaths due to AIDS, the population of Malawi would be about 16 million in 2010 but, because of AIDS, the population will be about 14 million (National AIDS Commission, 2003). This indicates a population growth rate of about 2.4 percent a year, compared with around 3.2 percent without AIDS. Thus, although AIDS will have an impact on the population size, the population will keep growing.

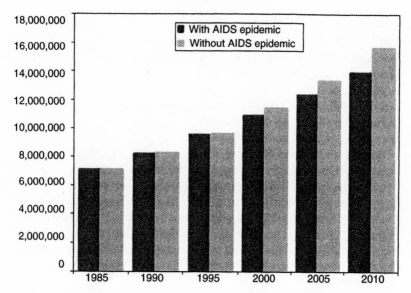

Figure 3.4   Population projections for Malawi with and without AIDS
1985–2010
Source: Estimates of the prevalence of infection and the implications, National AIDS
Commission, 2003b.

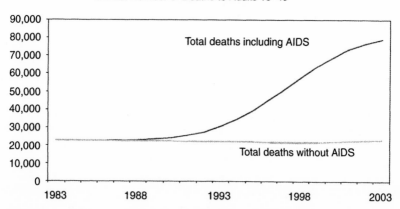

Figure 3.5   Impact of AIDS on adult mortality in Malawi, 1985–2003
Source: Estimates of the prevalence of infection and the implications, National AIDS
Commission, 2003b.

Increasing mortality rates[5]

The National AIDS Commission estimated in 2003 the contribution of AIDS deaths to mortality of people aged between 15 and 49 years in Malawi for the period between 1983 and 2003 (National AIDS Commission, 2003). They assumed that mortality in this age-range would have remained the same between 1985 and 2003, at a level of about 22,000 deaths per annum. The annual number of deaths of people aged between 15 and 49 years was about 56,000 in 1998 and nearly 80,000 in 2003 (see Figure 3.5).

Infant and under-five mortality

Malawi has one of the highest infant mortality rates in the world. About 10 percent of infants born in Malawi die before their first birthday. Nearly 20 percent of children die before the age of five. Data from censuses and surveys conducted in the country over the past 20 years show that childhood mortality had (prior to the epidemic) been declining consistently (National Statistical Office, 1977, 1987, 1998; National Statistical Office and Macro International Inc, 1994; National Statistical Office and ORC Macro, 2001).

The US Bureau of the Census anticipated that the AIDS pandemic will increase infant and child mortality. In 2002, infant mortality was estimated at 87.2 per 1000 without AIDS and 106.1 with AIDS. Under five mortality is even higher – 155 per 1000 without AIDS and 184.7 with AIDS. (US Census Bureau, 2004).

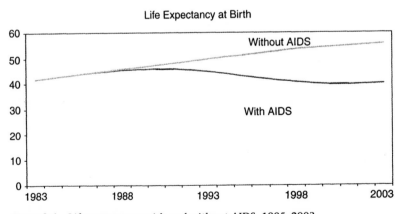

Figure 3.6 Life expectancy with and without AIDS, 1985–2003
Source: Estimates of the prevalence of infection and the implications, National AIDS Commission, 2003b.

Life expectancy

The life expectancy at birth is the average length of time that a new-born is expected to live under prevailing mortality conditions. The 1998 census estimated this to be about 40 years, the same level as in 1985. The trend as shown in Figure 3.6 clearly shows the deterioration in the health prospects of the Malawian population. Without AIDS the life expectancy was expected to be about 15 years higher than the present 40 years (National AIDS Commission, 2003).

Conclusion

Malawi continues to reel under the AIDS pandemic. The data presented in the first part of the chapter demonstrates that despite all efforts to reduce transmission of the virus, there are approximately 110,000 new infections each year. Prevalence rates are stabilising around 14.4 percent on a national basis. Prevalence is declining in only two sites: Lilongwe and Blantyre. The pandemic in Malawi follows global statistics with more women than men infected and prevalence rates higher in urban than rural areas and a higher proportion of orphans and vulnerable children in urban rather than rural areas. This has implications for policy and demonstrates the need to focus on poverty reduction and safety-net interventions in the relatively neglected urban slums where the impact of the AIDS pandemic is very serious and life is precarious, especially for the young.

In our discussion of drivers of the pandemic, we argue that gender inequality is important and young women in particular are vulnerable to infection. Most women have little control over their sexual behaviour and cannot refuse to have intercourse or insist on the use of condoms. Unless this changes, the pandemic will continue to gather momentum. Children and adolescents are especially at risk of infection. High risk sexual behaviour, multiple sexual partners and limited use of condoms, combined with high rates of prevalence of sexually transmitted infections also drive the pandemic. A widespread sense of hopelessness also undermines incentives to change high risk sexual behaviour. Poverty drives the pandemic as poor women and children are forced into transactional sex in order to get money to survive. They are often fully aware of the risks but have no choice. The imperative for short-term survival in a desperately poor environment forces people into behaviours that place them at direct risk of infection.

This also has important policy implications as Malawi faces food crises almost annually. The last food crisis demonstrated the direct correlation between the lack of food and the need for the vulnerable to engage in high risk sexual behaviour in order to get food. This is a lesson that wealthy decision makers have yet to fully appreciate. People who live below subsistence in normal years cannot absorb a 30 percent reduction in production without it having devastating consequences for life and health.

Income inequality, low levels of wealth and political transition all drive the pandemic and contribute to infection rates which are consistently higher in urban rather than rural areas. This implies that HIV-infection rates will continue to remain high in Malawi without effective policies to improve governance, promote social cohesion and promote more equity in the distribution of wealth.

Malawi's population structure with 45 percent of the population less than 15 years old, high fertility rates and low life expectancy also creates the conditions to drive the pandemic as a high proportion of the population is sexually active. High rates of population mobility, including the separation of men from their families, also increase high risk sexual behaviours.

Finally, there is need for a re-think of how to implement a more inclusive approach to prevention programmes. The majority of programmes to prevent transmission of HIV are implemented by the Ministries, non-governmental organisations or community-based groups. Yet traditional authorities, traditional healers and the leaders in the faith communities are very influential in Malawi. There has been insufficient emphasis on understanding Malawi's specific cultural context in the design and implementation of programmes for prevention, care and support. There is an urgent need to intensify the dialogue with and provide support to traditional authorities and the faith communities to enable them to play a more constructive role in the fight against HIV/AIDS.

Notes

1. The National AIDS Commission (2004) draws information from the age and sex distribution of the reported AIDS cases. The Commission acknowledges that reported cases represent only a small proportion of all AIDS cases; nevertheless, they provide useful information about the HIV/AIDS pandemic.
2. Cohesion refers to the cultural homogeneity of a society, and is a product of good governance and strong civil society.
3. The gini-coefficient provides an indication of how equitable the distribution of income is across the population. The lower the level of the gini-coefficient, the lower the level of inequality, and the higher the level of the coefficient, the higher the degree of inequality.
4. The higher HIV-prevalence rates are confirmed in every urban area in Malawi. In Blantyre City, the urban infection rate is 27.8 percent compared with 18 percent in Blantyre Rural. Infection rates in Lilongwe City are

23.5 percent compared with 7.2 percent in Lilongwe Rural. For Zomba, the comparative figures are 26.2 percent and 18 percent. In Mzuzu, the figures are 19.8 and 8.2 percent (National AIDS Commission, 2004).

5. The authors commissioned a background paper by Dr Nyovani Madise on the Demographic Consequences of AIDS in Malawi. We acknowledge her input.

Bibliography

Barnett T. and Whiteside A. (2002) 'AIDS in the Twenty-First Century: Disease and Globalisation', Basingstoke: Palgrave.

Hickey C. (1999) 'Explaining Observed Patterns of Sexual Behaviour: Phase Two, Longitudinal Study, Final Report', Zomba, Centre for Social Research, University of Malawi.

Kumwenda N.I., Taha T.E. and Hoover D.R. (2001) 'HIV-I incidence among male sugar workers at a sugar estate in rural Malawi', AIDS 2001 Jun 1; 2 (2) 202–8.

Lewis S. (2002) 'Lunchtime Speech October 4th 2002', Office of the Special Envoy for AIDS in Africa.

Madise N. (2004) 'The Demographic Impact of AIDS in Malawi', Unpublished Background Paper commissioned by the authors.

Ministry of Health (2000) 'Malawi Demographic and Health Survey', Lilongwe, Malawi.

Munthali A., Kadzanzira J. and Mvula P. (2003) 'Formative study on prevention of mother to child transmission of HIV', Lilongwe, Malawi.

Munthali (2004) 'Background Study on Adolescent Sexual and Reproductive Health', Background Paper commissioned by UNFPA for a study on 'Protecting the Next Generation: Understanding HIV Risk among the Youth' UNFPA, New York.

National AIDS Commission (2003) 'Estimates of prevalence of infection and implications', Lilongwe, Malawi.

National AIDS Commission (2004) 'HIV and AIDS in Malawi: 2003 Estimates and Implications', Lilongwe, Malawi.

National AIDS Commission in collaboration with partners and stakeholders (2003) 'Joint Review of the HIV/AIDS National Strategic Framework and Operations of the National AIDS Commission', Lilongwe, Malawi.

National Statistical Office (2001) 'Malawi Demographic and Health Survey 2000', Lilongwe, Malawi.

National AIDS Commission (2004) *National HIV/AIDS Estimates 2003*, Lilongwe, Malawi.

National Statistical Office (1977) *Malawi Population and Housing Census Final Report*, Zomba.

National Statistical Office (1987) *Malawi Population and Housing Census Final Report*, Zomba.

National Statistical Office (1998) *Malawi Population and Housing Census Analytical Report*, Zomba 1998.

National Statistical Office and Macro International Inc. (1994) *Malawi Demographic and Health Survey 1992*, Lilongwe and Calverton, Maryland.

National Statistical Office and ORC Macro (2001) *Malawi Demographic and Health Survey 2000*, Lilongwe and Calverton, Maryland.

Pathfinder International (1998) 'Assessment of Youth Reproductive Health Needs in Malawi', New Orleans, Louisiana, United States of America; Tulane University School of Public Health.

Rimal R.N., Tapia M. Bose K., Brown J. and Mkandawire G. (2004) 'Exploring Community Beliefs, Attitudes and Behaviors about HIV/AIDS in Eight Malawi BRIDGE Districts', Centre for Communication Programmes, Johns Hopkins University, Baltimore MD.

Shah M.K. (2004) 'What is dead does not fear decay: The impact of HIV/AIDS on Primary Education in Lilongwe and Zomba Districts', Care International, Lilongwe, Malawi.

UNICEF (2004) 'Regional Report of the Secretary General of the United Nations', Task Force on Women, Girls and HIV/AIDS in Southern Africa. Lilongwe, Malawi.

UNAIDS/WHO (2005) 'Epidemiological Fact Sheet on HIV/AIDS and Sexually Transmitted Infections, 2004' accessed on-line http://www.who.int/GlobalAtlas/PDFFactory/HIV/EFS_PDFs/EFS2004_MW.pdf retrieved on 1st June 2005).

UNAIDS (2004) 'Global AIDS Epidemic', Geneva, UNAIDS.

US Census Bureau (2004) 'The AIDS pandemic in the 21st Century', Washington DC, U.S. Government Printing Office, International Population Reports WP/02–2.

Zulu E.M. (1996) 'Social and cultural factors affecting reproductive behaviour in Malawi', Unpublished dissertation, Population Studies Centre, University of Pennsylvania.

4

The Impact of the AIDS Pandemic on the National Economy and Development

Alan Whiteside and Anne Conroy

The focus of this chapter is the relationship between poverty, the economy and hunger. The chapter opens with an outline of Malawi's economy including human development indicators, economic growth levels, aid dependence, the crippling level of external and internal debts and employment statistics. The second part of the chapter addresses the impact of AIDS on children and the elderly. The issue of how AIDS impacts on children has not been given sufficient priority in the planning of national responses. We review data to demonstrate the growing number of orphans in Africa and in Malawi, who are increasingly at risk from exploitation and disease. Finally, we examine the impact of AIDS on agriculture and livelihoods. The AIDS pandemic almost guarantees household poverty in an economy where household labour is the major economic resource available. Food security for such households depends on the availability of labour to perform husbandry tasks on time – if these are delayed, productivity declines and the household is pushed into a downward spiral of poverty.

The Malawi case study: the economy

Earlier chapters have shown the desperate poverty of Malawi. To recap, 41.7 percent of Malawians live on less than one dollar a day, and 65.3 percent are below the national poverty line (UNDP, 2004a). In monetary terms it is one of the poorest and smallest economies in the world (UNDP, 2003). Life expectancy at birth is less than 40 years of age, and few Malawians get more than a very basic education (UNDP, 2002; 2004a). Twenty-five percent of Malawi children are malnourished and only 57 percent of the population have access to an improved water source (World Bank, 2004). Two-thirds of households are unable to consume the recommended calorie intake levels. Subsistence agriculture makes up to half of all household incomes. In real terms the economy has declined in size since 1993[1] (Figure 4.1) while population grew at 3.1 percent between 1975 and 2001.[2]

Malawi's economy is dominated by agriculture (although the contribution of agriculture has fallen recently – from 44 percent in 1980 to 36 percent in 1998) (World Bank, 2000). Nearly 85 percent of the

Table 4.1   Malawi and African economies

	Pop. density people per sq km	Gross national income $ billion 2002	GNI per capita $ 2002	PPP GNI per capita $ 2002	GDP % growth 2001/2002
Malawi	114	1.7	160	570	1.8
Ethiopia	67	6.5	100	780	2.7
Mozambique	24	3.6	200	990	7.7
South Africa	37	113.4	2500	9810	3
Tanzania	40	9.7	290	580	6.3
Zambia	14	3.5	340	800	3.3
Zimbabwe	34	NA	NA	NA	–5.6

Source: UNDP, 2004

Table 4.2   Selected social and demographic indicators in Malawi and other countries, 2003

	Malawi	Tanzania	Zambia	Mozambique	South Africa
% Population below poverty line (US$1 per day)	65	35	73	54	–
Per capita income (US$)	160	280	340	210	2780
illiteracy rate (%age of people aged 15 and above)	38	21	20	60	14
Life expectancy at birth (years)	38	43.1	36.9	41	46
Infant mortality (per 1000 live births)	113	104	102	101	52

Source: World Bank Group, 2004

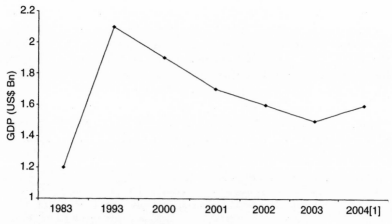

Figure 4.1   GDP (US$ bn) in Malawi, 1993–2003
Source: Economist Intelligence Unit (2004).

population live in rural areas. These rural people depend on agriculture for their livelihood. The majority of Malawians have little prospect of ever obtaining a formal sector job, and even if they do it is likely to be low-paid. Eighty-seven percent of working-age Malawians work in agriculture (most in subsistence agriculture). Between 1980 and 1991 (the last year for which there are data) monthly earnings in current US$ in agriculture fell from $20 to $16 (World Bank, 2002). It will be hard to improve domestic savings without a substantial increase in rural incomes.

Unsurprisingly, domestic savings are low. The percentage of GDP going to domestic savings between 1991 and 2001 averaged 5.6 percent (in Botswana it was 30 percent and in Mozambique, 7.1 percent). The trend moreover is downwards, with average savings falling from 12.1 percent in 1990 to 7.3 percent in 2000 and to 2.5 percent in 2002 (African Development Bank, 2003). There is little external investment, with total foreign direct investment in 2000 being US$27 million – less than 0.5 percent of the sub-Saharan African investment (World Bank, 2002). A balanced economic development will require an increase in both domestic savings and inflows of foreign investments.

Macro-level impacts of AIDS

In high HIV-prevalence countries, the combined negative effects of AIDS on all sectors of the economy and public finance are likely to have tangible macro-economic impacts. There is insufficient research on the impact of AIDS on the macro-economy, partly because it is difficult to separate out the negative impact of AIDS on economic growth from other sources of macro-economic instability[3] (Mills and Shillcutt, 2004). Malawi was the subject of one of the first attempts to model the macro-economic impact of AIDS[4] (Cuddington and Hancock, 1994 a, b). The long-run economic costs of AIDS may be devastating to the national economy[5] through:

- Destroying human capital, particularly of young adults.
- Weakening and breaking down mechanisms that generate human capital and investment in people, through loss of income and the death of parents.
- Giving rise to a new generation with little education and knowledge, and therefore less able to raise their own children and invest in their education.

AIDS and the private sector

The private sector in Malawi includes the manufacturing sector and accounts for 11.6 percent of GDP. The sector faces many constraints (even without the effects of AIDS) and, as noted earlier, there has been little new investment (and considerable disinvestment). The reasons include the unfavourable macro-economic environment, poor economic infrastructure, low labour productivity, high rates of taxation and inadequate funding for investment promotion (Malawi Ministry of Economic Planning and Development, 2005).

AIDS significantly increases the cost of business through an increase in direct, indirect and systemic costs. In addition to the immediate impact of ill-health and the death of employees at all levels, AIDS may indirectly affect the overall business environment of companies through the following mechanisms:

- Reduced government efficiency leading to the slower issuing of licences or approval of applications.
- Less efficient services, such as electricity supply, transport and infrastructure if public finance is diverted to health.
- Increased crime and poorer governance. These and other problems could encourage skilled professional staff to migrate and worsen the direct skill shortage due to HIV/AIDS.
- The reduced efficiency of the public health system could increase pressure on employers to provide private health insurance for their employees (Whiteside and Sunter, 2000).

Table 4.3   Costs of HIV/AIDS on a tea estate in Malawi, 1995–1996

Description	Total Cost (US$)	Related to HIV (%)	Cost of HIV (US$)
Provision of medical services	34,526	25	8,632
Funeral Costs	1,438	75	1,079
Death in service	7,271	100	7,271
Absence	23,056	25	5,764
Total	66,291		22,746

Source: Jones (1997)

As profitability declines, investment and growth also fall – with direct consequences for the economy. Businesses will shut down, reducing employment opportunities and tax revenue. At the firm/sector level, AIDS is equivalent to an additional payroll cost; it increases the cost of doing business. The Centre for International Health (CIH) at Boston University's School of Public Health looked at six formal sector enterprises in South Africa and Botswana (Rosen *et al.*, 2004). The analysis showed that, under a conservative set of assumptions, HIV/AIDS among employees added between 0.4 and 5.9[6] percent to the annual salary and wage bill of the firms. HIV-positive employees are also expected to be less productive than their healthy colleagues. Data from a tea plantation in Kenya, where workers were paid according to the weight of tea picked, showed HIV-positive individuals picked on average 3.6 kg/day of tea less 2–3 years prior to death, 5.1 kg/day less one year prior to death and 9.3 kg/day less approaching death. In the three years leading up to death HIV-positive individuals used between 3.4 and 11.0 more days sick leave, depending on the stage of illness (Fox *et al.*, 2004; Jones, 1996).

Jones (1996) looked at an urban-based industry in Blantyre and found that the cost of HIV/AIDS was estimated to be between 1.5 and 6.0 percent of operating profit. Another study on a Malawi tea estate (see Table 4.3) showed costs related to HIV accounted for 3.4 percent of the estate's gross profit during the 1995/96 fiscal year. The costs are determined by the levels of both employee benefits and of skilled labor necessary for production (Jones, 1997).

Impacts on the public sector and the development process

The productivity of many public sector jobs is difficult to measure (as many governments involved in privatisation have learnt). Public sector employees may be able to take more leave and be less productive than their private sector counterparts when illness strikes without the risk of losing their jobs. Important government sectors (notably health and social welfare) face increased demand for services at the same time that their capacity is being reduced by the ravages of HIV/AIDS. Malawi's annual losses of government staff rose almost six-fold between 1990 and 2000, primarily due to premature AIDS deaths (Malawi Government and UNDP, 2002). A study of deaths amongst teachers and health care workers in Malawi in 1999 showed that the major cause of death was TB (typically precipitated by HIV/AIDS) (Harries *et al.*, 2002). HIV/AIDS undermines public sector institutional capacity, and its ability to mobilise resources and to implement programmes. Thus HIV/AIDS causes the development process, which is heavily dependant on public sector capacity, to stall.

NGOs and civil society organizations (CSOs) have an increasingly important role in the implementation of development programmes at the community level. James (2004) has shown how AIDS undermines the capacity of such agencies to implement programmes as increasing numbers of staff are affected by the pandemic – either through personal infection and ill-health, or through the need to care for infected relatives. The scale of infection has considerable organisational costs for NGO and CSO staff and volunteers in terms of increased sick leave, extra medical and funeral expenses, as well as the loss of learning and experience. NGOs in Malawi report that their meetings with the community are increasingly being disrupted by funerals, with programmes falling behind schedule and going beyond the budget. Micro-credit programmes have found it increasingly difficult to get groups to act on the basis of solidarity in the context of high HIV prevalence. There is also evidence that families affected by chronic illnesses drop out of community activities. These conspire to make the most marginalised groups increasingly invisible and isolated from development interventions.

The impact of AIDS on the vulnerable – children and the elderly

Across Africa, millions of children are experiencing deepening poverty, mental stress from witnessing the illnesses and deaths of their loved ones and a profound sense of insecurity. The scale of the crisis is terrifying. At the end of 2004, 11 million children living in sub-Saharan Africa had lost one or both of their parents as a result of HIV/AIDS. The orphan crisis in the region is just starting to unfold. By 2010, the number of orphans is expected to have grown to 20 million (UNICEF, 2004). In Malawi, Mozambique, Zambia, Zimbabwe, Botswana, Lesotho and Swaziland, between 15 and 19 percent of children are orphans (USAID, UNAIDS, UNICEF, 2002). There are currently 2.1 million children aged less than 15 years old infected with HIV worldwide (1,900,000 in sub-Saharan Africa). There were 630,000 new infections of children in 2003, while 490,000 had died of the virus worldwide (UNAIDS, 2004a).

In Malawi, 20,000 children are born with the virus every year and an estimated 83,000 children in Malawi are living with the virus (UNAIDS, 2004a). Of Malawian children under 15, 4.5 percent had lost their fathers in 2000 compared with 6.4 percent in 1992 (National Statistical Office, 2001). Compared to rural areas about one-third more children in urban areas have lost their parents, reflecting the higher HIV-prevalence rates in urban areas (Madise, 2004). In 1999, the Government of Malawi (based on a HIV-prevalence rate of 16 percent) estimated that there would be 770,000 AIDS orphans by 2010 and that the number would increase to 1.1 million by 2020.

Children who are orphaned are more likely to be malnourished, sick, abused and sexually exploited. They are at a greater risk of dying from preventable diseases and are less likely than other children to be fully immunised. This has implications for all children. As immunisation coverage decreases, the herd immunity (the overall immunity of children as a group) declines and all children become more susceptible to common childhood illnesses – which in the case of HIV-infected children can be fatal (Giese, 2002).

Orphans are likely to lose their chance for secondary school education as relatives may be unable or unwilling to pay the fees. Orphans are more likely than their peers to drop out of school (leaving them with fewer opportunities for growth and development). They end up in low paid, insecure jobs, or at worst, become involved in crime or prostitution (Badcock Walters, 2002). The gains in school enrolment and the investment that countries have made in education – recognised as providing the best escape from poverty – are being eroded (UNICEF, 2001).

The more difficult psychological needs of orphans are inadequately catered for in most instances. The suffering and deaths of parents cause severe trauma in their surviving children – which may be compounded by feelings of guilt, bewilderment, betrayal, anxiety, anger and despair (Jackson, 2002). The orphans may move in to live with a relative (who may be exhausted, stressed and desperately poor), and lose the close knit support of their birth family at a time of emotional distress.

The AIDS pandemic is worsening the poverty experienced by the poorest children and families. Children may have to start working in the fields at a very young age in order to replace adult labour lost to the disease. In the worst cases, households may be headed by a child who, somehow, has to care for younger siblings and relatives. As the AIDS pandemic advances and poverty increases, children are forced prematurely into work. The recent Malawi Government National Child Labour Survey[7] shows that 3.2 million children were working, with 1.4 million living as unpaid family workers (Malawi Ministry of Economic Planning and Development, 2005).

The AIDS pandemic also affects the elderly who lack savings and are often too old or tired to work. They have watched and grieved with dignity and dismay as one after another of their children died, leaving them without the traditional support of their family in their old age. Some parents have lost all their children to the AIDS pandemic. In some families, no one is left except the old and the young. The old have buried their children and are now burying their grandchildren.

Malawi is a 'nation living in grief' but also a country of great courage. As Kelly (2003) notes:

> Official reports lack the eloquence and conferences miss the experience. The wonder, the great wonder is that people here respond so magnificently...They are upholding human dignity and respect in circumstances that would daunt the most stout-hearted. They are bewildered, they are saddened, but they maintain their spirit. The common bond of suffering has made them more appreciative of each other. Their constant search for food, for medicine, for work, for money has made them resourceful. For all its ravages, they have not let AIDS break their spirit.

The impact of HIV/AIDS on agriculture and livelihoods

Labour scarcity at critical times almost guarantees household poverty in an economy where household labour is the major economic resource available. Food security for such households depends on the availability of labour – normally provided by members of the household – to perform husbandry tasks (land preparation, planting, weeding, fertiliser application). If these tasks are done late or to a poor standard, yields of the food crops that provide subsistence are compromised. If labour is diverted from agricultural production and the crucial husbandry practices delayed, then yields fall and food security is undermined.

HIV/AIDS makes an already precarious situation worse as it affects primarily those that are sexually active – the same age group that provides much of the labour for subsistence agriculture. Ill persons cannot work effectively but continue to need food. Many households are forced to work off-farm to generate income to pay for food – reducing home production further. Much investment in smallholder agriculture comes from remittances provided by family members working outside the home. If such a family member becomes ill, he or she returns home and the remittances (and the consequent investment) cease. A significant minority of smallholder households in Malawi are short of food well before the next harvest arrives. In a hungry household, labour productivity falls due to poor nutritional status and lack of energy. HIV-infected individuals have higher nutritional requirements than normal, particularly with regard to protein and energy. The nutritional stress is also likely to accelerate the transition from HIV to full-blown AIDS.

Female-headed households face the worst labour problems. Women do most of the agricultural labour in Africa and have to combine this with multiple pregnancies, child-rearing responsibilities and household responsibilities including collecting firewood and water, and preparing food. They also face serious problems in gaining access to financial markets. They have the 'double burden of care' as they are most likely to suffer from HIV/AIDS and are also responsible to care for people affected by chronic illness within the household. Apart from caring for the affected individual within the household, an enormous amount of time is spent travelling to hospitals and health centres and trying to get medication.

The whole community is affected by HIV/AIDS. Income is diverted to pay for health care and the cost of funerals, so less is available to pay for improved inputs to increase agricultural productivity. Assets are depleted and livestock are sold in a desperate attempt to meet health care requirements. This affects the long-term sustainability of smallholder households and compromises future income and food security. Communities are devastated emotionally and practically by the amount of time that is spent at the funerals (which may occur daily in many villages). Fields are deserted; rural infrastructure (such as terraces, conservation of communal catchments, and irrigation systems) deteriorates as time is devoted to burying the dead.

Richards (1985) has outlined how communities develop indigenous knowledge, particularly on how to adapt to circumstances and manage communal resources. When experienced farmers die, their knowledge of soils, climate and the community dies with them. The household may lose specialised knowledge on new, as well as traditional technologies, on prices and markets, and information on credit and saving opportunities. HIV/AIDS affects the agricultural development institutions, especially planning, research and extension services making it even more difficult to provide solutions to the crisis in smallholder agricultural productivity (this is will be examined further in the following section and in Chapter 5).

The impact of HIV/AIDS on agricultural production systems and rural livelihoods in the central region of Malawi

A study conducted in the central region of Malawi (Shah *et al.*, 2002) found that a significant minority of households suffer from chronic illness[8] and are unable to provide the labour needed for even low-productivity subsistence agriculture. Whatever resources, especially cash, the household has are used to pay for health care and funerals – further depressing production and leading to lower levels of household income and nutrition. As food security deteriorates, malnutrition increases.[9]

Between 22 and 64 percent of households in all study sites suffered from chronic sickness. The impact of chronic sickness included close relatives who were involved in taking care of the sick and paying for funerals. However, the most immediate impact of chronic sickness was the loss of labour. Over 70 percent of households affected by chronic sickness experienced loss of labour – which caused delayed agricultural operations (45 percent of households), leaving land fallow (23 percent of households), changes in crop mix (26 percent of households), and changes in sources of livelihood (23 percent of households). All these factors combined to depress agricultural productivity. Low crop yields and the burden of medical and funeral expenses forced many of the households affected by chronic illness to sell produce in distress or to borrow from other villagers. Households affected by chronic illness relied more on *ganyu* labour (off-farm casual work), which reduced further productivity on their own farms.

Illness during the peak agricultural season had an immediate and drastic effect on household productivity. In Dedza District, a family had twin sons in July, three months before the start of the agricultural season. One son died almost immediately while the other was chronically sick. The mother spent most of the time caring for the sick child, and did not work her *dimba* garden.[10] The father worked off-farm for *ganyu* and consequently neglected his own gardens. As a result, the harvest was less than 50 percent of the previous year when there was no chronic sickness in the household.

In another case, the household head fell ill with shingles[11] in February (early in the agricultural season). He had just planted his tobacco, maize and groundnuts, but was too ill to work the fields. The household had neither the income to buy fertiliser nor the labour to weed the crop. As a result, the harvest was less than half of the previous year. His wife had to sell her goats to pay for medical treatment. The oldest child had to drop out of school because there was no money for secondary school fees. The household, which also included five orphans, was usually reliably and routinely food secure. Within one year, everything changed. It could only produce enough food to feed itself for six months and eventually fell into food insecurity and poverty.

Prolonged sickness depleted more resources and kept other productive workers at home looking after the sick individual. This effect was compounded when more than one household member fell sick. When a women falls sick, her husband is usually able to take care of her garden. The woman is also more likely to leave the household to be cared for by her parents. When a man falls sick, his wife usually remains to care for him or accompanies him to the hospital. Agricultural production plummets as the husband does not work due to illness, and his wife has to devote most of her time to caring for him.

Labour was lost as time was spent either taking the patient to health centres of hospitals, trying to obtain medicines from pharmacies or attending frequent funerals. Scarce cash was diverted from purchases of fertilisers or seeds to paying for medicines, transport, food and funerals. Profitable (but typically labour and cash intensive) crops such as tobacco are replaced by low-productivity, low-input cassava and sweet potatoes. Land may have to be left idle as there may not be sufficient labour to prepare and plant even low-labour crops. In a country where there is intense competition for access to scarce land resources, households who leave land fallow are very vulnerable to losing their land. The poorest households may spend up to 60 percent of the agricultural season working off-farm. But the increasing surplus of *ganyu* labour (reflecting a growing desperation in the countryside) is depressing already pitifully low *ganyu* labour rates further. The spiral of declining food security and poverty is relentlessly heading downwards.

To survive, households have to turn to livelihood strategies that threaten their long-term prospects for breaking out of poverty. Their coping mechanisms increasingly include strategies that undermine resilience and ability to recover. The household's already minimal capital reserves will be depleted as they sell productive assets[12] – reducing the range of income earning opportunities. In addition, there may be insufficient labour and cash to exploit (or continue) off-farm income earning and trading activities. Instead, a household may have to turn to activities that deplete what few natural resources they have access to – such as selling wood or charcoal. As the vicious cycle of poverty intensifies, children are taken out of school and women may turn to extreme 'coping mechanisms' such as selling sex for survival. Distress sales of crops are most common in those households facing chronic illness.

The death of a husband in a patrilocal[13] village usually results in the dissolution of the household as the widow is expected to leave the village and return to her parents' village (often without her children who are cared for by her husband's parents). Men in matrilocal villages are expected to leave the village within a month of the wife's death. Separation, divorce and remarriage are common in households where a family member is chronically ill.

Conclusion

This chapter has outlined the multiple impacts of AIDS – all of which will exacerbate poverty. The first part of the chapter outlines key economic statistics including limited economic growth and increased indebtedness. AIDS will impact the macro-economy through reducing already low rates of national savings, increasing pressure on the national budget and reducing labour productivity. The AIDS pandemic also affects the government's ability to deliver goods and services, its efficiency and in some cases, its very existence (Barnett and Whiteside, 2002). An effective and functioning public sector is vital for developing essential goods and services as well as developing successful national AIDS responses. Before the epidemic, several worst affected countries were already struggling with daunting development challenges, excessive debt burdens and declining trade – all features of the poverty trap. AIDS undermines public sector efficiency as it increases calls on the government's resources and time, while at the same time eroding public sector capacity. Deaths among skilled and experienced professional staff and managers exacerbate already severe human resource constraints.

The AIDS pandemic has a devastating impact on children – the future of the continent. AIDS increases the number of orphans and vulnerable children often beyond the coping capacity of the extended family. Children start to suffer when their parents become ill; the psychological impact of seeing parents suffer and die is often unbearable. The orphans and other vulnerable children, including children forced onto the streets, may become 'household heads' responsible for their younger siblings. This forces many into child labour – which is a significant phenomenon in Malawi. The AIDS pandemic also has a devastating impact on the elderly who are most likely to suffer from poverty as they do not have formal sector employment and have limited options to generate income from agriculture or off-farm employment. The communities are trying to respond to the growing number of orphans and vulnerable children but may be overwhelmed by the enormity of the task.

The AIDS pandemic undermines the agricultural sector from which 85 percent of the population derive their livelihoods. We have drawn on detailed field-level research to show how AIDS exacerbated poverty through multiple pathways. Malawi illustrates many of the issues which AIDS exacerbates unless there is innovative and timely intervention. There are investments – in irrigation, in input and output markets, for example – that can serve to boost productivity, increase income nationally and locally, and reduce the vulnerability to drought. Such investments could break the cycle of poverty that is driving the AIDS epidemic and provide an environment in which AIDS interventions may work. Economic growth and escaping the poverty trap requires investments. It is only possible to pull yourself up by your bootstraps if you have boots.

Notes

1. The economy, somewhat unrealistically, is expected to grow at around four percent annually for the couple of years following 2004 unless further drought-related food crises intervene.
2. Population growth is projected at 1.9 percent between 2001 and 2015 (UNDP, 2003). This lower population growth rate is assumed to take the impact of AIDS into account. According to the US Census Bureau it would have been 3.2 in the absence of AIDS (US Census Bureau, 2004).
3. These include, but are not limited to, high inflation and interest rates that undermine incentives for investment and growth. Other structural impediments to growth include limited internal markets, high external and internal transport costs, poor supporting infrastructure, expensive utilities and lack of security.
4. This work showed that when a Solow growth model was used, annual GDP growth rates reduced by 0.2–1.5 percent, and annual GDP per capita growth would decrease by 0.1–0.3 percent. With a more sophisticated dual labour model annual GDP growth was reduced by 3 to 9 percent and annual GDP per capita growth by 0 to 3 percent.

5. See Bell C., Devarajan S. and Gersbach H. (2003). *The Long-run economic costs of AIDS: theory and an application to South Africa.* Washington: The World Bank. The model overstates the impact of AIDS because it does not consider human resilience, adaptability, and the fact that people will not simply wait for the epidemic to affect them but will respond.

6. The variation is largely a result of differences in end-of-service benefits.

7. The survey was funded by the International Labour Organisation, International Programme for the Elimination of Child Labour-Statistical Information Monitoring Programme on Child Labour (ILO/IPEC-SIMPOC) in the ILO Office in Geneva.

8. During the fieldwork, researchers used the term 'chronic sickness' rather than HIV/AIDS as there is still some reluctance to discuss HIV/AIDS openly in Malawi (reflecting the stigma that surrounds HIV/AIDS). The study aimed to generate information useful in the design of appropriate practical intervention strategies that could, and should, be adopted to mitigate the catastrophic impact of HIV/AIDS on agricultural production in Malawi.

9. Protein and energy malnutrition as well as micro-nutrient deficiencies.

10. A *dimba* garden is a fertile wetland where households can cultivate crops during the dry season (May to November) and is an important component in many household food security and nutrition strategies.

11. A common early symptom of HIV/AIDS.

12. Typical items sold include livestock (especially goats), carts, radios, bicycles and roofing sheets.

13. A patrilocal village is where the land is passed through the male; a matrilocal village is where the land is passed through the female.

Bibliography

African Development Bank (2003) African Development Report 2003, Oxford: Oxford University Press.

African Development Bank *et al.* (2003) African Economic Outlook, Paris: OECD.

Barnett A (1999) 'HIV/AIDS and the African Agrarian Crisis: Which Way Forward?' In: Mutangadura, Jackson and Mukarazika (eds). 'AIDS and African Agriculture', Harare, Zimbabwe.

Badcock Walters P. (2002) 'Education' in Gow J. and Desmond C. 'Impacts and Interventions: The HIV/AIDS Epidemic and the Children of Southern Africa', University of Natal Press.

Barnett A., and Whiteside A., (2002) 'AIDS in the Twenty First Century: Disease and Globalization', Palgrave.

Bell C., Devarajan S. and Gersbach H. (2003) 'The Long-run economic costs of AIDS: theory and an application to South Africa'. Washington: The World Bank.

Bollinger L., Stover J. and Palamuleni M.E. (2000) 'The Economic Impact of AIDS in Malawi', The Futures Group International, July 2000, also at www.policyproject.com/pubs/SEImpact/malawi.pdf

Bonnel R. (2000) 'HIV/AIDS and Economic Growth: A global perspective', *Journal of South African Economics*, 68(5): 820–55.

Cohen D. (1999) 'Sustainable Development and the HIV Epidemic in Africa', In: Mutangadura, Jackson and Mukarazika eds, 'AIDS and African Agriculture', Harare, Zimbabwe.

Cuddington J. and Hancock J. (1994a) 'Assessing the impact of AIDS on the growth path of the Malawian economy', *Journal of Development Economics*, 43: 363–8.

Cuddington J. and Hancock J. (1994b) 'The Macroeconomic Impact of AIDS in Malawi: a Dualistic Labour-Surplus Economy', *Journal of African Economies*, 4(1): 1–28.

Economist Intelligence Unit (EIU) (2005) 'Malawi Country Report', January 2005, London.

Fox M., Rosen S., MacCleod W. and Wasunna M. (2004) 'The Impact of HIV/AIDS on Labour Productivity in Kenya', *Tropical Medicine & International Health*, 9(3): 318–24.

Giese S. 'Health' in Gow J. and Desmond C. (2002) 'Impacts and Interventions: the HIV Epidemic and the Children of South Africa', UNICEF and University of Natal Press.

Harries A.D., Hargreaves N.J., Gausi F., Kwanjana J.H. and Salaniponi F.M. (2002) 'High death rates in health care workers and teachers in Malawi', *Transactions of the Royal Society of Tropical Medicine and Hygiene*, 96(1): 34–7.

Hunter S.S. and Williamson J. (2000) 'Children on the Brink 2000', Washington DC: The Synergy Project.

Jackson H. (2002) 'AIDS Africa: Continent in Crisis', SAFAIDS, Harare, Zimbabwe.

James R. (2004) 'Dodging the Fists: The Crushing Blows of HIV/AIDS on Leaders in Malawi', INTRAC Praxis Paper.

Jones C. (1996) 'Brown and Clapperton Limited: The Cost Implications of HIV/AIDS', JSI-STAFF Project, Lilongwe, Malawi.

Jones C. (1997) 'What HIV cost a tea estate in Malawi', AIDS Analysis Africa, 7(3): 5–7.

Kelly M.J. (2003) 'Dying Day by Day: Facing AIDS with Dignity and Courage in Southern Africa', In: Africa Magazine, Kiltegan Fathers, Co. Wicklow Ireland.

Lowenson R. and Whiteside A. (1997) 'Social and Economic Issues of HIV/ AIDS in Southern Africa: A Review of Current Research', Harare, SAfAIDS Occasional Paper 2.

Madise N. (2004) 'The Demographic Impact of AIDS in Malawi', Unpublished background paper.

Malawi National Statistical Office (2001) 'Population Projections', Zomba, Malawi National Statistical Office.

Malawi Government and UNDP (2002) 'The impact of HIV/AIDS on human resources in the Malawi Public Service', Lilongwe, Malawi.

Malawi, Ministry of Economic Planning and Development (2001) 'Economic Report', Lilongwe, Malawi.

Malawi, Ministry of Economic Planning and Development (2004) 'A Growth Strategy for Malawi: Part One Overview and Macro-Economic Environment Strategy', Lilongwe, Malawi.

Malawi, Ministry of Finance (2005) 'Budget Statement', Government Printer, Lilongwe, Malawi.

Malawi, Ministry of Economic Planning and Development (2005) 'Economic Report 2005', Government Printer, Lilongwe, Malawi.

Mills A. and Shillcutt S. (2004) 'Communicable Diseases' in Bjorn Lomborg ed. Cambridge: Cambridge University Press. 'Global Crises, Global Solutions'.

Richards P. (1985) 'Indigenous Agricultural Revolution: Ecology and Food Production in West Africa'. Boulder, Colorado: Westview.

Richards P. (1999) 'AIDS and African Smallholder Agriculture' in Mutangadura, Jackson and Mukarazika eds, 'AIDS and African Agriculture', Harare, Zimbabwe.

Rosen S., Vincent J.R., Macleod W. and Fox M. (2004) 'The Cost of HIV/AIDS to Businesses in Africa'. *AIDS*, 18(2): 317–24.

Shah M.K., Osborne N., Mbilizi T. and Vilili G. (2002) 'The impact of HIV/AIDS on agricultural productivity and rural livelihoods in the Central Region of Malawi'. Care International, Lilongwe, Malawi.

Timaeus I. and Jassen M. (2003) 'Adult mortality in sub-Saharan Africa: Evidence from demographic and health surveys', Paper presented to the Conference on Empirical Evidence for the Demographic and Socio-economic Impact of AIDS, Durban, South Africa.

UNAIDS (1998) 'HIV/AIDS in the Workplace: Forging Innovative Business Responses', UNAIDS Technical Update, July, Geneva, UNAIDS Best Practice Collection.

UNAIDS (2000) 'Africa's children at the forefront of the AIDS pandemic', UNAIDS Focus in *SAfAIDS News* 8(3): 13.

UNAIDS (2004a) '2004 Report on the Global AIDS Epidemic', UNAIDS, Geneva.

UNAIDS (2004b) 'AIDS Epidemic Update', UNAIDS, Geneva.

UNAIDS (2003) 'AIDS Epidemic Update', UNAIDS and WHO, Geneva.

UNDP (2002) 'Poverty Reduction Strategy Paper for Malawi', UNDP, Lilongwe.

UNDP (2003) Human Development Report 2003', Oxford: Oxford University Press.

UNDP (2004) 'Human Development Report', Oxford: Oxford University Press.

UNDP (2004a) http://hdr.undp.org/reports/global/2004/pdf/hdr04_HDI.pdf

UNICEF (2001) 'The Progress of Nations', UNICEF, New York.

UNICEF (2004) 'Africa's Orphaned Generations', UNICEF, New York.

US Census Bureau (2004) 'International Population Reports WP/02-2, AIDS Pandemic in the 21st Century', US Government Printing Office, Washington DC.

USAID, UNAIDS and UNICEF (2002) 'Children on the Brink 2002: A joint report on orphan estimates and programme strategies', TvT Associates/The Synergy Project for USAID, UNAIDS and UNICEF, Washington DC, July 2002.

Whiteside A. and Sunter C. (2000) 'AIDS: The challenge for South Africa', Human and Rousseau Tafelberg, Cape Town.

World Bank (2002) 'Malawi Multi-Sectoral HIV/AIDS Project MAP: Orphans and Vulnerable Children Mission', Lilongwe, Malawi.

World Bank (2003) 'Malawi: Country Economic Memorandum: Policies for Accelerating Growth', Report No. 25293 MAI. The World Bank, Washington DC.

World Health Organization (2001) 'Macro-Economic Commission on Health: Investing in Health for Economic Development', WHO, Geneva.

World Health Organization (2002) 'Global burden of disease estimates 2002', World Health Organization, Geneva.

Whiteside A.W. (1985) 'Some Aspects of Labour Relations between the Republic of South Africa and Neighbouring States. Part 1: Legislation and Agreements', Manpower Studies No. 1, Human Sciences Research Council, Pretoria.

Whiteside A.W. (1986) 'Some Aspects of Labour Relations between the Republic of South Africa and Neighbouring States. Part 2: Economic Implications', Manpower Studies No. 2, Human Sciences Research Council, Pretoria.

Whiteside A. and Sunter C. (2000) 'AIDS the Challenge for South Africa', Human & Rousseau/Tafelberg, Cape Town.

Whitworth A. (2004) 'Malawi's Fiscal Crisis: A Donor Perspective', Department for International Development, Lilongwe, Malawi.

World Bank (1998) 'AIDS Assessment Study 10: Malawi', Washington DC.

World Bank (2000) 'World Development Indicators 2000', Oxford: Oxford University Press.

World Bank (2002) 'African Development Indicators 2002', The World Bank, Washington.

World Bank (2003) 'World Development Report', Oxford: Oxford University Press.

World Bank (2004) 'World Development Indicators', Washington DC: World Bank.

World Bank Group (2004) 'Country "at a glance" reports: Malawi, Tanzania, Zambia, Mozambique, South Africa', World Bank, Washington DC.

5

The Collapse of Agriculture

Malcolm Blackie and Anne Conroy

Tradition and African smallholder cropping stems

Africa is a continent of huge diversity. Soils, farming systems and rainfall patterns vary enormously both across the continent as a whole, and within countries. We focus on smallholder agriculture in southern and eastern Africa where the dominant smallholder cropping systems are based on maize. It is the productivity of these systems that are of concern to this book. The trends and patterns found in this region have their echoes in other parts of the continent and thus provide a useful proxy for understanding change elsewhere in Africa.

The food security of resource-poor households is critically dependent on the productivity and sustainability of maize-based cropping systems. Maize accounts for 60 percent or more of the cropped area in much of southern and eastern Africa. It has become the staple food of the region, accounting for about 50 percent of the calories consumed. In Malawi, maize is the main crop in nearly 90 percent of the area and contributes 80 percent of daily food calories. Most farm households use family resources, especially labour, to grow their maize. Animal (mainly ox) traction may be used to prepare the land and help with weeding. In Malawi, where grazing is scarce, human labour using hand-held hoes is the predominant power source. Increasingly, maize is grown on the same land year after year, possibly sparsely intercropped with beans, groundnuts, cowpeas or pumpkins.

Many traditional African agricultural systems were based around extended fallows and the harvesting of nutrients stored in woody plants. The site to be cultivated was cleared by cutting and slashing plant growth, and then by burning the dried plant material (Blackie and Jones, 1993; Blackie, 1994). The ash from the burned plants added some fertility but the main effect was on weeds. A hot burn from bulky plant material produced a weed-free seedbed which enabled a crop to be grown with the minimum of labour. Extensive exploitation of land by a few families characterised these systems. For example, in the *chitemene* slash-and-burn system in the *miombo* woodland of northern Zambia, land was fallowed for 50–70 years, followed by cropping in the centre of the clearing for a few years (Araki, 1993). Today, in most arable areas of Malawi, Zimbabwe and Kenya, fallowing has almost disappeared from the now sedentary agricultural system. The length of the fallow period continues to decline significantly in Zambia, Mozambique and Tanzania. Continuous cropping with maize or another food crop (sorghum or cassava, for example) is the norm.

There is a single consistent outcome from an agricultural economy based on inadequate fallows and extensive, low-input cultivation – crop yields decline and soils erode. Buddenhagen (1992) estimates that, discounting erosion effects, the weathering of minerals and biological nitrogen fixation will enable the production, at most, of 1000 kg of grain per hectare per year on a sustainable basis in the tropics. Loss of soil through erosion (and soils cultivated with annual crops in the upland tropics are very prone to erosion) will reduce this level considerably. Farmers locked into low-crop productivity systems (per unit of land) have little option other than to open new land for agriculture.

No 'silver bullet'

African agriculture in the early twenty-first century is a highly complex system where a single component rarely has a consistent overriding influence. Improved varieties, which demonstrate impressive yields on research stations, often fail to replicate their performance on farmers' fields. Pests, diseases, rainfall and soil fertility combine to produce a risky and variable production environment. The poor find themselves trapped in low-input, low-risk, low-productivity systems with few consistently reliable options for pulling themselves out of poverty. Biophysical signals within and between cropping systems substantially check the success that can be enjoyed by any single component of the system.

African farmers, as their counterparts in other regions, have shown considerable talent for innovation and ingenuity. They have developed complex cropping systems to fit environments ranging from the slopes of Mt. Kenya to the fringes of the Sahara, each with its unique mix of biotic and abiotic constraints. Many can be characterised as low-risk, low-input, long-fallow systems. Poor soils, short and unreliable growing seasons, and a challenging array of pests and diseases favour strategies that do not involve high inputs of labour, land and cash – which are stable in bad as well as good years, and which are productive within the normal resources available to a farming household.

An important part of addressing the poverty agenda in Africa is the development of predictable and significant improvements in farming systems using soils which are very low in fertility and subject to the further stress of periodic drought. The focus is not just one of increasing yields. New technologies must perform reliably and consistently in improving yield stability and safeguarding the investments of land, labour, and what little capital is available, of some of the world's most vulnerable people.

DeVries and Toennissen (2001) set the scene graphically:

[The reality] is that of a single mother whose primary means of income is a one hectare plot of unimproved land on an eroded hillside … . From each harvest she must provide for virtually all the needs of her family throughout the year, including clothing, health care, education costs and housing. Because she can afford few purchased inputs, the yield potential of her farm is low … perhaps 2000 kilograms of produce …

In the course of a given season, innumerable threats to the crops appear … . The impact of drought plus whatever combination of pests and diseases attacking the crop in a given year can often reduce the average harvest on her farm by perhaps 50–60 percent, to 1000 kilograms of produce. *At this level of productivity, the family is on the edge of survival.* [emphasis added]

Several factors are evident from this analysis. The family can shift from the 'edge of survival' to relative food security through the elimination of existing losses. The gains from such a strategy are significant and are sufficiently attractive to poor households – while most in need of such technologies are those least able to pay for them. Reliability and consistency of performance are as important as absolute yield improvements and thresholds. A single mother hoping to harvest a ton of rice on a hectare of depleted upland soil can ill-afford to lose 100 kg of her harvest to a crop pest or disease. Moreover, she has so many demands on her very limited resources of cash and labour that she needs to know, as far as it is possible, that any investment she makes in crop improvement will be worthwhile.

Poor farmers in Africa do not want to be poor. The reason so many are living on the 'edge of survival' is that too many of their traditional

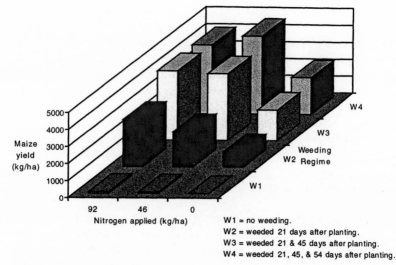

Figure 5.1   Interaction between weeding and fertiliser use in maize
Source: Kabambe & Kumwenda, 1995.

approaches to agricultural production are breaking down. The fundamental productivity issues faced by most African farmers (who are smallholders) are often those for which agricultural experts have few, if any, realistic answers. Nor can the farmer turn elsewhere for counsel. In a period of unprecedented change, farmers find that their traditional wisdom provides limited guidance (Lele, 1992; Eicher, 1999; Blackie, 1994). In stark contrast with Asia's food challenge of the 1960s and 70s, improving food security in Africa will require the improvement of a broad range of farming systems.

Thus we see that there is no simple answer to improving cropping system productivity in Africa – change will require action on several fronts. Smallholders across the continent have been mining nutrients from their soils consistently for the past 30 years or more. Byerlee *et al.* (1994) note that what smallholders in Africa need are improved seeds, combined with complementary technologies for maintaining soil fertility and increasing labour productivity. In Figure 5.1, the interaction between weeding and fertiliser use is well illustrated. If the crop is not weeded at all (W1), even with very high rates of fertiliser, the crop yields dismally. By contrast, weeding twice gives significantly more yield with less fertiliser (W3 and 46 kgs of nitrogen) than weeding only once and double the fertiliser (W2 and 96 kgs of nitrogen). However, weeding is a highly labour-intensive operation which coincides with high labour demands in other parts of the farming system.

To help clarify the difficulties faced by smallholders in Africa as they struggle to feed their families, we will look, somewhat anecdotally, at an individual household. Lack of cash dominates the choices available to the African farm family of today. Two major costs faced by many smallholders in producing food are labour and the inputs of seed and fertiliser (including home-produced fertilisers such as composts which are highly labour-intensive). We will focus on labour, as without labour, no crop will be produced.

Labour may be provided by the family, it may be bought from other farmers, or it may be sold to others for food or cash. Often the household is headed by a woman, with small children. The older children may be at school, or have moved to town. If she is fortunate, her husband and children living away will send cash or kind to help support the rural household. If not, she will have to support herself and her children from what she can grow or sell. She will be living on a piece of land that has been cultivated many times before. What inherent fertility was there has long been extracted from the soil. Weeds, including the devastating *Striga*,[1] will have established themselves and will compete strongly with whatever she plants for light, water and soil nutrients.

If she has access to a hectare or more of land, she may produce enough to feed herself and her family if her health is good and the weather favourable. But the start of the rains brings diarrhoea and malaria. Often, illness to herself or her children will result in her planting her crop late. With a poor rainy season (Africa and drought are synonymous) her crop may fail. The odds are that in some years, she will find herself unable to produce enough food for her family's needs. She will need to go out to work for neighbouring farmers who will then feed or pay her (and any children that work with her) for the days that she puts in. Typically this work will be planting, weeding or fertilising the neighbour's crop – which means that her own is left unplanted, unweeded and unfertilised until later in the season. Late planting and poor weeding mean a poor harvest and once again she finds herself without food before the crop comes in.

This is the downward spiral that creates much of African poverty. Malawi illustrates an advanced case of this scenario with some 60 percent of rural households (and 41 percent of the total population) producing less than they need to feed themselves through the year. Improved seeds may have a high yield potential but, unless the plant is fed, it will never reach that potential. Feeding the plant involves adding fertility to the soil – from purchased mineral fertilisers, from manures and composts or from a combination of both. In most parts of the world, mineral (also called inorganic or chemical) fertilisers play a major role in maintaining or increasing soil fertility. On average, African farmers use around 7 kgs of fertilisers per hectare. This low level of use (well below soil nutrient replacement needs) is, in part, caused by the cost of fertilisers. Fertiliser is the most costly cash input used by the typical smallholder, and in many countries its real price is rising each year. But an expensive input can be profitable if used efficiently. In the developed world, farmers have reached a high degree of scientific knowledge and skill in their use of fertilisers.

In fact, farmers in much of Africa receive advice on the use of fertilisers that actively discourages its use. Fertiliser recommendations typically ignore soil and climatic variations found in smallholder farming areas, are either incompatible with farmer resources (which we know are severely limited), or are inefficient (which drastically affects the profitability of fertiliser use). Organic sources of fertility can come from adopting suitable crop rotations (especially those involving legumes), the addition of animal manure, and appropriate intercropping. But these rarely (under the conditions faced by many smallholders in sub-Saharan Africa), are able to add sufficient fertility to the soils to replace losses from cropping. There are other important constraints to this approach. As pressure for arable land rises, cropping encroaches into areas previously used for grazing. The availability of animal manure declines as livestock are squeezed out.[2] Even in the best areas, the supply of animal manure and its quality is usually inadequate to maintain soil fertility on its own. Leaf litter from trees can make significant contributions in areas close to woodlands – but deforestation associated with the demand for arable land, and for building and firewood, work against this option as the population rises. Composted crop residues are used in wetter areas and where crop biomass production is relatively high, but composts are rarely sufficient for more than a modest part of the cultivated area.[3] Furthermore, these technologies require a substantial labour commitment on the part of farmers and this puts them beyond the reach of the many labour-poor farm families.

Land, agricultural productivity and land policy

So far, we have looked at agricultural decline in Africa mainly from the perspective of the household. We now turn to some of the key institutional obstacles to a productive agricultural sector. In many countries in sub-Saharan Africa, access to land heavily influences national policy. In southern Africa, most notably Zimbabwe in recent years, land access has totally dominated the political agenda. But even in countries with a less evident legacy of colonial land policy, the sustainable use of land is becoming a critical issue as farmers spread out into protected watersheds and other ecologically-sensitive areas. Using the Malawi case, we will show how the accretions of an ill-focused land policy compromise the potential for breaking out of poverty into a food-secure future.

Understanding the evolution of land policy in Malawi is crucial to understanding food insecurity. Struggles over land have profoundly formed the national consciousness (Cross, 2002). Surprisingly, as land availability per capita in Malawi has fallen, the outcome has not been agricultural intensification but rather land degradation, falling production per unit area of land, and the consequent impoverishment of the majority of the population. Malawians have simply been too poor to access the means to increase productivity per unit area as farm sizes have fallen.

The first President of the Republic of Malawi, Dr Hastings Kamuzu Banda had a vision for Malawi of an economy based on labour-intensive agricultural exports[4] produced by large scale 'modern' farms. Smallholder agriculture was perceived as 'backward'. Land policy was deliberately aimed at stimulating the growth of the large-scale estate sector. A significant amount of land was alienated from the smallholder to the estate sector. The resources needed to finance the expansion of the estate sector were extracted from the smallholder sector via implicit taxation of smallholder export crops. By the end of the 1980s, the amount of land transferred from the small holder sector to the estate sector was in excess of 700,000 hectares (Cross, 2002). The principal beneficiaries were members of the political elite, party functionaries and richer smallholders, many of whom failed to use the land effectively.

The effects on smallholders (and especially the rural poor) have been devastating with many smallholder land holdings too small to support the families that live on them, and some rural households effectively landless. Recent survey data indicates that 72 percent of smallholder households cultivate less than one hectare and 41 percent cultivate less than 0.5 hectares (Malawi Government, 2003) – too small at current levels of productivity and farming systems to achieve food security. The environment also has suffered. Forest cover has declined from 26 percent to 19 percent of the total land area over the past 25 years with attendant problems associated with the management of watersheds (World Bank, 2003). The World Bank (2003) suggests that harvested crops annually remove a net 75,000 tonnes of soil nutrients, causing further environmental degradation, and compromising family livelihoods and food security.

Macro-economic policy reform: a Malawi case study of disaster

A major tool used to create favourable change in developing countries in recent years has been macro-economic policy reform. Krugman (1999) has pithily reviewed the mixed outcomes from many such endeavours and we will not attempt to develop his discussion further. Here we focus again on the Malawi case and show how inconsistencies and a lack of logical rigour in the imposition of structural reforms have exacerbated an already threatening situation of national food insecurity and poverty.

In the first years following independence in the early 1960s, Malawi's economic growth was largely based on two key interrelated factors:

- Tobacco production by the estate (large scale) sector.
- The introduction of fertilised hybrid maize (using subsidies to disguise the real cost of production) to the wealthier farmers in the smallholder sector.

But growth across the agricultural sector was highly uneven, with smallholders playing a minor role. Widespread poverty and ecological decline resulted despite the best efforts of the Banda government to conceal these facts. By the mid-1980s there was compelling evidence that, despite the well-stocked ADMARC[5] retail maize markets, tens of thousands of Malawian households were too poor to buy this maize. In the face of national surpluses, chronic malnutrition afflicted nearly half of Malawian children.

In response to a deteriorating macro-economic situation, the Malawi Government introduced a structural adjustment programme in late 1979 with support from the World Bank and International Monetary Fund (IMF). A series of such programmes continued throughout the 1980s and 1990s supported by successive IMF standby arrangements and World Bank financed structural adjustment loans. The (entirely laudable) aim was to redress the policy bias against smallholder agriculture. The production of smallholder exportable cash crops (tobacco, groundnuts and cotton) was encouraged by increasing the producer prices offered by ADMARC. Maize prices were held down as a further incentive to farmers to shift to export crop production. Maize fertiliser subsidies were targeted for removal (Harrigan, 2003). An agricultural adjustment credit approved in 1990 included the partial liberalisation of burley tobacco production to allow smallholders to grow this lucrative export crop.[6]

The structural adjustment exercises were intended to remove market distortions that encouraged too many resources being devoted to maize production and that inhibited smallholders from participating in crop markets. Price incentives alone however were not sufficient to generate the needed supply response. The need to develop complementary but essential policies to address technological, land and credit constraints faced by smallholder households remained largely ignored (Harrigan, 2003). The main causes of food insecurity and stagnation in Malawi are the failure to implement reforms to address basic questions of declining land availability, fragmentation of holdings, and the decline in soil fertility in the smallholder sector.

In 1987, three simultaneous events catapulted Malawi from a routine national food surplus to regular national shortages. The cassava mealy bug decimated the staple crop of Malawi's northern lakeshore population; drought ravaged the Shire Valley; and Malawi became a safe haven for large numbers of Mozambicans fleeing a devastating civil war. Long accustomed to buying low-priced maize in ADMARC markets in the hungry season, Malawians suddenly found themselves queuing for rationed supplies; a household's accustomed monthly maize consumption cost the equivalent of 40 days' wages. With maize weighted heavily in the consumer price index, inflationary pressures mounted.

This set the stage for the long and continuing slide in the value of the Malawi kwacha and made more difficult and painful the opening of the economy to market forces. There followed an extended period of intermittent food crises with donors providing extensive food aid. Following the great drought of 1991–92 and the collapse of the credit system, donors started to provide emergency free distributions of seed and fertiliser to maintain maize production. Even with an overvalued currency and a high fertiliser subsidy, few households found the use of fertiliser on maize (based on official recommendations for its use) an economic option. The sharp devaluation of the Malawi kwacha in the 1990s drove fertiliser prices beyond the reach of almost all maize growers.[7]

Market and crop pricing reform

Prior to 1987, ADMARC was a monopoly buyer and seller of essential farm inputs and selected farm outputs in smallholder areas. Its policy had two main elements:

- Farm inputs (especially fertiliser) were subsidised and maize prices controlled through maize-pricing policies which ignored differentials imposed by distance from market (prices normally are higher further from the market) and season (prices fall at harvest and then rise as stocks are used up until the next harvest comes in).
- The costs of these subsidies were covered by paying smallholder producers of export crops (tobacco, tea and sugar) significantly less than the market price – an implicit export tax.

In 1987, ADMARC lost its monopoly in the domestic market as private traders were licensed and allowed to operate in specified markets. In 1996, the need for licences was withdrawn. The response to market liberalisation was mixed. In remote areas, the closing of ADMARC depots was not always followed by the entry of private traders – leaving farmers facing greater uncertainty and higher transaction costs. In areas with better infrastructure, increased competition often led to increased farm-gate prices for smallholders.

The prices of all crops (except maize) were decontrolled in 1996. From that date, the maize market (theoretically) operated within a price band. ADMARC was to intervene when prices in markets went outside the band. In practice, ADMARC never had the resources to defend the price band, and producer prices fell below the floor in years of good harvest and consumer prices were over the price ceiling in years of deficit.[8]

The liberalisation of burley tobacco production in 1994 was a major reform intended to inject cash into the smallholder economy. There was a major supply response by smallholders who were at last given the opportunity to grow and market Malawi's most lucrative crop. Many smallholders had considerable experience of burley and flue-cured tobacco production as tenants to estate growers or through 'illegal' cultivation during the Banda era. Smallholder tobacco production increased from 35,000 tonnes in 1995 to 85,000 tonnes in 1998, with smallholders responsible for more than 70 percent of total production (Harrigan, 2003). However, despite the initial success of tobacco liberalisation, the programme stalled as returns from tobacco production began to fall. This has affected not only those families growing the crop but also their neighbours through the reduced opportunities for *ganyu* labour for poor smallholders.

No comprehensive analysis of the costs and benefits of market liberalisation has been undertaken. Major beneficiaries are probably wealthier smallholders in the higher potential areas best served by infrastructure. There is evidence of high rents extracted by private traders from vulnerable smallholders through arbitrage between the low post-harvest and the higher 'hungry season' prices – but the practice of *ganyu* which many of the vulnerable use to survive the hungry season is just as exploitative. Informal cross-border maize trade has developed considerably. This trade contributed significantly to ameliorating the food crisis in 2002–2003 when private traders were able to import maize at significantly lower cost than the Government.

But in the reform process, ADMARC was left stranded as a loss-making parastatal without a clear mission, mandate, or budget. It was still expected to fulfil important social functions (maintaining food security reserves, providing markets in remote districts), while at the same time operating at a profit. The agency could no longer generate surpluses from the taxation of smallholder export crops to subsidise losses incurred in making food security interventions (including the management of the national strategic grain reserve). It could not afford to maintain a presence in low-volume markets, often leaving farmers without a marketing channel. ADMARC's social functions were nominally paid for on a reimbursement basis by the Treasury. In practice, reimbursements were not made, leaving ADMARC with severe cash flow problems. This in part, led to ADMARC selling the national grain reserve without authority in 1997 and 2001.

The apparent positive outcomes of reform include better market services for those living in areas with reasonable infrastructure. There is little (beyond the development of cross border trade) to suggest that the many farmers who are remote from good roads and other essential infrastructure have benefited significantly from the changes. ADMARC, in trying to meet clearly conflicting goals of social responsibility and corporate profitability, has fallen into practices that have been unhelpful in terms of national development and food security.

The market reforms helped increase cropping diversity in smallholder systems. There has been an increase in smallholder production and marketing of a range of crops including paprika, pulses, groundnuts and cassava. The best outcomes were where there was complementary support to both production and marketing through smallholder farming associations.[9] Despite maize market liberalisation, maize prices moved upwards[10] (except in 1999–2000 and 2000–2001 – years of exceptional surplus due to the Universal Starter Pack Programme and expanded Agricultural Productivity Investment Programme[11]). As food, particularly maize, takes up such a large proportion of poor Malawians expenditures, rising maize prices have meant declining real incomes for most Malawians. The benefits from burley market liberalisation were largely limited to wealthier smallholders – male-headed households with a mean holding size of 1.6 hectares and access to credit (Orr, 2000).[12]

Fertiliser subsidies

In the Banda era, fertiliser subsidies for maize production were used to shore up national food production. But blanket subsidies of this type are very inefficient ways of helping the poor – providing many opportunities for the wealthy and the well-connected to capture the real benefits. Fertiliser subsidies were, therefore, earlier targeted in Malawi's reform process as part of the implementation of the second Structural Adjustment Loan in the mid-1980s and the Government committed itself to complete removal of fertiliser subsidies by 1989–1990. In any event, the rising import costs of fertiliser as a result of devaluation made the costs of policies to promote growth through fertiliser subsidies fiscally unsustainable.

Other national changes also had their own effects. The country was moving towards a more conventionally democratic political system. A significant casualty of political change was the smallholder credit system that delivered the subsidised seed and fertiliser to a minority of larger smallholders. The credit system used draconian measures to ensure that all loans were repaid. When the ruling party changed, so did the ability of the government to collect credit repayments.[13] The credit system suffered blows from other sources as well. After the 1991–1992 drought, there was an entirely reasonable moratorium on credit repayments – it was impractical as well as inequitable to demand credit repayments from families on the edge of survival. Farmers learned fast that credit did not always have to be repaid. A policy of post-drought credit expansion to boost fertilised hybrid maize and restore grain reserves also brought in new and less credit-worthy borrowers. What was intended to be an expanded credit programme in reality became a large free inputs programme for the final round of credit recipients. Whereas before 1990, the quantity of fertiliser not paid for did not exceed 5 percent in any one year of the total used by smallholders, by 1996 this had risen to over 50 percent (Whiteside and Carr, 1997).

But the tragedy was that neither the Malawi Government nor donors had anticipated how fundamentally the twin events of the collapse of the credit system and the increased cost of fertiliser would affect food security. Once improved maize seed and fertiliser technology were priced beyond the cash means of most smallholders, the outcome was disastrous. The 1996–1997 supply of marketed maize (after a good growing season) fell precipitously, the village level purchase price of maize quadrupled, and there was widespread hardship amongst the poor section of the population. The liberalisation of markets (agreed generally as essential to Malawi's future growth) was rapidly becoming discredited amongst the public by the high consumer price of maize and by the conspicuous rents evidently being extracted by private traders. The economy was experiencing all the downside effects of liberalisation, but few of its benefits. A food crisis was looming in 1998.

The deteriorating food security situation in 1998 threatened to undo completely the impressive progress made in laying the policy framework for growth. High maize prices were creating powerful inflationary pressures, compromising household food security, promoting labour unrest and fuelling demands for higher wages. Emergency maize imports contributed to the Government's runaway expenditure that further fed inflation. Interest rates rose sharply and the kwacha collapsed, undercutting productive investment and further driving up the cost of fertiliser for the next crop. With the looming food crisis (and the associated high consumer prices for maize meal and large-scale theft of drying maize from fields), households were eating an unusually high proportion of the crop as green maize – with consequently less available for the following year's consumption. This was the same scenario that was played out again in 2002 and 2003. Famine was averted in 1998 by the introduction of the Universal Starter Pack Programme (see Chapter 9) but, under donor pressure this promising initiative was emasculated from a powerful development intervention into a limited and moderately successful safety net programme for the poor.

Many Malawians express nostalgia for the settled times of the 1970s. In this period, according to popular myth, food was always available, there was little crime, and it was a time of optimism and progress. But we have seen how the policies of that period laid the ground for the major problem that afflicts Malawi today – a perennial food crisis. Every year, it seems, food is either in short or desperately short supply. Food insecurity at the national and at the household level dominates the development of policies. Fear of national food shortages paralyses action at many levels. The effects are often contradictory and counter-productive. Reforms carried out at the macro-level have failed to reach their potential largely because the ever-present threat of a food crisis drives much of what is implemented as policy. Needed long-term change is lost in the urgency of dealing with immediate real or perceived crises.

It was evident then, and remains true today, that Malawi needs urgently to implement a strategy for broad-based and vigorous income growth, within a non-inflationary environment. A strict policy of non-intervention in the market comes at an unacceptably high cost. While, in the longer term, high maize prices may allow for greater invest-ments at the farm level and thus lead to increased productivity, the tragic famines of 2002 and 2003 suggest that it is quite possible that many Malawians would not survive to benefit from these changes.

The collapse of agriculture reviewed

The message of this chapter is that African farm families face a dreadful series of choices. The technologies which they are recommended to use are incomplete, often uneconomic, and do not provide a reliable and effective road from poverty. Reforms carried out at the macro-level fail to reach their potential because there is such poor understanding, on the part of planners, as to how they play out in real life.

Add into this unpromising mix the devastating effects of HIV/AIDS, and it is entirely possible to view the situation as impossible. Most fam-ilies in Africa are poorer and hungrier than they were 50 years ago. Those living in poverty are over 50 percent of the total population, the number of stunted (physically and mentally) children is increasing as food becomes scarcer, and life is shorter and more difficult than ever before.

Africa is a very diverse place. It has many problems to which there is no single solution. The data and the evidence which form the core of this chapter derive from the particular ecological, historical, and insti-tutional problems of southern Africa, with detailed illustrations from the Malawi case. The real world situations portrayed provide funda-mental lessons in terms of approach and understanding that can be widely applied throughout the continent. The limited geographic focus enables an in-depth analysis of the development process. It enables the interactions between the various factors to be examined and for the lessons of time and experience to be learned.

Too much of what passes as development literature for Africa is poorly rooted in reality. Outside support for African development is falling – not because the problems are solved, not because funds are being diverted elsewhere, but because of a growing recognition that existing models have failed, and that new strategies are slow in being implemented. National development resources, modest from the outset, are increasingly scarce as treasuries struggle to reconcile demands for debt repayments, recurrent costs and political expectations. There is a growing consensus amongst development agencies in Africa that a 'new way' must be found to help Africa. There is little agreement as to what that new way is, or how it should be implemented in an environment of weak national governments, a flawed national policy formulation process, and conflicting priorities – between African governments and their peoples, between donors and African governments, and amongst the donor community itself.

The story told here is one of the need for a long-term commitment to agricultural development. There are so few models in Africa (although they exist widely elsewhere) of successful smallholder development. Since most elite Africans regard subsistence agriculture as the fate they have escaped from, few have a sense of the unlocked potential in smallholder agriculture. Too few educated Africans, escapees from the ghetto of rural impoverishment, are convinced that agricultural change can really be a key to sustainable development.

A new way is indeed possible which we will explore in later chapters – the agricultural story is developed in Chapter 9. The talent to drive change in Africa is there. It can be found in the work developed by (mainly, but not exclusively, African) friends to the continent. Subsequent chapters will show that that, given the opportunity, change can be created – not driven by outsiders but by Africans themselves, firmly linked to the best in international skills and talents.

Notes

1 *Striga spp.* are a species of parasitic weeds of maize, sorghum and related crops. The plant attaches itself to the root system of the host plant and lives off the nutrients that should be going to make grain. *Striga spp.* will produce millions of seeds each year if allowed to flower, and the seeds can last for many years in the soil before germinating. It is particularly problematic to low fertility soils and can almost wipe out the crop. Control of the parasite is extremely difficult.

2 This is more of a problem in the monomodal rainfall areas of southern Africa – where the long dry season makes zero grazing techniques difficult or impossible for smallholders – than in the bimodal rainfall areas of eastern Africa.

3 And, like manures, quality is often poor.

4 Notably tobacco which was highly profitable at the time.

5 ADMARC, the Agricultural Development and Marketing Corporation, was a Malawi parastatal marketing board with monopoly powers to trade in small-holder farming areas. The explicit objective of ADMARC was to protect smallholders from exploitation by private traders. As subsequent sections will show, its track record, while mixed, was not entirely unimpressive.

6 The Special Crops Act of 1964 prevented smallholders from growing the high-value burley and flue cured varieties of tobacco. This together with production quotas served as the main means of allocating opportunities and distributing wealth in the country.

7 The removal of subsidies is widely believed to be the main culprit for the rise in fertiliser prices. In fact, it had a minor effect compared to that of devaluation.

8 This system changed with the establishment of an autonomous National Food Reserve Agency (NFRA) in 1999. The NFRA was originally intended to play a major role in price stabilisation, but once it was clear that this would require significant resources when none were made available, its role was changed to one of holding import buffer stocks in case of an emergency.

9 The most successful of these is the National Association of Smallholder Farmers in Malawi (NASFAM).

10 High maize prices benefit surplus producers, but have an adverse impact on the majority of smallholders who are net-deficit producers, and the urban poor.

11 These are detailed in Chapter 7.

12 Burley tobacco production is not suitable for the most land-constrained and poor smallholders (those on less than 0.5 hectares) due to rotation requirements.

13 The Banda government had used draconian measures to ensure credit repayment and, as a result, had an impressive repayment record (although a dreadful human rights one).

Bibliography

Araki S. (1993) Effect on soil organic matter and soil fertility of the *chitemene* slash-and-burn practice used in northern Zambia. In: Mulongoy K. and Merckx R. (eds) *Proceedings: Soil Organic Matter Dynamics and Sustainability of Tropical Agriculture*. Wiley-Sayce, Chichester, UK, pp. 367–75.

Blackie M.J. (1994) 'Maize productivity for the 21st century: The African Challenge', *Outlook on Agriculture* 23: 189–95.

Blackie M.J. and Jones R.B. (1993) 'Agronomy and increased maize productivity in eastern and southern Africa.' *Biological Agriculture and Horticulture 9*, 147–60.

Buddenhagen I. (1992) 'Prospects and challenges for African agricultural systems: An evolutionary approach', Paper presented at the Carter Lecture Series on Sustainability in Africa: Integrating Concepts. University of Florida, Gainsville, USA.

Byerlee D., Anandajayasekeram P., Diallo A., Gelaw B., Heisey P.W., Lopez-Pereira M., Mwangi W., Smale M., Tripp R. and Waddington S. (1994) *Maize Research in Sub-Saharan Africa: An Overview of Past Impacts and Future Prospects*. CIMMYT Economics Working Paper 94–03, Mexico, D.F.

Cross S. (2002) 'Customary Land Tenure, Taxes and Services Delivery in Rural Malawi: A Review of Institutional Features of Rural Livelihoods', Centre for Development Studies, University of East Anglia.

DeVries J. and Toennissen G. (2001) *Securing the harvest*, Wallingford: CABI.

Eicher C.K. (1999) *Institutions and the African Farmer*, Third Distinguished Economist Lecture, CIMMYT, Mexico, D.F.

Harrigan J. (2003) 'U Turns and Full Circles: Two Decades of Agricultural Reform in Malawi: 1981–2001,' *World Development 31* (5): 847–63.

Kabambe V.H. and Kumwenda J.D.T. (1995) 'Weed management and nitrogen rate effects on maize yield in Malawi', in: Jewell D., Waddington S., Ransom J. and Pixley K. (eds) *Maize research for stress environments*, CIMMYT, Harare, Zimbabwe.

Krugman P. (1999) Pop Internationalism, Cambridge: MIT Press.

Lele U. (1992) *Aid to African Agriculture*. Baltimore, USA: Johns Hopkins.

Malawi Government (2003) Survey of land cultivation, see p. 156.

Orr A. (2000) 'Green Gold? Burley Tobacco, Smallholder Agriculture and Poverty in Malawi', *World Development* 28 (2): 347–63.

Whiteside M. and Carr S. (1997) 'Services and policies needed to support sustainable smallholder agriculture in Malawi', Report to the Overseas Development Administration, UK. mimeo

World Bank (2003) 'Country Economic Memorandum: Policies for Accelerating Growth,' *Report No. 25293*, World Bank, Washington DC.

6

Economic Isolation

Anne Conroy and Jeffrey Sachs

Poor infrastructure equals low economic growth

Infrastructure contributes to economic growth in a number of ways. Good infrastructure helps lower input costs for goods and services, reduces transaction costs (thus facilitating trade), and leads to wider market opportunities. It also plays a role in developing human capital (particularly through better health and education) and in improving the natural environment. In direct terms, investment in infrastructure can provide higher returns to the scarce resources of land, labour and capital. But, while infrastructure and the services that flow from investments in infrastructure are critically important, they are a necessary but not sufficient condition for growth.

At a national policy level, infrastructure is routinely placed as a top priority for development. For example, the Heads of State Implementation Committee of the New Partnership for Africa (NEPAD) put agriculture, infrastructure and health as their uppermost priorities at the May 2003 meeting (IFPRI, 2003). The link between the provision of basic infrastructure services and poverty alleviation is widely acknowledged. However, investments in infrastructure are costly in terms of finance and resources. The level and type of infrastructural development needs to be suited to the local capacity to sustain it and to make full use of its potential. In much of Africa, the ability to develop infrastructure in rural areas is closely linked to growth in the agricultural sector. Off-farm employment opportunities are heavily dependent on infrastructure services (Halcrow, 2005).

We have seen that Malawi is very poor. Most villages are isolated from even the most basic infrastructure of roads and electricity. This puts farmers and business people in these villages at a considerable disadvantage. Where people live close to a well-used road, there is usually a reasonable transport connection to the local administrative centre (BOMA).[1] There will be regular traffic – minibuses, personal vehicles, matola,[2] bicycles and ox carts – that can be used to transport goods to markets with greater competition from buyers and hence, obtain better prices. Without access to adequate roads, it is difficult for the poor to enter the market economy other than under very disadvantageous terms.

Tera (2004) conducted detailed surveys of villages' access to transport in rural Malawi.[3] In all villages surveyed, most goods were transported by 'head load' (on a person's head). Heavy loads were carried by ox carts – an expensive and slow means of transport. All villagers cited the poor maintenance of secondary roads as a major constraint. During the Banda era of one-party rule (1964–1994), local people contributed substantially with their own labour to road repairs. An annual April Youth Week was dedicated to this purpose, creating a sense of community responsibility for the maintenance of road infrastructure. This externally imposed spirit of self-help unsurprisingly did not survive the new democratic (and less draconian) administration which took over from President Banda. Road infrastructure is now fully undertaken by public works programmes funded by different donor agencies – with insufficient resources and erratic funding. Food (or inputs) for work programmes have been recently developed which provide an incentive-based model for mobilising communities (especially the youth) to contribute to local infrastructure development and maintenance in the winter season. Such programmes need imaginative strengthening and expansion to provide opportunities for the poor to help themselves out of poverty.

The Tera (2004) survey of seven villages outlined the impact of economic isolation of villagers' lives. Some 70 percent of the respondents interviewed were farmers. The study found a direct relationship between access to a trading centre and the number of people involved in non-agricultural income-generating activities. Respondents noted that the condition of the roads had not improved significantly in the last 30 years. On average, people walked more than 12 km to reach a hospital and between 2 and 5 km to reach a health centre. Primary schools were generally accessible within 1 and 1.5 kilometres of the villages; the major problem in accessing a school was if students had to cross a stream or river during the rainy season. Water sources and grinding mills for maize were generally within walking distance. Most women spent up to two hours per day collecting firewood – their main energy source.

While most villagers walked to the market, school, health centre and water points, around 50 percent of respondents had access to bicycles and there is a growing business in hiring bicycles. However, the availability of other transport services such as cars, motorcycles and donkeys was severely limited in all of the villages visited. The poor condition of the roads connecting the villages with the main roads was the major reason for the absence of motorised transport. Most of the villages surveyed were only accessible to trucks with a load capacity of 1 to 3 tonnes. Only one village was accessible to a 10-tonne lorry. Even in villages more accessible to major trading centres, only 20 vehicles came to the village each week. In many, typically only a single vehicle a day would pass through.

Most roads were maintained only once or twice a year, and few of the villagers participated in such maintenance programmes. A minority of villagers participated through MASAF (the Malawi Social Action Fund), CADECOM (the Catholic Development Committee), GTZ (the German Aid Agency), and WFP (World Food Programme – food for work). Such programmes paid villagers for carrying bricks, water, stones, sand and soil to the work site, as well as for moulding bricks. In return, participants received wages or food. The decline of the self-help spirit is a major constraint to sustainable maintenance of infrastructure.

In terms of local priorities for infrastructure, the survey showed that electricity, water,[4] and roads were the top items. These were followed by a desire for improved services in health, education (both in terms of cost and quality[5]) and markets. Finally villagers sought loans, local employment opportunities and technical help in starting new businesses (Tera International Group, 2004).

Transport

Internal

The domestic road, rail and water transport systems follow the country's north-south axis. The main road network consists of a hinterland main road from Karonga in the north to Nsanje at the southern tip. Parallel to this road is the lakeshore road starting from Balaka in the southern region passing through the lake ports of Chipoka, Salima, Nkata Bay and connecting with the hinterland spine to Mzuzu. Smaller roads connect districts, rural centres and other areas to these two main north-south trunk roads.

Malawi's total road network is 15,451 km in length. Main and secondary roads account for only 6482 kilometres, and only 25 percent of the road network is paved. While 80 percent of the main roads are paved, a mere 9 percent of the secondary road network and less than 1 percent of the tertiary and district roads are all-weather roads. Thus much of the district road network is impassable in the rainy season, isolating farmers from inputs and markets. As road maintenance has declined, even dry-season access can be difficult. Many transporters simply refuse to use any but the main roads. Financial assistance from the European Commission's Road Maintenance Initiative (partially funded through a fuel levy) has allowed for some road rehabilitation and modest investments in new roads.

Although recent estimates suggest that there are only six vehicles per 1000 people, Malawi has one of the worst road accident rates in the world (EIU, 2004), mainly due to a combination of the poor state of the roads and a failure to enforce road safety laws.

External

Malawi is a land-locked country with a small internal market and far from the ports of South Africa and Tanzania. The nearest (and potentially cheapest) port of Nacala in Mozambique needs significant upgrading and investment in essential infrastructure (the port and railway line) if it is to handle increased trade. Malawi exports are relatively small volumes of primary products (principally tobacco, tea, sugar and cotton). Tobacco, sugar and tea represent approximately 80 percent of Malawi's export earnings, with tobacco accounting for 70 percent of foreign exchange earnings and around 37 percent of GDP.

Freight charges are amongst the highest in the southern African region. When the heavy internal costs of transport are factored in, Malawian goods carry a substantial transport overhead before reaching world markets, severely limiting competitiveness:

- Airfreight charges for cut flowers from Malawi to Europe are 25 percent higher than in Zambia, and 55 percent higher than in Kenya (Tera International Group, 2004).
- Of the 61 developed and developing countries surveyed, Malawi had the fourth highest proportion of transport costs as a percentage of the landed cost of goods of all exports (Radelet and Sachs, 1998).

The effects of these costs are not well understood by either the donors or the Government. A major outcome is that there are very few opportunities for Malawian businesses to compete successfully in world markets (DFID, 2005). As Radelet and Sachs (1998) note, the evidence suggests that countries with high shipping costs find it difficult to promote export-led development, even if they reduce tariffs, remove quantitative restrictions and follow prudent macro-economic policies. Firms in such geographically isolated countries are forced to reduce wage costs to compensate for the higher transport costs in order to compete in the world market – making it unlikely that they will be able to replicate the East Asian model of growth based on the export of labour intensive goods. Thus, the inevitable conclusion is that growth in Malawi will have to come, not from increasing exports, but from raising production and demand within Malawi. This will require a strong focus on improving agricultural productivity to lay the foundation for growth.

Malawi has four main borders through which international freight is routed: Mchingi on the Malawi/Zambia border, Mwanza on the south-west Malawi/Mozambique border, Nayuchi on the south-east Malawi/Mozambique border, and Kaporo in the north on the Malawi/Tanzania border. Mwanza remains the dominant trading route. It caters for Beira and other southern African ports, as well as traffic to and from the southern African region in general. The use of the Nacala route has increased since the mid-1990s as the railway is being progressively upgraded. Formal trade through Mchingi and Kaporo is decreasing, but they remain important as informal trading posts.

The choice of logistical chains used to deliver exports often depends on existing relationships rather than the overall cost efficiency of the routes. Freight forwarders consider other important factors such as the expense of moving low volumes, the availability and security of storage and warehousing, the potential for back-loading full containers as opposed to returning with empty loads, road regulations regarding axle loads and their enforcement, and the efficiency of customs compliance procedures.

To illustrate with Malawi's main export of tobacco: Smallholder tobacco producers contract local transporters to carry tobacco to the auction floors.[6] The trucks often have to wait for several days, if not weeks, before being allowed to off-load tobacco at the auction floors. Farmers are charged for waiting costs. The principal tobacco buyers (Limbe Leaf, DIMON and Stancom) determine the export routes and make the arrangements with export freight firms. Approximately 60 percent of the tobacco goes to Europe, 25 percent to the United States and 15 percent to South Africa and Asia. The nearest (and potentially cheapest) port is Nacala but if the crop is sent through this port (or through Beira) it has to be sent in containers due to the high levels of humidity (and delays) at these ports. If sent using the longer route to Durban, cheaper, bulk transport can be used (Tera International Group, 2004). Globally, it has been calculated that a one-day's delay in transit is equivalent to a 0.8 percent tariff for the importing country. Thus a 10-day delay in Nacala port would increase the price of goods by 8 percent (DFID, 2005).

The high costs of exporting from Malawi is also made worse by difficulties related to customs procedures, such as import and export procedures, licensing and quarantine regulations, transport formalities and the need for insurance. Transit formalities and export documentation are complex and time consuming. As an example, the Malawi Revenue Authority Offices are located at some distance from the tobacco auction floors. As all tobacco must be inspected prior to export, and customs officers rarely have transport of their own, each tobacco exporter has to arrange to meet and collect a customs officer each time a consignment is ready for despatch. Delays are common and costly.

There are some amazingly simple interventions which could help reduce delays. Border posts often close after dark if the power fails. This can cause considerable congestion at times when exports are leaving and essential imports such as fertilisers (and maize in years of food shortage) are coming in. The provision of stand-by generators to ensure that all border posts have reliable electricity 24 hours a day could make a real impact on reducing costs. The removal of restrictions on the use of foreign-registered vehicles would increase competition and reduce prices in the freight sector[7] (DFID, 2005).

Energy

Fuel wood, both firewood and charcoal, provides about 91 percent of the total annual primary energy demand. Fuel wood demand was estimated at 18.37 million cubic meters in 2000 and is growing by around 6 percent per year (EIU, 2004). About 80 percent is consumed by households; the remainder is used by agri-industries, particularly for curing tobacco and tea. Fuel wood consumption has contributed to severe deforestation – the rate of deforestation is estimated at 40,000 hectares per year (EIU, 2004), leading to environmental degradation and, in particular with respect to the energy sector, the silting of rivers and dams and consequent damage to national electricity-generating capacity.

Malawi's electricity supply is very unreliable, and wealthier households, offices and businesses increasingly rely on standby generators. Although four new hydro-electric power stations have been opened on the Shire River since 1989, low water flows, owing to drought and high levels of silting, have hindered their operations. The national Electricity Supply Corporation of Malawi (ESCOM) cannot keep up with the demand for electricity. It generates insufficient resources for investment and development despite increases in tariffs over recent years. ESCOM is exploring the possibility of importing power from Mozambique with a planned power connection to be established in 2009 (EIU, 2004). This will ease shortages and allow the coverage and reliability of electricity services to increase.

The national demand for coal is estimated at 74,000 metric tonnes per year. Production at the main Mchenga coal mine is still below potential peak output due to limited investment and financial constraints. The coal mine was privatised in 1999 which should help attract new investments. However the mine is located in the far north of the country, well away from Malawi's major industrial centres in the south (EIU, 2004). All petroleum is imported – mainly through the Northern Transport Corridor (Dar Es Salaam – Mbeya). Fuel imports through the ports of Beira and Nacala will increase once the needed investments in new fuel storage capacity has been completed.

Other key infrastructure

There are only eight fixed-line telephone and 13 cellular phone subscribers per 1000 people. Only three persons per 1000 have access to the internet (UNDP, 2005), typically using slow and unreliable dial-up connections. Access to information technology – a critical driver of change in today's global economy – is poor. Malawi also performs very badly in terms of research and development. Without a significant increase in investments in secondary, vocational and tertiary education, and increased access to information about science and technology, it will be impossible for Malawi to overcome the constraints imposed by economic isolation.

The regulatory and taxation environment

The investments needed for successful infrastructural development require a clear, reliable and equitable regulatory and taxation environment. Investors (whether from the donor community or private sector) are easily discouraged from investigating options in a remote, isolated country if the investment climate is unwelcoming. The Department of Economic Planning and Development in collaboration with the National Action Group conducted a thorough analysis of the principal constraints to economic growth in Malawi (Department of Economic Planning and Development and National Action Group, 2003). Poor macro-economic conditions were the biggest constraints to private sector investments and trade. Major issues were poor access to and the high cost of finance, and weaknesses in the legal and regulatory environment.

The effects of poor macro-economic conditions and instability are seen in high real interest rates, relatively high inflation, unpredictable exchange rates and weak domestic demand. The burden of taxation on legitimate businesses has steadily grown as the Government seeks to bridge an unsustainable budget deficit. The taxation system is also highly complex involving multiple taxes (corporate tax, personal tax, surtax, withholding tax, provisional tax, minimum turnover tax and a whole array of charges and levies). Even businesses concerned to meet their tax obligations fairly find themselves penalised:

> Legitimate businesses in Malawi now have to be tax experts and devote considerable resources to managing their tax position to avoid undue penalties. Yet the non-tax paying, formal/informal sector for which many of the taxes and draconian penalties are designed to catch, are seen simply to bribe their way out if they are caught. The taxation system is therefore overly complex, subject to arbitrary change and costly for businesses and government to manage. (Department of Economic Planning and Development, 2003, p. 28)

There are weaknesses in the legal and regulatory environment and a lack of consistency in applying rules. Delays in processing permits and weak coordination between different Government Ministries to support investors have cost Malawi heavily over the years. The regulatory environment is perceived to be 'non-supportive' of the growth and well-being of existing business, but favouring green field investments. Attitudes of the public service are perceived as negative or, at best, ambivalent to business, despite the importance of the private sector to domestic revenue collection.

The commercial legal system is inefficient and costly due, in part, to severely limited capacity within the Judiciary. There are no dedicated commercial courts or small claims courts where minor cases could be dealt with quickly or cheaply. Mechanisms for dealing with land encroachment issues are absent. For a country heavily dependent on trade, Malawi simply does not have adequate skills to negotiate trade agreements. Mauritius, which has no real competitive advantage in sugar when compared to Malawi, managed to negotiate preferential access for 400,000 metric tonnes of sugar into the European market, compared with Malawi's 20,000 metric tonnes.

These core problems are compounded by weak dialogue between the public and private sectors. The Department for Economic Planning and Development (2003) reports that:

> Consultation processes have generally been very weak, with the public sector going through the motions while the private sector has become unwilling to invest enough time, energy and resources to see it through. When there has been consultation, there has been a failure to really listen and appreciate the perspective of the other side resulting in misunderstanding, false perceptions and frustration. There are signs that this can be reversed but it has meant that the private sector has tended to work as a series of independent and relatively weak subsector lobbies with limited real influence on policy.

Responding to the need for change

This state of affairs has started to change with the National Action Group playing a far more significant role in policy dialogue and formulation, but there is a continuing need to ensure that the lines of consultation remain open and are followed consistently. Where consultative processes have worked well, progress has been made. Where they are neglected – as when, in mid-2005, the government decided to engage in a major importation of fertilisers without any real effort to involve the local private sector – the consequences for the whole economy are grave. In this case, for instance, local importers (who provide most of the fertilisers used on export crops) inevitably held off placing orders until the government explained how it was going to use its own imports. The result will be that agricultural exporters will almost certainly be short of fertilisers for the 2006 growing season, with knock-on effects on yields and quality. A coordinated effort involving both local importers and the government could have easily avoided this problem.

President Mutharika's new administration has focused on strengthening macro-economic management to provide a climate conducive to growth and investments. It has also attempted to strengthen dialogue and collaboration with the local private sector. As a result of this commitment to sound economic management and a drive against corruption, the International Monetary Fund approved a Poverty Reduction and Growth Facility (PRGF) in early September 2005. The PRGF facility is worth US$55.9 million and will run from July 2005 to June 2008. The PRGF has a strong focus on improving fiscal discipline and promoting macro-economic stability. Additional aims of the programme include improving private sector access to finance, developing the rural economy and increasing spending on healthcare, education and infrastructure. The programme also aims to help the private sector by lowering fiscal borrowing, which is expected to reduce real interest rates. There is also emphasis on developing rural areas, promoting export diversification and strengthening rural infrastructure (EIU, September 2005). But the PRGF programme follows the path of every previous structural adjustment or poverty reduction programme in Malawi in setting targets which are not achievable. The constraints to meeting these targets need more careful analysis and interpretation if the targets are to be meaningful. The evidence from previous efforts suggests that many of the targets may be overly-optimistic.

Despite the strong commitment to succeed, the principal threat to the successful implementation of the programme is, once again, a food crisis – which will almost inevitably put everything off-track. We know that the economy is dominated by agriculture which accounts for 40 percent of GDP (EIU, July 2005). In the 2005–2006 budget, total revenue (including external support) is forecasted to rise by 45 percent to MK116.2 billion Kwacha (US$967 million). Although donor assistance is projected to increase following the approval of the PRGF facility, it is unlikely that all of it will be disbursed, especially if political instability increases. Furthermore, the scope for increasing domestic revenue collection is limited both by the small size of Malawi's formal economy and the effect of drought on the mainly agriculturally-dependent business sector.

The environment for investment is very poor; net foreign direct investment as a proportion of GDP is 1.3 percent (UNDP, 2005), other private flows are negligible. Domestic interest rates are very high as the Reserve Bank is trying to keep monetary policy tight in order to try and reduce inflation. The bank lending rate is 25 percent and the scope for reducing this is likely to be constrained by mounting inflationary pressure. Higher food price inflation increased year-on-year inflation to 15.9 percent in June 2005 (EIU, September 2005). Food price inflation will increase throughout the year due to the food crisis and an estimated 4.8 million people in need of food aid. Economic growth will continue to be strongly influenced by the performance of the agricultural sector as a result of the lack of economic diversification and exploitable natural resources. The Economist Intelligence Unit (2005) predicts Malawi's growth in 2005 at just over 1 percent as a result of the food crisis.

The poor economic performance has also resulted in exchange rate depreciation – always a problem in a highly indebted country. The total external debt is estimated at US$3.23 billion in 2004, compared with a total GDP of US$1.5 billion. The Malawi Kwacha exchange rate with the US dollar fell sharply from MK108 in March 2005 to MK124 in late June 2005. The Economist Intelligence Unit (EIU) anticipates that the exchange rate will continue to depreciate towards the end of the year as central bank intervention in the market will prove too costly to maintain (EIU, September 2005).

In the external sector, the value of exports is expected to fall from an estimated US$476 million in 2005 as the drought will negatively impact on the tobacco crop (the main source of export revenue). There are also reports that low prices on Malawi's auction floors have driven some farmers to smuggle tobacco out to neighbouring countries where prices are higher (EIU, 2005). Imports are likely to rise sharply in 2005 due to the need to increase maize imports for the humanitarian relief programme and also through informal cross-border trade.

Tourism receipts, the main source of service credits, are expected to increase modestly, but the services account will remain in deficit as trade-related costs will keep services debits high. Interest payments on medium and long-term external debt will be reduced under the IMF-World Bank's Heavily Indebted Poor Countries Initiative, but the reduction in external debt payments will be modest. Inflows of donor aid are expected to rise in 2005 and 2006 – assuming that the country remains stable and the Government continues to implement donor-guided reforms. The Economist Intelligence Unit predicts that the current account deficit will increase to 14 percent of GDP in 2005, before decreasing to 10.6 percent of GDP in 2006 (EIU, September 2005).

Conclusion

This chapter has demonstrated the critical importance of infrastructure in promoting economic growth. The majority of the Malawian population live below the poverty line in villages isolated from markets and lacking the most basic economic and social infrastructure. Goods are transported by 'head load' or oxen to the main roads. The poor state of the roads and lack of income inhibits growth and diversification in rural areas. There is also a decline in the spirit of self-help and national programmes to maintain infrastructure at the community level. Different donor-funded initiatives in the area of public works compensate to some degree, but there is a need to build up national programmes for infrastructure maintenance and to strengthen the self-help spirit.

At the national level, very high internal and external transport costs remain a threat to growth. Malawi's road networks are severely limited with the majority of roads in poor condition despite the efforts of the National Road Authority's Road Maintenance Initiative. The Nacala Port is potentially the cheapest external transport route, but it needs significant investments in upgrading essential infrastructure both at the port and along the railway line. Malawi's geographical isolation and long distances to ports inhibit prospects for export-led growth and poverty alleviation – this is illustrated by the difficulties and delays experienced by tobacco producers getting their produce to local and international markets. The long distances to ports, limited competition, processing delays and high costs also limit prospects for export diversification.

Apart from very high internal and external transport costs, Malawi lacks other basic economic infrastructure including reliable power supply. There is also poor access to telecommunications, the internet and information technology which is the driver of growth in today's global economy.

The Department of Economic Planning and Development in collaboration with the National Action Group – a group including Malawi's leaders from the business and the private sectors – conducted a comprehensive analysis of constraints to growth in 2003. It clearly outlined the key constraints and made constructive recommendations on how to address them. This again demonstrates that the national authorities working in collaboration with representatives from the private sector, living and investing in Malawi, have a clear understanding of the constraints and issues that must be addressed. As in all other sectors (health, education, food security etc.) their work demonstrates the importance of consultation, collaboration and joint efforts to identify priorities and implement key actions.

The chapter concludes by providing an overview of key macroeconomic variables. Despite the efforts of the new administration to strengthen macro-economic management, the critical constraints remain unaddressed. There is limited potential to improve the quality of key services (essential for poverty reduction) because of the very high burden of domestic debt and limited resources. A new Poverty Reduction and Growth Facility was approved by the IMF in late August 2005, leading to the resumption of balance of payments support by Malawi's principal donor partners. However, the new administration faces key challenges in responding to the food crisis – which was declared a National Emergency in mid-September 2005. The food and political crisis is likely to dominate events in the short term, undermining prospects for economic growth as the country now has to focus its efforts on survival.

Notes

1 British Overseas Military Administration is the name of the former colonial administrative units. This term is used widely in modern Malawi for Government.

2 This is the equivalent of paying to ride on a Government or private vehicle. It is an important form of informal transport, especially for the poor and in areas poorly served by public transport.

3 The villages are Santhe in Kasungu District, Ngolome in Mchinji District, Chagunda in Salima District, Sakhome in Phalombe District, Tiimbenawo in Chickwawa District, Migana in Chikwawa District and Mkando in Mulanje District.

4 Sixty-seven percent of Malawians had access to an improved water source in 2002 (UNDP, 2005). The Ministry of Water Development states that the recommended improved water point density should be four water points for every 1000 people – so one water point should serve 250 people (Malawi Government, 2005). Access to clean water may be reduced by the number of non-functional or unmaintained water points. There is a need for increased investment to ensure that the population has access to clean water and to maintain existing water points through a more intensive involvement of communities in water management. Only 46 percent of the population has access to improved sanitation services (UNDP, 2005).

5 Primary Education has been free in Malawi since the advent of multi-party democracy. There is almost universal access to education. Ninety percent of children in urban areas attend school compared with 80 percent in rural areas. Despite the increase in enrolment, only 34 percent of primary school pupils completed up to Standard Five in 2004 (NB: there are eight standards in primary school so this indicates very poor completion rates.) A number of challenges continue to affect primary education including high dropout rates especially among girls, poor school environment and lack of teaching and learning materials. Secondary education has increased as a result of the expansion in primary education and the growth in private and Community Day Secondary Schools – but less than 30 percent of children have access to secondary school education (UNDP, 2005). As a result of the increase in

enrolment, the quality of secondary education has declined due to inadequate learning materials and the limited number of trained teachers, especially at the new Community Day Secondary Schools. The constraints are exacerbated at the tertiary level where just over 1000 Malawians graduate from tertiary education institutions every year. The low level of participation in secondary, vocational and tertiary education acts as a major constraint to building capacity in all professional fields and economic diversification.

6　The main tobacco auctions are held in Lilongwe. The Blantyre/Limbe auctions are secondary centres.

7　To the annoyance of the powerful and well connected domestic trucking lobby.

Bibliography

Department for Economic Planning and Development and National Action Group (2003) 'Draft Consultation Document: A Growth Strategy for Malawi: Part One, Macro-Economic Environment Strategy', Lilongwe, Malawi.

Department for International Development (2005) 'Stimulating Growth in Malawi and the role of agriculture and social protection', Draft for Discussion, a paper in support of the Malawi Economic Growth Strategy. DFID, Lilongwe, April 2005.

Economist Intelligence Unit (EIU) (July 2004) 'Malawi Country Profile', Regent Street, London.

Economist Intelligence Unit (July 2005) 'Malawi Country Report', Regent Street, London.

Economist Intelligence Unit (September 2005) 'Malawi Country Report', Regent Street, London.

Halcrow Group Limited (2005) 'Agriculture and Infrastructure Linkages', Working Paper prepared for the Department for International Development.

IFPRI (2003) 'Revitalising the Drive for Rural Infrastructure', IFPRI Forum, September 2003 (available on-line: www.ifpri.org/pubs/newsletters/ifpriforum)

Malawi Government (2005) 'Malawi: Millennium Development Goals: Progress Report for the United Nations Millennium Summit 2005'.

Ministry of Economic Planning and Development and National Action Group (2003) 'A Growth Strategy for Malawi: Part One, Overview and Macro-Economic Environment', Draft Paper, Lilongwe, Malawi.

Radelet S. and Sachs J.D. (1998) 'Shipping Costs, Manufactured Exports and Economic Growth' (available on-line: at www2.cid.harvard.edu.hiidpapers/shipcosts.pdf)

Tera International Group Inc. (2004) 'Malawi Transport Cost Study, Policy Review Report', Report Prepared in collaboration with the Ministry of Transport and Public Works, the International Bank for Reconstruction and Development and the Road Maintenance and Rehabilitation Project, Lilongwe, Malawi.

United Nations (2005) 'Human Development Report: International Cooperation at a Crossroad: Aid, Trade and Security in an Unequal World', United Nations, New York.

World Bank (2003) 'Malawi: Country Economic Memorandum: Policies for Accelerating Growth', Report No. 25293, Washington DC.

7

Malawi and the Poverty Trap – A First Person Account

Anne Conroy

Introduction

This chapter is a first hand 'insider' perspective on the recurring food crises that have plagued Malawi over the past decade. The policy blunders (by both the Government and the donor community), and the associated politics of a government struggling to break out of famine and its inability to focus on development needs are analysed and discussed. The administration was desperately trying to deal with the long-ignored problem of poverty – while building its own capacity for good governance, and at the same time losing many of its most skilled and experienced personnel to disease, death or emigration. These would be major challenges for any government.

In Malawi, despite the high hopes of the electorate (and Malawi's friends throughout the world) after the removal of Dr Banda's one-party state, some of the less desirable outcomes have been corruption, the abuse of power and the interruption of the process of democratic transition. As technocrats focused on trying to take the country out of crisis, the political leadership was distracted in an attempt to amend the Constitution to allow President Muluzi a third term of office. This attempt was opposed by civil society and the faith communities, and ultimately failed. The absence of strong direction from the top allowed the macro-economic management to deteriorate. The major donors, concerned at the looming crisis, suspended balance of payments support – and the economy crumbled. The budget went into severe deficit and domestic debts rose to unsustainable levels.

Unsurprisingly, most Malawians wanted this awful set of events to come to an end. But the opposition to President Muluzi's United Democratic Front (UDF) party was fragmented, and after elections in

May 2004, a minority Government under the leadership of President Mutharika came into power. It did not get off to an easy start. The UDF was unhappy that President Mutharika had abandoned his colleagues in the UDF to form a new party, the Democratic Progressive Party. The Malawi Congress Party (MCP) remained resentful of its loss of power that it had enjoyed for so many years under Dr Banda. The MCP had the greatest number of seats (but not a majority) in Parliament and chose to challenge the election result – delaying the start of the new parliamentary session. The unexpected death of the respected Speaker of Parliament delayed the Budget Session of Parliament which held up the IMF approval of a much-needed Poverty Reduction and Growth Facility.

While the new Government has tried to address corruption and to restore budget discipline, it also has to deal with the problem of its inheritance of unsustainable levels of domestic debt and arrears to the private sector. The on-going political tension undermines the Government's ability to assume clear leadership and respond to both long- and short-term development challenges. Of these, yet again, the most urgent is food. The 2005 harvest was the lowest in a decade – partly because seeds and fertilisers reached most farmers too late, and the rains ended prematurely. Probably between 4.2 million and 4.8 million Malawians are in need of humanitarian assistance before the 2006 harvest comes in. Once again Malawians face the prospect of famine. The challenge, which we will examine in the second part of this book, is to create policies that will allow Malawi to break out of this increasingly desperate cycle of chronic food insecurity, broken only by years of famine. But before embarking on that analysis, we will first look at the lessons from the past.

From food insecurity to famine: the 2002 food crisis

In Chapter 5, we traced the events leading to the collapse of agriculture in Malawi. Smallholders were, in effect, taxed out of the most profitable segments of agriculture, and national food security was shored up using an unsustainable system of subsidies and credit packages which benefited the wealthier smallholders. The majority of the population grew poorer (and more malnourished) year by year – but dissent was subdued by a draconian political machine. As is the way of such things, the cracks could not be covered up forever and, as indicated in the first chapters of this book, Malawi took a more democratic path. A casualty of that change was the already precarious national food security situation.

Widening access to improved agricultural technology

In 1998, as we saw in Chapter 5, famine was looming. Food prices were escalating well out of the reach of the poor and the much needed economic liberalisation was in danger of collapse. With support from The Rockefeller Foundation, a team of national and international scientists, economists, and development workers put together a highly innovative package to avert the coming famine. It was based on the hypothesis that Malawi's immediate priority was to bring down food prices, reduce inflation and ensure that most Malawians had access to reasonably priced food. We will describe this effort in more detail in Chapter 9. In brief, all smallholders in Malawi were given a small pack of the correct maize seed and fertiliser for their area – enough to plant 0.1 hectares. This 'starter pack' (as it became known[1]), would at the very least provide enough to take the average family through the hungry season. It was not the only programme as the Malawi government had developed a grain reserve strategy, holding stocks against poor years. NGOs and church groups were heavily involved in a variety of food security and agricultural development exercises. Efforts were being promoted by various agencies to help smallholders diversify their cropping systems away from maize monocropping.

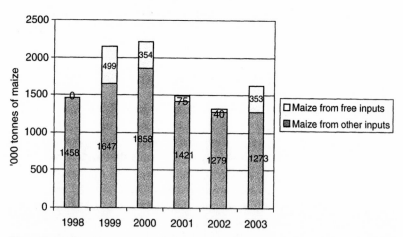

Figure 7.1   Starter pack/TIP contribution to total maize production, 1998–2003
Source: Ministry of Agriculture crop estimate survey data, from FEWS. Estimates of maize produced with free inputs (SP/TIP contribution) are from the evaluation surveys.

Figure 7.1 shows the contribution of the Starter Pack/TIP Programme to overall maize production from 1998 to 2003. In Chapter 5 we saw how the collapse of the agricultural credit system, combined with the removal of all subsidies on production resulted in low harvests in 1997 and 1998. The Government then had to divert scarce foreign exchange to import maize – which arrived late and which was so expensive that landed sales had to be subsidised. With the implementation of the Starter Pack, total maize production increased from just below 1.5 million metric tonnes in 1998 to over 2 million tonnes in 1999 and 2000. Food prices came down benefiting the poor. Abundant food allowed the government to focus on development priorities.

Despite the Starter Pack Programme's evident success, the donor community was opposed to any programme that provided untargeted subsidies for food production. They insisted that the programme should be scaled down to a 'safety nets' programme targeting 1.5 million smallholder households in 2001. As a result, production fell to just over 1.5 million metric tonnes. The donor community subsequently insisted that the programme be scaled down further in 2002 to 1 million smallholder households. Total maize production was 1.3 million metric tonnes and the food gap was estimated at 600,000 metric tonnes. Grain prices tripled in the markets.

Managing grain reserves

The Malawi Government had a second major programme in place to help ensure national food security – the Strategic Grain Reserve (SGR). It purchased grain in good years, and stored it in a modern complex in Kanengo outside Lilongwe, with the intention of selling it in years of shortage. A grain reserve consists of specific import buffer stocks held as security against a poor harvest. The purpose of a grain reserve is to allow time to arrange imports in an orderly fashion. The grain reserve is not a substitute for a failed harvest. This appears a very simple strategy – but is costly to implement (large sums of public money are tied up in grain for indefinite periods) and is potentially open to abuse (stored grain may be sold off or just disappear without proper explanation).

The maize harvest in 2002 was 1.3 million metric tonnes and the Malawi Government predicted a food crisis. Furthermore, the grain reserve had been sold off, which seemed a surprising policy in the circumstances. In the initial debate about the food crisis, donors and the international press focused on the sale of the grain reserve rather than on the shortfall in production. There were heated and ill-informed debates over the role that the grain reserve could and should have played in alleviating the immediate crisis.

The salient facts are indisputable. Prior to 1999, the SGR was managed by ADMARC on behalf of the Malawi Government. A technical committee comprising the Ministries of Finance, Economic Planning and Development, Agriculture, and Statutory Corporations provided technical oversight. The technical committee also included DFID, the European Commission and USAID to ensure that there was transparency in all decisions related to grain reserve management. All purchases for and sales from the grain reserve were on the basis of open competitive tenders.

This arrangement worked effectively. However, the Malawi Government was required as conditionality for a World Bank loan[2] to establish the National Food Reserve Agency (NFRA) as an independent autonomous agency. The assumption was that grain reserve management – a crucial component of national food security – was best left to the private sector and could be undertaken with limited oversight or technical support. The NFRA was established in 1999 with the mandate to manage the grain reserve, stabilise prices and be fully autonomous in its operations. The technical committee was thus dissolved.

The Malawi Government expected that capital requirements for the NFRA – estimated at US$35 million – would be included in the Structural Adjustment credit. But IMF policy conditionality limited the resources that the Government could use to intervene in the maize market. The budget did not include any resources to intervene in the grain market. As a result, the NRFA was set up in 1999 without the resources to perform its mandate, hire competent staff, or to establish operating or accounting procedures. In that year, with a bumper harvest following the successful Starter Pack programme, the government instructed ADMARC to buy 160,000 metric tonnes of grain, financing this from a local bank loan equivalent to US$28 million at interest rates of 46 percent. There was evident confusion between ADMARC's responsibility for domestic grain marketing and NFRA's responsibility for managing the import buffer stock. ADMARC owned most of the grain storage facilities and could sell grain without NFRA's knowledge or approval. There was no proper agreement between ADMARC and NFRA for grain reserve management or for separating ADMARC's grain sales from those of NFRA.[3]

Ignoring the warning signs

In early 2000, it was clear that there would be another bumper harvest due to the Universal Starter Pack and the government was pressured to

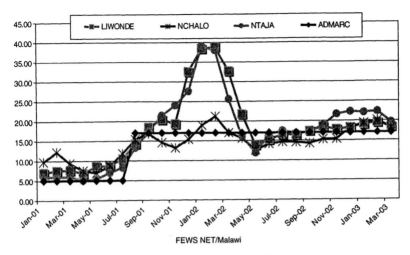

Figure 7.2   Local market prices for maize in the southern region
Source: Ministry of Agriculture and Irrigation, FEW NET/Malawi.

sell the grain to clear the expensive bank loan. By June of the following year, the entire maize reserve had been sold, mainly on the domestic market.[4] But that year was a poor harvest year (just over 1.5 million metric tonnes) and NRFA had to import 134,000 metric tonnes of maize to meet consumption requirements. The total cost of these imports was US$29.5 million and it was financed by an external loan, repayable within one year. Movements in grain prices are probably the most reliable indicator of an impending crisis. Figure 7.2 shows that grain prices increased significantly from as early as July 2001. This should have alerted the donor community to the impending crisis.

The significance of the fall in the maize harvest was downplayed by the donor community who argued that the increased output of cassava, sweet potatoes and Irish potatoes would compensate for the fall. This was due to the reported increases in yields of cassava and sweet potatoes which appear unrealistic (see Figure 7.3). Unreliable production estimates lead to unrealistic assumptions about consumption. World Bank (2003) notes that if the crop estimates were correct, Malawi would have produced between 3400 and 3900 kilocalories per day per capita between 2000 and 2003. The average for sub-Saharan Africa is only around 1500. Data from the Integrated Household Survey indicates that average consumption is only 1818 calories per day. This gives a consistent picture of very low overall food availability and calorie consumption. The Integrated Household Survey

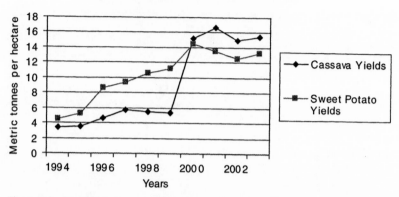

Figure 7.3 Yields of cassava and sweet potatoes, 1994–2002
Source: Ministry of Agriculture and Irrigation, National Crop Production Estimates.

data demonstrate that households living below the poverty line (65 percent of total) consume an average of 1428 calories per day whilst ultra-poor households (28 percent of total) consume an average of 1165 calories per day (Government of Malawi, 2000).

The evidence, when dispassionately analysed, suggest that the reported growth in production of root crops was not reliable. Furthermore, an expansion in production of alternative crops does not compensate for a national shortfall in maize production. This is because during February (the hungriest month) alternative food crops – cassava, sweet potatoes and rice – are not available in most households as they are harvested later in the year. Ironically, the availability of non-maize staple foods accentuates the maize shortage rather than offsetting it in the hungry season (Nyirongo C., Msiska B., Myetseni H., and Kamanga F. with Levy S., 2003).

Raising the alarm

While the donor community were downplaying the crisis, the Department of Disaster Preparedness, Relief and Rehabilitation also failed to raise the alarm. It was left to the NGOs, civil society groups, and the faith communities to raise the alarm. The Malawi Economic Justice Network mobilised activist groups including the Catholic Commission for Justice and Peace and pressurised the Government to declare a state of disaster. They issued a press release stating that 'hunger had reached crisis proportions in Malawi' and calling for urgent action to address the crisis by both the government and the international community.

At the beginning of 2002, approximately one-third of the population was in need of food aid and President Muluzi declared a state of disaster on February 27th 2002. Despite considerable initial delays in recognising the existence of a food crisis, the eventual response was exemplary. The government, donors and other stakeholders collectively addressed the issue of how to implement a relief operation for 2–3 million Malawians. Capacity constraints were identified at the outset. The Malawi Government and donors agreed to work with leading Non-Governmental Organisation (NGOs) and civil society institutions operating at district levels. Eventually, lives were saved and all concerned deserved the credit. The humanitarian relief operation demonstrated that where there is political will and commitment by all stakeholders, programmes can be implemented successfully.

Lessons from the 2002 famine

Budget disruption

Levy (2004) noted that:

> The maize imports in 2001 and 2002 cost Malawi dear in terms of foreign exchange reserves. Foreign exchange reserves fell sharply after August 2001. This was partly due to the use of foreign exchange to import maize, and partly as a result of the suspension of balance of payments support following concerns about governance.

The decision to import maize had grave macro-economic consequences (Whitworth, 2004). The combination of financing through domestic credit expansion, and the running down of foreign reserves led to exchange rate depreciation,[5] increased inflation and had a consequent adverse impact on investment and growth. Substantial increases in Treasury Bill Stocks crowded out private sector investment through high interest rates. Furthermore, the Malawi Government now had a substantially increased debt to service, and debt payments competed with discretionary public expenditure in subsequent years.

The donor community pledged just over 200,000 tonnes of maize for the humanitarian relief programme, leaving (in the Malawi Government's view) a dangerously large gap in the national food supply. The government decided to purchase and import itself some 250,000 tonnes of maize, financed by commercial borrowing and using procedures that did not fulfil donor requirements.

However, the delivered cost of maize imports put it well beyond the purchasing power of the poor and vulnerable. Most of the maize was bought at prices that ranged between US$210 and US$236 a tonne. With interest payments and internal distribution costs added, the break-even sale price to consumers was around MK28 per kilogram, compared with a pre-food crisis price of around MK15 per kilogram. The Government then decided to subsidise all maize sales (as opposed to targeting subsidies at the poor). But even the subsidised maize was too expensive and only 44,000 tonnes were sold. A stock of over 200,000 tonnes was still held by government when the 2003 harvest came in.[6]

At the same time, there was continuing tension between the Malawi Government and the donors regarding the financial management of the Strategic Maize Reserve. With plans in hand to improve the management of NFRA, there were two clear choices for the donors – they could help pay for the maize that had already been imported (this was the choice of most technicians in government as it was clear that most of the grain could not be sold even at subsidised rates) or else re-stock the SGR with additional grain imports. The donor community chose the latter. They were not willing to pay for imports that did not follow their own procurement rules. The outcome was a substantial balance in the SGR plus a large overhang of unsold commercial maize imported separately by the government. Some of this grain was eventually exported at a loss to Zimbabwe.

Disruption to on-going programmes

The 2002 Malawi food crisis took much of the limited management capacity within the country away from core development activities. For example, the Ministry of Health was criticised for not attending the Food Crisis Task Force meetings regularly. They responded:

> We are trying to save lives. Hundreds of thousands of children out there are malnourished. That's our responsibility. You can't expect us to spend time in Lilongwe in meetings when children are dying out there.[7]

The Ministry of Agriculture and Irrigation chaired a Multi-Sectoral Food Crisis Task Force very ably. Senior managers and advisors from key ministries, representatives from the donor community, the United Nations, the private sector and Non-Governmental Organisations spent a significant part of the year coordinating the response to the food crisis. Key government officials who were involved in the Joint Food Crisis Task Force spent most of their time during that year managing the food crisis. There is general agreement that it was handled competently, although there were occasions when better follow-up and decision taking at the political level were needed.

At the height of the 2002 food crisis in Malawi, 3.2 million people throughout the country were being fed. The Vulnerability Assessment Committee identified the worst affected areas. District and Village Relief Committees identified the most vulnerable households at the village level. As 65 percent of the population live below the poverty line and consume less than 1500 calories per day even in 'normal years', and poor families in Malawi spend 76 percent of their income on food (Malawi Government, 2000), it was very difficult to identify the most vulnerable 32 percent of households for targeted food distribution in villages. Notwithstanding these difficulties, there is general agreement that the targeting mechanism was relatively effective. Mechanisms were also put in place to monitor food aid distribution through civil society and a Parliamentary Committee. The food distribution was done in an orderly manner with few incidents. There were mechanisms for dispute resolution and rapid follow-up by the Chair of the Non-Governmental Consortium that organised relief distribution at the district levels.

In addition to the generalised food distribution programme, the government and NGOs implemented a supplementary and therapeutic feeding programme targeted at 295 Nutritional Rehabilitation Units and 165 Mother and Child Centres. The programme focused on under-five severely malnourished children admitted to Therapeutic Feeding Centres (TFCs) and their carers. The programme also supported moderately-malnourished children and pregnant and lactating women identified to be at risk and who were attending maternal and health centres. At the beginning of its operation, 62,240 children received supplementary and therapeutic feeding, and by December 2003, the number had increased to 82,419 (Phiri, 2004).

The 2002 food crisis captured the attention of the international press and high-profile visitors. Almost every week there was a senior delegation from one donor mission or other, UN Special Envoys and members of the international press. This served to raise the profile of the food crisis, mobilising international support. But it also created additional strains on overworked technocrats and Malawi's political leadership. They had to attend high-level meetings and diplomatic functions rather than focusing their energies on responding to the food crisis.

Disruption to household coping mechanisms

Prior to the 2002 food crisis, the majority of the population in Malawi were already consuming less than 1500 calories per day and few households had any assets to sell. The Integrated Household Survey reported that just over one-third of all households owned a bed with the majority of the population sleeping on mats on the floor (Malawi Government, 2000). Less than a half of households owned chairs and tables – people sit on the floor and eat out of a single pot with their hands. Few households own a radio, although most have access to one through the chief, village headman or neighbours. Ownership of a bicycle is a sign of wealth. Anyone in employment earning around US$60 per month was envied for their secure employment and income. When poverty is this serious, there is virtually no scope for normal coping mechanisms that promote resilience.

Kamowa (2002) documented Malawian coping strategies during the food crisis. These included consuming maize bran (usually fed to livestock), rationing food and going without food for several days at a time. Other strategies involved selling their few remaining assets and early distress sales of crops. There was increasing absenteeism by pupils because children were too hungry to attend school or had to help parents find food. There was also a significant increase in anti-social behaviour and increased violence during disputes. The traditional social structure started to break down – the elderly and the orphans were neglected and there was an increase in transactional sex and high-risk sexual behaviour.

The United Nations, in partnership with the government, conducted a reproductive health and HIV/AIDS vulnerability assessment in areas affected by the 2002 food crisis (United Nations Humanitarian Response Team (UNHRT) and Ministry of Health (MoH), 2002). The purpose of the survey was to assess the reproductive health needs of the population and the capacity of the health system to respond to the crisis. The survey showed that 70 percent of households reported a negative impact of the food crisis on their daily lives. The majority of households had reduced food consumption and children dropped out of school due to malnutrition. There was also an increase in consumption of non-traditional foods, an increase in unsafe sexual practices and households sold off their assets.

The food crisis rapidly became a humanitarian emergency. There was a 36 percent increase in TB cases (a good proxy for HIV since co-infection exists in over 80 percent of cases). The under-five CMR was 3.8 (greater than two is considered a humanitarian emergency). Antenatal clinic attendances fell sharply (UNHRT, 2002).

Young men cited instances where girls were pressurised into having sex in exchange for food. Young women reported that many of them had multiple sexual partners during the food crisis in order to increase food availability for the family. They also reported instances where young women were forced by their parents into prostitution in order to obtain food. Adult men reported an increase in mobility as they attempted to find opportunities for off-farm employment. This led to an increase in the number of sexual partners for both men and women (men reported that their wives were also more likely to engage in extra-marital sex while they were away). However, adult women who left the village overnight in search of work said they did not engage in extra-marital sex (UNHRT, 2002).

The United Nations Humanitarian Response Team (2002) reported the following statistics in areas worst affected by the food crisis:

- The number of patients presenting with sexually transmitted infections increased by 31 percent during the food crisis.
- There was a marked decline in the number of women delivering at health facilities.
- There was an increase in malnutrition and anaemia among pregnant women.
- Teenage pregnancies increased by 93 percent, spontaneous abortions by 62 percent, and complications due to abortion by 153 percent.
- The number of cases of anaemia increased by 96 percent and the frequency of haemorrhage increased by 153 percent.

Focus group discussions revealed that there was a significant increase in gender-based violence during the food crisis. There was a reported increase in the frequency of children being taken out of school in order to work in bottle stores (where they usually fall into prostitution). There was also an increase in the number of girls forced into early marriage and an increase in domestic violence, especially in polygamous households. Overall levels of violence increased during the crisis as people were beaten up (sometimes fatally) when they were caught stealing food.

The humanitarian crisis increased vulnerability to HIV/AIDS by increasing the pressures for unsafe sexual practices, increasing the incidence of risk pregnancies, increasing the tendency for gender-based violence, aggravating the food insecurity of HIV-positive individuals and weakening immune systems. The food crisis also reduced incentives for health-seeking behaviour because people were too weak to travel to the health centres.

The health sector was not in a position to respond adequately to the impact of the crisis on the sexual and reproductive health of individuals and HIV/AIDS through prevention, care, treatment and support. The report concluded that 'without prompt attention to the sexual and reproductive health needs within the context of the humanitarian response, the impact of the food crisis will be extended well beyond the duration of the food shortage by increasing the burden of ill-health, particularly in the area of maternal and newborn health, HIV transmission and AIDS deaths' (United Nations Humanitarian Response Team and Ministry of Health, 2002).

Deterioration in macro-economic management and governance after 2002

The cost of maize imports and the distractions of ensuring a third term of office for President Muluzi caused a collapse in macro-economic management until after the 2004 elections. Non-priority expenditure (including external travel, state residences, foreign affairs, defence, the National Intelligence Bureau and special activities) increased significantly. Domestic debts increased from MK9.5 billion at the end of 2001 to MK54.4 billion by July 2004 – when it represented around 30 percent of GDP (Whitworth, 2004). As a result of the increase in domestic debts, interest payments on domestic debts increased from 9.1 percent of total expenditure in 1998–1999 to 28.4 percent of expenditure in 2003–2004. Maize operations alone accounted for MK6.7 billion in 2002–2003 or 13.1 percent of expenditure and 4.3 percent of GDP. This squeezed expenditure on priority-protected pro-poor expenditure[8] to only 8 percent of total expenditure in 2003–2004.

As a result of the increase in the share of the budget used to finance domestic debt payments and maize operations, the share of discretionary expenditure in the budget declined from 59 percent of the budget in 1998–1999 to 31.3 percent of the budget in 2003–2004 (discretionary expenditure represents the resources that are available to implement programmes and provide public services). At the time of the 2004 Presidential Election, the economy was on a path to ruin.

The atmosphere in the run-up to the 2004 Election was also very tense. Most political parties had fragmented due to power struggles. Veteran politicians broke away to form new alliances or parties.

Gwanda Chakwamba broke away from the Malawi Congress Party to form the Republican Party (RP). Brown Mpingangira broke away from the United Democratic Front (UDF) to form the National Democratic Alliance (NDA). Vice President Justin Malewezi left UDF to stand as an independent presidential candidate. The Alliance for Democracy (Aford) split into two – Aford and the Movement for Genuine Democratic Change (Mgode). Aleke Banda, formerly of UDF formed the People's Progressive Movement (PPM).[9] There were concerns that the UDF candidate, Dr Bingu Mutharika, was a 'Third Term in disguise'. Most Malawians believed that this would lead to a continuation of economic mismanagement that had started in 2002. Religious leaders and civil society organisations encouraged the opposition to unite but they refused to do so, and a total of five presidential candidates[10] stood in the election.

President Bingu Mutharika was elected to power. Former President Bakili Muluzi retained the Chairmanship of UDF and negotiated with the Republican Party and the National Democratic Alliance to provide a fragile majority for UDF in Parliament. President Mutharika asserted himself and started a high-profile drive against corruption, and gradually distanced himself from the UDF. As a result he won support from the population but alienated the former President and his party. A split was inevitable – President Mutharika left UDF. Rather than remaining aloof from party politics, he chose to form a new political party – the Democratic Progressive Party (DPP). The majority of UDF MPs who held cabinet positions, some opposition and independent MPs joined DPP, but do not command a majority in Parliament. Frequent changes in allegiance and political parties have further disillusioned an electorate already losing faith in democratic politics. The current political tension and the regrettable exacerbation of tension between Christians and Muslims do not serve the national interest. The Public Affairs Committee[11] is trying to mediate between political leaders, but many are not prepared to prioritise national interest over their own political agendas. This leads to a climate of uncertainty which is destructive and undermines the potential for the government to focus on development priorities.

Politics and fertiliser subsidies

Assuring food security was a key theme in the 2004 election campaign. The Malawi Congress Party promised to implement a universal fertiliser subsidy – a return to the nostalgic 'peaceful' time of Dr Banda.

The UDF originally planned the budget around a Universal Starter Pack Programme (at a cost of around US$40 million), but then changed to a 'universal fertiliser subsidy' where all fertilisers would be sold at MK1400 per bag.

Most politicians favoured a 'universal fertiliser subsidy' because the major beneficiaries are those who are already using fertilisers. An untargeted fertiliser subsidy allows the richest farmers to gain access to fertilisers below the world market price. The disadvantages of a generalised fertiliser subsidy are that it actively excludes the poorest smallholders (the majority) who cannot afford to buy inputs even at a subsidised rate. Generalised fertiliser subsidies have a negligible impact on poverty as the principal beneficiaries are those who already purchase inputs. Furthermore, the costs to the government can quickly spiral out of control since the government does not control the international price of fertilisers, the exchange rates and fertiliser demand. Subsidised fertilisers create major incentives for cross-border trade, and uncertainty regarding government intentions seriously disrupts trade as importers and farmers wait to see the amount of the subsidy before placing orders.

Between May and October 2004, fertiliser prices increased significantly and it was soon clear that there were not sufficient resources programmed in the budget to provide the planned 'universal fertiliser subsidy'. The private sector was responsible for close to 100 percent of fertiliser sales in 2004–2005. The delay in sales during the critical months of July and August delayed the whole import pipe-line as fertiliser companies finance subsequent imports from earlier sales. As fertiliser imports were disrupted, it became apparent that the government could not afford a 'universal fertiliser subsidy' and there was a policy reversal in favour of an Expanded Targeted Inputs Programme around September 2004. The government then signed contracts with the private sector in the middle of October for the delivery of fertilisers to farmers over a 3-month period.

The contracts were too late and fertilisers were delivered late to smallholders – some arriving as late as January. The fertiliser market was also disrupted by uncertainties and as a consequence, commercial imports of fertilisers were also delivered later than usual. This was long after the crops were established, thus reducing yield response to the fertilisers. Once the fertilisers were delivered, the rains stopped at a critical stage of crop development leading to a food crisis.

The fact that Malawi would face a food crisis was obvious in mid-February 2005. The President met all donors resident in Malawi in late

February to early March to request assistance for humanitarian requirements. However, the Malawi Government was reluctant to declare a State of Emergency. It feared that the opposition would politicise the food crisis and blame the government. It also appears that senior representatives in the donor community advised the government not to declare a State of Emergency. Heads of donor missions were interviewed by the local press to reassure the population that the situation was under control and that they should not panic. This reassurance was reinforced continually during meetings of the Food Crisis Task Force and also informally. In response, the government sought to confirm the data. The Second Crop Estimates released at the end of March confirmed that crop production would decline by over 40 percent. The Malawi Vulnerability Assessment Committee (MVAC) confirmed that between 4.2 and 4.8 million people were in need of humanitarian assistance in May (MVAC, 2005). They presented two scenarios. Under the first scenario of relatively stable prices, there is need for a minimum of 270,000 metric tonnes of food aid. Under the second scenario which assumes a rapid increase in maize prices, the MVAC assesses total food aid requirements at close to 400,000 metric tonnes. The Food and Agricultural Organisation/World Food Programme (FAO/WFP) mission confirmed that the Second Round Crop Estimates possibly over-estimated production and noted that production in 2005 was the lowest for over a decade. Despite this evidence, the Malawi government and the donor community were reluctant to launch a formal international appeal until late August 2005.

Possible explanations for the delay in launching the international appeal include the fact that the government and donor communities were focused on getting back on track with the IMF and were cautious of potential adverse consequences of declaring a state of emergency in advance of the budget session of Parliament in July. They were concerned about potential pressures on the government to import commercial maize thus undermining the budget and foreign exchange reserves. Instead, they started planning the humanitarian programme and probably assumed that the full requirements of the humanitarian programme would be met even without launching a formal emergency appeal.

The Department of International Development (DFID), the European Union and the Norwegian Government were the first donors to provide assistance. Together with the Malawi Government, they pledged sufficient resources to finance 150,000 metric tonnes of maize for the humanitarian relief programme in early March.[12] As a result of resource constraints for logistics, DFID proposed to use its Logistics Unit (formerly for the Targeted Inputs Programme) for food aid distribution rather than the higher-cost World Food Programme. Under this arrangement, the World Food Programme will handle logistics in the worst affected south, while DFID will handle logistics in the less affected central and northern regions piloting a voucher scheme. In addition to food aid, the Malawi Government intends to expand the public works programme. The public works programme should supply between 25,000 metric tonnes of maize. There have been few pledges since late March – Ireland, France and Italy have pledged modest support to the World Food Programme.[13]

The United Nations Office for the Coordination of Humanitarian Affairs launched a 'Flash Appeal' for Malawi in the first week of September 2005. The Appeal calls for some US$51 million for emergency humanitarian assistance. The United States Agency for International Development (USAID) responded with a pledge of 23,500 metric tonnes, Japan 4251 metric tonnes and France 2424 metric tonnes. This implies that total commitments for the humanitarian relief programme are 209,000 metric tonnes against a minimum requirement of 270,000 metric tonnes in the Vulnerability Assessment Committee of scenario one. The scenario one estimate for total food aid assumed that maize prices would range from MK19–23 per kilogram.

The second scenario of the Vulnerability Assessment Committee assessed food aid requirements at close to 400,000 metric tonnes based on maize prices of MK33–MK40 per kilogram. It is clear that Malawi is moving towards the second scenario. The Famine Early Warning System Network/World Food Programme (FEWSNET/WFP) assessment of November 2005 has recorded that maize prices are already in excess of MK33 per kilogram in 16 out of Malawi's 26 districts.[14] The food security situation is clearly deteriorating rapidly and there is a need to scale up and intensify interventions and mobilise additional resources for the humanitarian relief programme. The situation is serious especially in the south and central regions where some households are consuming only maize bran and boiled mangoes.

The UN Appeal also called for US$37 million for emergency agricultural assistance. At the end of September 2005, total pledges for the Appeal were just over US$12 million. The major donor was DFID which increased balance of payments of support by US$8 million to be allocated for agricultural inputs. Ireland, Sweden and Luxembourg also pledged support for the agricultural input component of the Appeal.

Apart from financial constraints, it is apparent that the food aid pipeline is running into difficulties. Some of the companies that responded to the initial tenders to supply maize to Malawi have withdrawn from their tenders – finding more lucrative markets elsewhere in the region. International transport routes are severely congested leading to long delays in fertiliser and maize imports. The poorest and most vulnerable Malawians will pay the price of donor policy to undermine programmes to support agricultural production and scale down the Strategic Grain Reserve and the failure of Malawi's politicians to defend national policies for food security. The economy is crippled by unsustainable levels of external debts built up over years of structural adjustment lending, and internal debts due to the excesses of the previous political regime. The forthcoming food crisis will fuel the AIDS pandemic and undermine health. The pledges made at the Gleneagles Conference ring rather hollow as the poor in Malawi will die of hunger in the early part of 2006.

Notes

1 The original starter pack contained 'best bets' – the recommended (and economically profitable) maize seed and fertiliser for a given area and was given to all smallholders. The designers felt it was impossible to distinguish the poor from the desperately poor in Malawi and that it was important to involve the farming leaders. After two years, the starter pack became a Targeted Inputs Programme or TIP aimed at helping the very poor to survive. The essential link to high quality technology was lost.

2 The Fiscal Restructuring and Development Programme (FRDP II).

3 These failings were noted in an audit report of May 2003. The auditors also concluded that NFRA made major losses through poor grain management and handling procedures, confused lines of authority, decision making and reporting (Economic Resources Ltd., 2003). The poorly designed privatisation of the SGR forced by the donor community removed all technical oversight over a crucial aspect of national food security, increasing opportunities for political manipulation of the grain reserve.

4 There are legitimate concerns about the transparency of grain sales from the SGR. These were not done on the basis of competitive tenders. Some of the grain was not paid for, and the proceeds of the sale were not used to offset the bank loan. Twenty-eight thousand metric tonnes of grain were exported to Kenya.

5 The Malawi kwacha fell to MK108: US$1 at the end of August 2003, compared with MK65: US$1 two years earlier at the start of the food crisis.

6 And when the debt of over US$75 million was due to be paid to commercial banks.

7 Theresa Banda, Senior Nutritionist in the Ministry of Health and Population reporting to the National Food Crisis Task Force.

8   This is expenditure targeted to priority pro-poor expenditure; for example expenditure on training medical staff and drugs, provision of teaching and learning materials, and water and sanitation.
9   This was the only new party to win seats at the election.
10 Dr Bingu Wa Mutharika (United Democratic Front), John Tembo (Malawi Congress Party), Gwanda Chakwamba (Mgwirizano Coalition), Brown Mpingangira (National Democratic Alliance), and Justin Malewezi (independent candidate).
11 The Public Affairs Committee (PAC) is a respected civil society institution comprising all faith communities. Its mandate is to promote public interest, mediate in political disputes and conduct civic education.
12 The Malawi Government tendered for 20,607 metric tonnes to replenish the Strategic Grain Reserve (SGR), and also purchased grain options of 40,000 metric tonnes. DFID financed a tender for 49,900 metric tonnes, and the European Union financed a tender for 10,000 metric tonnes of maize for replenishment of the SGR. The European Union also provided US$4,825,000 for distribution costs to the World Food Programme, and an additional US$5,900,000 under Envelope B finance. Norway financed 6500 metric tonnes of maize through a tender and also provided US$2,000,000 in distribution costs to the World Food Programme (United Nations Development Programme Brief on Humanitarian Assistance, 2005).
13 Ireland has pledged US$603,000 to the World Food Programme, and Italy US$114,000.
14 Balaka, Blantyre, Chikwawa, Chiradzulu, Machinga, Mangochi, Mulanje, Neno, Phalombe, Zomba, Ntcheu, Dedza, Salima, Nkhotakota, Kasungu and Mzimba.

Bibliography

Economic Resources Ltd. (2003) 'Audit Report on the National Food Reserve Agency', Commissioned by the Malawi Government, Lilongwe, Malawi.
FEWSNET/WFP (2005) 'Report of the fieldtrip on the food security situation in the Southern Regions, Lakeshore Areas, and Northern Region', Unpublished Draft, Lilongwe.
Kamwona O.W. (2002) 'Living in the Abyss: Hunger in Mchingi', Unpublished paper for Save the Children (UK), Lilongwe, Malawi.
Malawi Government (2000) 'National Economic Council: Analysis of the November 2000, Integrated Household Study'.
Malawi Vulnerability Assessment Committee (2005) 'Vulnerability Assessment Update and Scenario Programming', Lilongwe, Malawi.
Levy S. (2004) 'Financing and Macro-Economic Impacts: How Does the Starter Pack Compare?' In: 'Starter Packs: A Strategy to Fight Hunger in Developing Countries', by Sarah Levy (ed.), CABI Publishing, UK.
Nyirongo C., Msiska B., Myetseni H., and Kamanga F. with Levy S. (2003) '2002–03 Extended Targeted Inputs Programme (ETIP)', Evaluation report for the Department for International Development.
Phiri A. (2004) 'Assessment of the Malawi Government strategy to address the 2001–02 food crisis: First draft report', Emergency Drought Recovery Programme.

United Nations Development Programme (2005) 'Unpublished Tables on Food Aid Commitments', UNDP, Lilongwe.

United Nations Humanitarian Response Team Malawi (2002) 'Reproductive Health and HIV/AIDS Vulnerability Assessment', United Nations Country Assessment Team (UNPFA, UNICEF, WHO, WFP, Ministry of Health and Population Reproductive Health Unit), Unpublished Paper, Lilongwe, Malawi.

Whitworth A. (2004) 'Malawi's Fiscal Crisis: A Donor Perspective', Unpublished Discussion Document, DFID Malawi.

World Bank (2003) 'Malawi: Country Economic Memorandum: Policies for Accelerating Growth', Report No. 25293 MAI.

8
Breaking Out of the AIDS and Disease Crisis

Anne Conroy and Justin Malewezi

Introduction

We will examine Malawi's attempts to prevent transmission of HIV by traditional measures (information, education and communication, behaviour change and condom promotion). We will show that, despite these interventions, infection rates remain stubbornly high. The reason is that, in Malawi as elsewhere, the fight against AIDS is too narrowly focused and ignores the broader societal drivers of the pandemic (which include poverty, poor nutrition, exploitation of vulnerable children, and gender inequality). We will also examine Malawi's attempts to mitigate the impact of the pandemic. The data will show that, despite heroic efforts, human and financial limitations mean that the country is reacting to the health and AIDS crisis, rather than breaking out of the pandemic.

Focus will be given to the major challenges for the health sector in responding to the crippling burden of highly infectious diseases where resources (both financial and human) are severely limited. We will examine issues regarding the national health policy, including the design and implementation of the Essential Health Care Package, and the transition to the Sector-Wide Approach (SWAP), investments in human resources, and the scaling-up of best practice from the community level. In the context of HIV/AIDS, there are issues of the management and treatment of sexually transmitted infections, blood safety and the prevention of mother to child transmission. The transparent and equitable scaling-up access to treatment, including the management of opportunistic infections and anti-retroviral therapy, presents major challenges under the difficult constraints faced by the Malawian health system.

Finally, we will show that a poor country such as Malawi simply cannot, by itself, muster the resources and skills necessary to curb the effects of the disease. The global pandemic of HIV/AIDS and burden of infectious disease in poor countries requires a global response. The international community needs to comprehend and implement key priorities if the health and AIDS crisis in Malawi – and in Africa – is to be defeated.

Malawi's responses to the HIV/AIDS pandemic

The initial response by Malawi to the AIDS pandemic was slow. The first case was diagnosed in 1985. But the conservative administration of Dr Banda was reluctant to acknowledge the threat posed by the disease or to allow for public debates on the subject. AIDS was buried by silence. To their credit,[1] and despite the absence of political commitment, the technicians in the Ministry of Health established a National Committee for HIV/AIDS in 1986 and developed an AIDS Control Plan (with the help of the World Health Organization) in 1987. The initial response to the pandemic focused on bio-medical interventions, with a focus on blood screening and the development of Information, Education and Communication (IEC) messages.

Following the first World Conference of Health Ministers in 1988, where Health Ministers acknowledged that AIDS was a serious epidemic that threatened development, Malawi established the National AIDS Control Programme in 1989 to coordinate all AIDS-related activities in the country. The AIDS Control Programme developed the first 5-year plan (1989–1994) which continued the focus on prevention through blood screening, and through promoting awareness and behaviour change. Voluntary counselling and testing sites were set up, but the overall impact of the plan was limited by human resources constraints, inadequate funding and lack of political leadership.

With the advent of multi-party democracy in 1994, President Bakili Muluzi acknowledged that Malawi faced a serious pandemic. There were public discussions of HIV/AIDS in the media. A Cabinet Committee on AIDS and Health was established under the leadership of the Vice-President. A Strategic Planning Unit was established under the National AIDS Control Programme in 1998 to manage the process of developing a multi-sectoral response to the AIDS pandemic. This led to the National Strategic Framework for AIDS Prevention and Care, launched by President Muluzi in 1999. The National Strategic Framework focused on core elements of prevention. These included promoting voluntary counselling and testing (VCT), information, education and communication (IEC), behaviour change, the promotion of correct and consistent use of condoms, management and treatment of sexually transmitted infections, prevention of mother to child transmission and blood safety.

Voluntary counselling and testing (VCT)

Access to VCT services is a key element of the prevention strategy, with demand rising sharply as the services become available. Just over 92,000 people (only about 3 percent of sexually active Malawians) accessed VCT services in 2002. The HIV Unit of the Ministry of Health and Population anticipate that the number of people accessing VCT services will increase to 450,000 in 2006. This is based on an estimate that some 84 percent of sexually active Malawians will want to know their HIV status (Ministry of Health and Population, 2004). Access to VCT services is limited by capacity within both the public health sector and associated NGOs. Existing facilities need to be upgraded to national standards before new ones are opened.[2] VCT services are also constrained by lack of resources. Essential supplies, reagents and test kits are often out of stock, due largely to the absence of a national ordering system for supply replenishment. Reporting formats need to be standardised to enable data to be aggregated and compared (Ministry of Health and Population, HIV Unit, 2004a). There are gender considerations also – while women are more likely to be HIV-positive, they are less likely to come forward for VCT services due to fear of stigmatisation (National Aids Commission *et al.*, 2003).

Information, education, and communication (IEC)

Information and education alone rarely translate into behaviour change. Malawi developed a behaviour change strategy that was based around in-depth and participatory analysis of the realities of traditional beliefs and practices (including sexual and reproductive health). The National IEC Committee has broad representation, is inclusive, and works with the faith communities in the area of prevention. There is particular emphasis on the modification of cultural values, beliefs and practices that facilitate spread of HIV. For example, there is now a greater collaboration between hospitals and traditional initiators on the circumcision of children. A culture of acceptance of People Living with HIV/AIDS (PLWHAs) has been promoted.

There has been a substantial increase in the availability of IEC materials in local languages and in the coverage of HIV/AIDS issues in the media (radio, newspapers, Television Malawi, billboards and posters).

The Demographic and Health Survey (National Statistical Office, 2001) reported that, while knowledge of HIV/AIDS is almost universal, this did not translate to an in-depth understanding of the methods of preventing transmission of HIV. Seventy-two percent of respondents suggested 'avoiding sex' and 63 percent reported 'using condoms' as key strategies to prevent transmission. Only 23 percent of respondents cited 'limiting the number of sexual partners' while a small minority recommended 'not sharing razor blades' or 'ensuring that injections were made with clean needles'. Despite some progress towards increased openness about HIV/AIDS, only 21 percent of adults had ever discussed the issue of HIV/AIDS with their partners (National Aids Commission *et al.*, 2003).

Changing sexual behaviour among children is arguably the most important intervention to prevent transmission as 50 percent of new infections occur in young people aged 15 to 24 (National Aids Commission, 2003a). However, the many children living in poverty are not always in a position to decide freely about sexual behaviour. Few have in-depth knowledge of the facts of sexual health. Behaviour change strategies can be blocked by sexual abuse as well as violence, poverty, stigma, culture and gender inequality. These issues have been examined in depth in Chapter 3 – the AIDS pandemic.

Prevention strategies

Reducing the spread of the virus

A major element in the prevention of HIV is the promotion of condom use. Despite a 15 percent increase since 1996, the 34 percent condom-use rate for sex with a non-regular partner is alarmingly low (Demographic and Health Survey, 2000). While 42 percent of women and 20 percent of men report that they could get a condom if they wanted to, there are important logistical bottlenecks in condom supply at the district and health centre levels. Supply availability is estimated at 19 million annually – seriously inadequate in a country where the sexually active population is estimated to be around 5–6 million. Support for condom social-marketing needs to be intensified for all age groups. The Ministry of Health is piloting the female condom programme with its own staff and intends to expand it to other ministries and public sector institutions in the near future.

Despite considerable efforts to reduce transmission of the virus, there are 110,000 new infections in Malawi every year. Prevalence rates are stabilising around 14.4 percent (National Aids Commission, 2003a, 2003b). The National Aids Commission (2003a, 2003b) estimates that the majority of infections (about 88 percent) are transmitted through heterosexual contact. Although the probability of transmitting AIDS in a single act of intercourse is quite low, a number of factors increase the risk dramatically. The two most important are the presence in either partner of a sexually transmitted infection (STI) such as syphilis or gonorrhoea, and having multiple sexual partners. STIs may be partly managed through better access to health facilities and the promotion of condoms. Reducing the number of sexual partners, however, requires help from the community leaders as well as other influential groups.

Engaging influential groups in the fight against HIV/AIDS

The Malawi Government has recognised the need to include traditional authorities and the faith communities in the fight against AIDS. Three groups have great potential to reduce the spread of HIV – the traditional authorities, the traditional healers and the faith communities. These groups are extremely influential, especially in the rural areas. Traditional authorities perceive that the advent of democracy has encouraged a more permissive society. They also see that their authority has been weakened especially among young people in society. They feel that young people have too much freedom, as children now 'affirm their rights' and 'no longer respect their parents'. In the past, elders instructed children about sexual norms, but this rarely happens today. None of the other mediums of information on sex education are particularly effective in informing young people on issues of sexual and reproductive health.

Traditional authorities have been exposed to messages about HIV prevention and care. They are slowly amending the harmful cultural practices that fuel transmission of the virus. However, they could be more effective especially if they could influence the discourse and language surrounding HIV prevention messages. There is a rich culture in Malawi. Cultural messages could be adapted in the fight against HIV/AIDS. However, the traditional authorities appear to be sidelined and are not seen as central in the fight against HIV/AIDS. In order to involve them in the national campaign against HIV/AIDS, traditional authorities need to be engaged with the issues in a culturally sensitive manner and be empowered to lead the fight against the disease.

Traditional healers also play a central role in peoples' lives and form an important part in the complexity of traditional practices and traditional authority. Traditional healers are the first point of contact in cases of illness for many people, especially in rural areas. They deal not only with physical but also spiritual well-being. Most have a sound basic understanding of HIV transmission and know that AIDS is an incurable disease. Their herbal treatments can help alleviate some of the symptoms of opportunistic infections associated with HIV/AIDS.

Traditional healers are widely consulted by those with STIs as there is considerable stigma and discrimination associated with STIs in Malawi. This is related to a general avoidance of open discussion of sexual issues, STIs and HIV/AIDS. These traditional healers could help break these barriers and work with the formal health system by referring patients to health centres for treatment of STIs.

The faith communities could also play a more constructive role in HIV prevention and care. The Malawi Government recognised this and convened a high-level Government Faith Community Consultation on HIV/AIDS in February 2001. This consultation involved the senior leaders of all churches and other faiths in Malawi. However, this important meeting excluded women and young people who are the most vulnerable to HIV transmission.

The outcome was an agreed Common Action Statement to reduce stigma and discrimination, promote voluntary counselling and testing (VCT), and strengthen programmes to keep the youth informed on HIV/AIDS issues. The Government agreed to support the faith communities in emphasising the importance of abstinence and mutual faithfulness. However, the government also promotes condoms as a proven technical approach to HIV prevention. Unfortunately, differences of opinion between the government and the faith communities on condom use dominated the consultations. The failure to reach common ground, or even to respect differences on this issue, remains unresolved to this day.

The government and the faith communities agreed to develop theological approaches that emphasise love, compassion and hope in dealing with the AIDS pandemic. Issues surrounding the AIDS pandemic and the sensitivities of the faith communities must be addressed. The faith communities will continue to have great influence in the lives and deaths of all Malawians, and need to find a role that is as constructive and compassionate as possible. Developing an active role for the faith communities and traditional authorities in the fight against HIV/AIDS remains an important challenge. It is also one that requires dedication, honesty and moral courage from all concerned if it is to succeed.

Impact mitigation

Community home-based care

The demand for community home-based care[3] outstrips resources and capacity. As the HIV pandemic increases the number of people who are symptomatic and in need of clinical and palliative care, much of the responsibility for care of the sick and orphans falls to the community – and increasingly to the faith communities. Seventy-five percent of community groups providing home-based care are supported by faith-based organisations (National Aids Commission *et al.*, 2003). There has also been an increase in the number of trained community-based health providers. The National Aids Commission has developed a curriculum and training materials. Unfortunately, many programmes and interventions in community home-based care do not meet the basic nutrition and hygiene needs of patients. Referral systems remain weak and over-stretched, and information systems are inadequate. There is a high drop-out rate of volunteers and rapid turn-over of care givers – possibly due to the limited financial, technical and material resources available to support community home-based care initiatives (National Aids Commission *et al.*, 2003).

Poverty is the chief factor limiting implementation of sustainable community programmes. Basic commodities such as food, soap and drugs are often unaffordable or unavailable. There is little psychological and spiritual support. Health staff may be unaware of home-based care programmes that patients could be referred to, and there are too few trained volunteers at the community level. Obtaining sufficient of the right food can be seriously problematic for the poor. HIV-infected individuals have higher nutritional requirements than normal, particularly with regard to protein (up to 50 percent above normal needs) and energy (up to 15 percent above the norm) (Haddad and Gillespie, 2003). But these individuals are also more likely to suffer from loss of appetite. This is made worse for the poor who are likely to be malnourished prior to being infected. There are also important indirect impacts at the household and community level. These may be brought about by, for example, a diminished capacity of caregivers to care for themselves, their young children and sick household members. In many poor households, even those unaffected by the pandemic, childcare may be compromised in the short term to ensure food security in the long term (Haddad and Gillespie, 2003).

Care of orphans

The AIDS pandemic impacts especially the elderly and the children. In Malawi, over 840,000 children under the age of 18 are orphans

(45 percent due to HIV/AIDS). 950,000 orphans and vulnerable children are in need of support (National Aids Commission *et al.*, 2003). The most recent projection is that there would be 770,000 AIDS orphans by 2010 and that the number would increase to 1.1 million by 2020 (National Aids Commission, 2003a; 2003b). There is a higher proportion of orphans living in urban rather than rural areas (reflecting the higher prevalence rates in urban areas[4]).

Although deaths from AIDS are concentrated among adults, children suffer directly from the loss of parents, other family members, teachers and sometimes their peers. This has a major psychological, social and economic impact on the children affected. The extended family may be so overwhelmed that care-givers cannot spend enough time with individual children to help them through their trauma – the most that can be done is to ensure that they are fed, housed and receiving some form of education. Adult deaths also affect the provision of services to children,[5] as well as children's human rights – including the right to health, development and survival, rest and leisure, and protection from sexual and other exploitations. The number of street children appear to be growing (there is very limited information on this group) and can be expected to increase due to HIV/AIDS, poverty and hunger. Children go on the streets for reasons such as child abuse, hostile home environments or broken families – but will often find themselves in an even more vulnerable situation. They are also at risk of being permanently alienated from society due to their lack of education and care. They may also turn to crime or commercial sex work making them very vulnerable to HIV infection (World Bank, 2002).

The Malawi Government has a National Policy on orphans and vulnerable children – the challenge is to mobilise the resources and capacity to implement the policy. The initial emphasis of the policy has been on capacity development to enable communities and households to provide care and support, through the use of available social capital and other resources. A system for orphan registration has been developed and is in place at the national and district levels. The Ministry of Gender estimates that 340,000 orphans and vulnerable children have been reached in the period 1999 to 2003 (National Aids Commission *et al.*, 2003).

Much remains to be done. Better institutional coordination mechanisms between the Ministry of Health and the National AIDS Commission, and between donors and the various stakeholders are needed. While the policy framework provides useful guidance, a national consensus on the best approaches to ensure that orphans have access to education, health and nutrition as well as protection from abuse, stigma and discrimination is urgently needed.

The health sector

The Malawi Government is committed to promoting access to health services in line with the Constitution and the Poverty Reduction Strategy. Formal health services are provided by four main agencies: the Ministry of Health and Population which has overall responsibility for 60 percent of health services, the Christian Health Association of Malawi (CHAM) which accounts for 37 percent of health services, while the Ministry of Local Government and the private sector account for the balance.

The most recent Health Plan (1999–2004) identified the major health challenges as high child mortality and morbidity, high maternal mortality and associated mortality, and morbidity due to infectious diseases, including but not limited to AIDS, tuberculosis and malaria. The Ministry of Health and Population concluded in early 2004 that 'while some progress has been achieved in the implementation of the 4th Health Plan, much work needs to be done to achieve the overly ambitious targets set for the planned period. Besides the biological causes of disease, socio-cultural, environmental and lifestyle factors also have a significant role in causing ill-health. Additional initiatives are needed to improve the social conditions of disadvantaged groups who mainly reside in the rural areas' (Ministry of Health and Population, 2004).

A number of important initiatives have been taken to support the implementation of the National Health Plan. Some health units have been given greater autonomy, such as the tertiary care hospitals, and the Central Medical Stores, which is responsible for drug procurement and distribution. There have also been attempts to decentralise decision-making to the districts. But the single most important change has been the development of the Essential Health Care Package (EHP). The following discussion outlines Malawi's attempts to follow international best practice through the adoption of the EHP and Sector Wide Approach (SWAP). It also discusses two innovative approaches that are essential – investment in human resources, and involving community leaders to reduce the level of maternal mortality, and to scale up access to sexual and reproductive health services for adolescents.

The Essential Health Care Package (EHP)

The design and implementation of the EHP is the core strategy for improving the overall health status of Malawians. The EHP focuses on those conditions and service gaps that disproportionately affect the health of the poor and disadvantaged populations. The EHP will be delivered free at the point of service in line with the Poverty Reduction Strategy. The EHP consists of the following services delivered at various levels of the health service:

- Control and management of vaccine preventable illnesses.
- Reproductive health services including family planning, safe motherhood and prevention of mother to child transmission.

The prevention and treatment of diseases (together with related complications) such as malaria, tuberculosis, acute respiratory infections, acute diarrhoeal disease (including cholera), STIs, HIV/AIDS, and eye, ear and skin infections).

The EHP also deals with the prevention and management of malnutrition, nutritional deficiencies and related complications, and with the treatment of common injuries. It involves the enhancement of the following support services:

- Essential laboratory services.
- Drug procurement, distribution and management.
- Information, education and communication.
- Pre and in-service training.
- Planning, budgeting and management systems.
- Monitoring and evaluation.

The Sector Wide Approach (SWAP)

The EHP is intended to provide a basis for a shared vision for the health sector, in terms of public and donor finance, with a Sector Wide Approach (SWAP) as the mechanism for sectoral planning. The two strategies are intended to improve the equity and efficiency of resource allocation. There is also the expectation that the EHP and SWAP will serve to mobilise additional resources around a Joint Programme of Work. The Ministry of Health and Population finalised the Joint Programme of Work in November 2003. The Joint Programme of Work and National Health Plan is based on the priorities of the Ministry for EHP and non-EHP implementation.

The Sector Wide Approach, based on the Joint Programme of Work, is intended to get all partners (government, donors, NGOs and other stakeholders – including CHAM and private sector providers) to work together to develop and operate the systems and structures for effective and equitable health service delivery. This move is a result of re-thinking the modalities of external support in order to ensure that it is used in the most effective manner.

The Malawi Essential Health Care Package is intended to provide the basis for a shared vision of the health sector in terms of what should be supported with public funds including external support. The SWAP is therefore:

- a mechanism for sectoral programming around the Ministry's core business of EHP service delivery, and,
- a means of enhancing donor co-ordination and joint working.

The SWAP process is relatively far advanced in Malawi with most bilateral and multilateral donors agreeing to 'basket funding' and a joint reporting mechanism. This allows the technicians in the Ministry of Health to focus on implementation and service delivery rather than constant negotiation with donor partners and responding to multiple requests.

Investment in human resources

Chapter 2 on the Health and Disease Crisis highlighted the fact that human resource is a critical constraint in expanding access to and improving the quality of health services. While most of the population of Malawi live in the rural areas, over 80 percent of skilled health staff operate in urban areas. Only 9 percent of current health facilities are ready to implement the EHP, and many rural health centres are manned by Health Surveillance Assistants with only 10 weeks of training (Ministry of Health, 2004b).

The Malawi Government is attempting to respond by implementing a Six-Year Emergency Training Programme focusing on training nurses, clinical officers and medical assistants. All training facilities are operating at full capacity. They also train technical staff, including pharmacy, laboratory and environmental health officers. But these efforts are ineffective in a situation where half of new staff is merely replacing those that are lost due to death or migration. Retaining staff within the public sector is a fundamental pre-requisite for implementation of the EHP – as well as expanding its activities into new areas such as increasing access to Anti-retroviral (ARV) therapy.

The human resources constraint also limits the potential to scale up treatment for AIDS. The Malawi Government has always stressed the need to invest in human resources as the pre-requisite for successful implementation of the Essential Health Care Package and roll-out of

ARVs. The British Department for International Development (DFID) has provided US$100 million over a 5-year period to expand training, supplement salaries to enhance staff retention and recruit additional medical staff as a temporary measure, while additional Malawian doctors and specialists are trained. This is a new and innovative approach, classified as a high-risk intervention. However, the increased support for human resources development provided by DFID and other partners under the SWAP is essential and deserves continued support. DFID's programme is bold and innovative, and is focused on increasing the quality of health services. Promoting progress implies that risks are taken, that the programme is supported and that lessons are learnt and applied throughout the region. The alternative is to accept the collapse of health services with the resulting impoverishment and suffering.

Scaling up best-practices from the community level

Malawi's Ministry of Health has implemented the Family and Reproductive Health Project in three districts of Malawi with support from the Canadian International Development Agency (CIDA) and the United Nations Fund for Population Activities (UNFPA).[6] The project was designed to 'increase the utilisation and quality of reproductive health, family planning and safe motherhood in Malawi through an improved relationship between the community and health service providers in the three districts.' The aim is to 'provide accessible, affordable and convenient, comprehensive reproductive health services to all women, men and young people through informed choices in order for them to attain their reproductive health goals and rights' (Twea, 2005).

Key elements of the programme included capacity building for all the community leaders and 'gate keepers' – including traditional authorities, group village headmen, village headmen and village health committees. Traditional Birth Attendants (TBAs) and medical staff, including medical assistants, health surveillance assistants (HSAs) and nurses/midwives, were also trained in STI syndromic approach, youth friendly services, gender issues, life-saving skills and infection prevention.

The programme disseminated information on family planning, safe motherhood, sexually transmitted infections, teenage pregnancy, dangers of abortion, and other sexual and reproductive health issues. It also focused on community empowerment and ownership, and built consensus around the fact that no one should deliver at home, that a *primo gravid* and high risk pregnant woman should relocate to the District Hospital from the eighth month of pregnancy, and untrained

TBAs should not conduct deliveries. The community enforced penalties if these were not followed. The communities also invested in 'bicycle ambulances' that could transport women to the nearest health centre in case of emergencies.

Youth clubs were established and youth counsellors were trained. The programme provided confidential counselling to young people on all issues related to sexual and reproductive health. Young people were able to express their views, ask questions, and obtain accurate information and family planning services. The programme was exceptionally successful. Outcomes include:

- A significant reduction in the number of maternal deaths. A maternal death audit at Makanda Health Centre revealed that maternal deaths declined from 14 in 2001 to one in 2005.
- A significant reduction in the number of abortions and negative cultural practices.
- An increase in the number of mothers delivering at health centres, rather than by traditional birth attendants, and increase in attendance at antenatal clinics and clinics for the treatment of STIs.
- An improvement in sanitation and hygiene at the health centres, and in the relationship between the community members and health workers.
- Increased demand for, and utilisation of, family planning services (Twea, 2005).

This programme demonstrates that change is indeed possible (at a modest cost) provided that there is a strong focus on the involvement of the community, traditional authorities and faith leaders. It succeeded in promoting gender equity and health-seeking behaviour. The results show the benefits of directly involving community leaders and the youth, and of prioritising the key interventions to reduce maternal deaths. There is much that can be gained by applying these simple principles across all sectors of development.

The health sector response to the AIDS pandemic

Blood safety and waste disposal

All blood in Malawi is screened for HIV and syphilis. The main challenges in this area are poor dissemination of the national policy on blood safety, and inadequate enforcement of standardisation and uniform testing of blood. The material, technical and resource capacity to implement approved guide-lines for blood safety needs enhancing, as do those for post-transfusion services (personnel, medical and laboratory equipment). Post-screening counselling for HIV-positive donors who would like to know their status also needs improvement. Epidemiological assessments are required so as to identify low risk groups for HIV in order to encourage them to donate blood regularly (McConville, 2004).

There is inadequate monitoring of, and no standards for, the disposal of medical waste. There are also concerns over maintaining standards of care in the absence of adequate supervision and in resource-constrained environments where hygiene and sanitation are very poor. District implementation plans do not yet include a budget for infection prevention. Syringes and needles may be reused, leading to HIV infection. This last can be addressed through providing auto-destruct syringes only and purchasing only the required number of needles and syringes with injectable medicine (McConville, 2004).

Mother to child transmission

Approximately 10 percent of all new infections in southern Africa are due to perinatal transmission. Malawi follows the southern African norm in this regard. Without any preventative measures, about 25–40 percent of babies born to infected mothers will themselves be infected. About 500,000 pregnant women in Malawi need antenatal care including HIV counselling and testing (National Aids Commission, 2003a; 2003b). Approximately 80,000 women need anti-retroviral therapy to prevent vertical transmission of the virus (National Aids Commission, 2004). In the absence of any intervention to prevent mother to child transmission, more than 20,000 children will be born with the virus every year (National AIDS Commission *et al.*, 2003).

By the end of 2003, comprehensive Prevention of Mother to Child Transmission (PMTCT) services were being offered at nine sites and partial services at seven sites in the country. Only 3 percent of mothers had access to PMTCT services. Major constraints included limited human, technical and institutional capacity. These are exacerbated by the limited capacity within the Ministry of Health and Population to provide technical oversight and also weak linkages with other support networks and service providers including Traditional Birth Attenders, community home-based care and associations of people living with HIV/AIDS.

Treatment strategies

Malawi has pursued treatment aggressively, while recognising that prevention and treatment are interlinked. It established a technical working group to explore options to introduce anti-retroviral therapy immediately after the Durban International AIDS Conference of 2000. This led to an ambitious proposal to roll out treatment to all HIV-positive eligible patients in advance of the United Nations General Assembly on HIV/AIDS in June 2001. The initial proposal planned to address the main constraints to the health sector's capacity to provide treatment and to manage opportunistic infections. It focused on investment in human resources, developing health services infrastructure, providing essential support to the implementation of the Essential Health Care Package and rolling out treatment. It called for an investment of US$1.6 billion over seven years. This was in line with the initial estimates of financial requirements for the Global Fund and subsequent analysis of resource requirements for the provision of comprehensive health services in Malawi. However, the Malawi Government was repeatedly told to scale back the investment programme, especially in the area of human resources, health systems support, management, monitoring and evaluation. As a result of all these cuts, Malawi submitted a proposal for just under US$300 million in the first round of the Global Fund.

In August 2002, the Global Fund approved Malawi's revised proposal for US$196 million to roll out treatment for HIV/AIDS to 25,000 patients. Fortunately, the momentum for providing treatment was accelerating and the World Health Organization approved the 'Three by Five' Programme.[7] The use of cheaper generic drugs was approved by the Global Fund. This allowed countries to increase the number of patients who could be treated with the available resources. Malawi, however, has argued consistently that providing satisfactory anti-retroviral therapy will require complementary investments in human resources and health sector capacity.

The Ministry of Health established a HIV Unit to provide treatment guidelines for ARVs, management and treatment of opportunistic infections, voluntary counselling and testing, and prevention of mother to child transmission of the virus. The Ministry recognises that widespread, unregulated access to ARV drugs will lead to the emergence of resistant strains – with terrible consequences for the individual and the nation. ARVs will be provided within a structured public health approach that will follow principles established by the Tuberculosis Control Programme.[8] The approach will also include

Directly Observed Therapy Supervised (DOTS) programmes by guardians to promote the high rates of adherence necessary to minimise the likelihood that resistant strains of virus will emerge. The public health approach of supplying free drugs will minimise the likelihood that patients will drop out because they cannot afford to continue with treatment.[9]

By the end of 2004, 59 hospitals were identified to provide treatment across the public sector, the Christian Health Association of Malawi (CHAM) and Malawi Defence Forces. The aim is to integrate ARV therapy into district health services. There will also be a public health campaign to inform the public that drugs will only be made available to eligible patients and to stress the importance of adherence. The Ministry of Health established several criteria for the delivery of ARV therapy. These include a commitment from the District Health Management Team, a dedicated room for VCT and the management of ARVs, reliable (uninterrupted) supplies of test kits, and the allocation of appropriate staff.

Despite the fact that all the training guidelines are in place and all the staff has been trained, there are potential constraints to achieving the goals agreed under the 'Three by Five' Initiative:

- The capacity of the health sector to deliver drugs in the light of serious human resource constraints.
- The capacity of the Central Medical Stores and its partners to provide sufficient drugs to meet the demand and to replenish stocks on a regular basis to ensure that there is no interruption in supply.
- Patient demand for HIV testing and ARV therapy (Ministry of Health and Population, HIV Unit, 2004c).

There are also issues of equity involved in the rapid scale-up of ARV therapy. The National HIV/AIDS Policy establishes the principle of equitable access to HIV/AIDS treatment and care regardless of gender, age, ethnic group and sexual orientation. There are also specific provisions for the poor and the vulnerable. The approach of using district hospitals and providing for follow-up at peripheral health centres should increase access by the poor. However, the challenges and needs remain enormous.

By the end of 2004, there were 13,183 patients on ARV in Malawi. The results were very encouraging. Of the patients that were started on therapy, 84 percent were alive, 8 percent were dead, and 8 percent were not followed up. Of those alive and on ARV, 98 percent are ambulatory and 85 percent fit for work. The results based on pill counts of 96 percent of patients show 95 percent or more adherence to therapy, and only 10 percent with major side effects (Harries, 2004) By the middle of 2005, 30,000 patients were receiving treatment. Sixty percent of those on ARV are women. There have been efforts to ensure equity in access to therapy, with the focus on delivery through district hospitals to increase access by the poor. Preliminary information on 'who gets ARV' in the public health sector suggests that treatment is being provided to the ordinary person.

Reflections on Malawi's attempts to break out of the AIDS and health crisis

The chapter has outlined Malawi's efforts to address the health and AIDS crisis. The country is implementing a broad range of policies to prevent transmission of the virus – including information, education, communication, behaviour change, voluntary counselling and testing, condom promotion and efforts to reduce transmission among the youth. However, these efforts are fragmented due to capacity and resource constraints. They are not succeeding in reducing infection rates. Infections rates will not decline unless the broader societal issues such as poverty, inequality, lack of social cohesion, gender inequality and food insecurity are addressed in a comprehensive manner. The fight against AIDS has to be broadened to include strengthening of political leadership and the more effective inclusion of and collaboration with influential groups, namely the traditional authorities, traditional healers and the faith communities.

Efforts have been made to mitigate the impact of the pandemic through the provision of community home-based care and support to orphans. Both are undermined by a lack of resources. The government and communities are trying to respond to the pandemic but are overwhelmed in their efforts to do so.

There are also huge challenges in addressing the overwhelming burden of infectious diseases and the AIDS pandemic. The government is attempting to provide comprehensive prevention and treatment of major infectious diseases, but with costs of around US$6.00 to US$8.00 per capita, it is an enormous challenge. There are high levels of attrition in the health sector resulting in a human resource crisis which represents the most serious constraint to the provision of basic health services and the roll-out of anti-retroviral therapy. The health sector has attempted to address challenges posed by the AIDS pandemic and focuses on the management and treatment of sexually transmitted infections, prevention of mother to child transmission and blood safety. However, all the programmes are limited by resource constraints and have limited coverage. Plans to manage and treat opportunistic infections and to roll out anti-retroviral therapy are well-advanced, with the aim of treating 80,000 people by the end of 2005. Despite Herculean efforts and a total commitment, many elements of the Global Fund Programme are running behind schedule including the prevention of mother to child transmission and community home-based care.

Like most very poor countries over-burdened by a health and AIDS crisis, Malawi is not breaking out of the trap. It is committed in attempting to implement comprehensive programmes for prevention and care, but all its programmes are affected by resource and capacity constraints with the result that the battle is being lost. Less than 5 percent of the population currently have access to programmes in VCT, PMTCT or anti-retroviral therapy. A small minority of orphans or those in need of community-based care are receiving comprehensive support. The communities are making valiant efforts but failing to make headway. Poverty and capacity constraints limit the potential for success. There is an urgent need for a new approach.

Health and poverty are closely related. Improving health reduces poverty, and reducing poverty improves health. This may seem self-evident, but it also implies that many of the most important strategies for improving health fall outside the health sector. It is important to improve nutrition, especially in a country where the majority of the population fail to meet basic nutritional requirements. It is also important to improve the infrastructure for technology and health including access to clean water, basic sanitation and good housing. There is also a need to promote gender equality as inequality drives the AIDS pandemic. Investments in education also improve health outcomes as literacy, especially female literacy, contributes to good health.

The international community should commit to providing adequate resources for research and development, particularly for neglected diseases. The Commission on Macro-Economics and Health noted the gross imbalance between research and development relative to the global burden of disease (World Health Organisation, 2001). This imbalance has been documented for over a decade. The Commission on Health Research and Development noted the '90/10 disequilibrium' and found that only 10 percent of the world's research and development spending is directed at the health problems of 90 percent of the world's population (Global Forum for Health Research, 1999). This must be addressed in order to reduce the crippling burden of ill-health in Africa.

There is need to focus on the principal communicable diseases including AIDS, tuberculosis and malaria. There is also need for invest- ments in human resources and strengthening health systems in order to address the burden of communicable diseases. All this will require additional resources and sustained commitment.

Addressing malaria will require additional resources to ensure that everyone sleeps under a bed net, ensuring that children obtain access to medical care on time and developing more effective drug regiments. Addressing the HIV/AIDS pandemic will require changes in sexual behaviour – reducing the number of sexual partners, especially concur- rent sexual partners, and increasing the use of condoms to prevent transmission of the virus. Running programmes to reduce transmission among high-risk groups are also important. The management and treatment of sexually transmitted infections is also a core strategy to reduce the probability of infection during intercourse.

None of this will be easy as it affects sexual behaviour, as well as gender and power relations in society. Changing sexual behaviour will not be possible without addressing the underlying drivers of the pan- demic including poverty, vulnerability, gender inequality, poor health and nutritional status, the lack of opportunities, and despair that fuel high-risk sexual behaviour.

Two other interventions are critical. The first is the expanded use of microbiocides that would allow women to protect themselves before sex. The second is the need to intensify research to identify an AIDS vaccine. This is a difficult challenge, but the world cannot abandon the quest for an AIDS vaccine as it represents the best chance of turning round the pandemic.

At the same time, there is a need to provide treatment for infected people in developing countries. It has been a long battle to convince the international community to support treatment. Without treat- ment, people in the developing world will die early and painful deaths. They need access to medical care that will markedly extend life and allow them to look after their children longer. Malawi has demon- strated that high rates of drug adherence can be achieved in resource- poor settings and that people can return to health and eventually to work. These results were achieved through the commitment and dedi- cation of all involved.

At the same time as a rolling-out treatment for AIDS, we must not neglect deaths from other causes. There is a need to move forward on two tracks. The first track is by investing in the health system to make it strong enough to deliver a comprehensive range of essential interventions. The other is by complementary investments in educational and broader institutional advances such as community involvement and reform of services to ensure that the poor can access health care. These investments in education and health care will also encourage people to reduce fertility as they have more confidence that their children will survive.

Transforming health is a fundamental component of economic development. It requires additional resources. In the words of the Commission of Macro-Economics and Health

> Fighting disease will be the truest test of our common capacity to forge a global community. There is no excuse in today's world for millions of people to die each year for the lack of US$34 per capita to cover essential health services. A just and far-sighted world would not let this tragedy continue.

If the Gleneagles Agreement of 2005 to double aid to Africa is serious, this must include increasing funding for health without delay as access to health services and medicine are the most fundamental of human rights. No one in the world should be denied access to health services.

Notes

1 Even to appear to dissent from President Banda's perspective could result in severe punishment, so it was no small decision to follow this path.

2 A recent survey conducted by the Ministry of Health revealed that 50 percent of existing sites offering VCT were not operating according to national guidelines before new ones were established (Ministry of Health HIV Unit, October 2004).

3 Community Home-Based Care is any form of care given to sick people in their own environment by their families and supported by skilled health workers, trained volunteers and communities to meet physical, spiritual, material and psychological needs (World Health Organization, 1993).

4 Urban prevalence is estimated at 23 percent (with a range of 19–28 percent) compared to rural areas 12 percent (with a range of 10 to 15 percent). HIV prevalence is also higher in the more urbanised southern region (approximately 20 percent) than in the less urbanised central and northern regions (approximately 10 percent).

5 The 1988 Population Census revealed 4.2 percent of the population were disabled, about 60 percent of them children. Few have access to social welfare activities (Madise, 2004).

6 The three districts were Nkhata Bay in the north, and Dedza and Mchingi Districts in the central region. The programme was funded by CIDA through

the Canadian Public Health Association (CPHA) to a tune of 500,000 Canadian Dollars. UNFPA also provided technical and financial support.

7 This programme is intended to provide access to treatment for 3 million eligible patients by the end of 2005. It is estimated that 2 million beneficiaries will be drawn from sub-Saharan Africa, the epicentre of the pandemic.

8 The successful Tuberculosis Control Programme is based on standardised diagnosis and case finding, standardised treatment, recording and reporting systems, management of drugs by paramedical officers and free drugs for all patients (Harries, 2004).

9 Prior to the provision of free drugs, the Lilongwe Lighthouse provided ARV treatment on a revolving drug basis. Drug default rates approached 40 percent. By contrast, where ARV therapy was provided free of charge in the Thyolo and Chiradzulu districts by Medicines Sans Frontiers, the default rate was less than 1 percent.

Bibliography

Global Forum for Health Research (1999) 'The 10/90 Report on Health Research', Geneva, Global Forum for Health Research.

Haddad L. and Gillespie S. (2003) 'Effective Food and Nutrition Policy Responses to HIV/AIDS: What do we know and what do we need to know?', FCND Discussion Paper No. 112, International Food Policy Research Institute, Washington DC.

Harries A. (2004) 'Power Point Presentation: Scaling Up ARV Therapy: Integration of TB and HIV', Lilongwe, Malawi.

McConville F. (2004) 'Prevention of HIV/AIDS in Malawi: Background paper for the visit of Peter Piot and Suma Chakrabarti to Malawi, February 2004', Lilongwe, Malawi.

Ministry of Health and Population, HIV Unit (2004a) 'Power Point Presentation to the Technical Working Group on the Health Sector Response to HIV/AIDS', National AIDS Commission, Lilongwe, Malawi.

Ministry of Health and Population (2004b) 'Human Resources in the Health Sector: Issues and Challenges', Lilongwe, Malawi.

Ministry of Health and Population (2004c) 'Joint Programme of Work', Lilongwe, Malawi.

National AIDS Commission in collaboration with partners and stakeholders (2003) 'Joint Review of the National Strategic Framework and Operations of the National AIDS Commission', Lilongwe, Malawi.

National AIDS Commission (2003a) 'HIV Sentinel Surveillance Report 2003', Lilongwe, Malawi.

National AIDS Commission (2003b) 'Estimates of prevalence of infection and implications', Lilongwe, Malawi.

National AIDS Commission (2004) 'HIV and AIDS in Malawi: 2003 Estimates and Implications', Lilongwe, Malawi.

National Statistical Office (2001) 'Malawi: Demographic and Health Survey', National Statistical Office, Zomba, Malawi, ORC Macro Calverton, Maryland, USA.

Twea S. (2005) 'Best practices and lessons learned: The family and reproductive health project', UNFPA, Lilongwe, Malawi.

World Bank (2002) 'Malawi Multi-Sectoral HIV/AIDS Project: Orphans and Vulnerable Children Mission', Lilongwe, Malawi.

World Health Organisation (1993) 'Global Plan of Action', Geneva, Switzerland.

World Health Organisation (2001) 'Macro-Economics and Health, Investing in Health for Economic Development', Geneva.

9

Breaking Out of Food Insecurity

Malcolm Blackie, Anne Conroy and Jeffrey Sachs

Introduction

In Chapter 5, we focused on the technical components of low agricultural productivity. Traditional African agriculture was based around robust, but low-productivity (per unit of land) farming systems. Returns to the scarce resources of labour and cash dominate the real choices open to African smallholders. We showed, using the Malawi case, the very real obstacles faced at both the national and the household levels in breaking out of poverty in an agriculturally dominated economy. But we ended on a positive note – there are difficulties aplenty but there are also real options for change. In this chapter, focusing on the real world experience of Malawi, we will demonstrate how opportunity can be created from despair.

Making fertilisers profitable

As we learned in Chapter 5, addressing the central issue of soil fertility was one of the keys to creating change. Crops will only yield well if they are fed adequately. Crops get their nutrition from the soil. If the fertility of the soil is not regularly and routinely replenished, crop yields (and food security) decline. An important component of dealing with this problem in much of the developed world has been through the use of chemical fertilisers. But such fertilisers will remain a high-cost item for African farmers for the foreseeable future, so profitability of fertiliser use depends heavily on making the best use of the limited amounts of fertilisers that the typical smallholder is able to purchase. The utility and economics of existing fertiliser recommendations, especially in the more risky climatic areas, has been questioned for many years.

Smallholder farmer practice in Zimbabwe reflects the need for substantially revised fertiliser recommendations. Rainfall markedly affects fertiliser use efficiency yet there is almost no guidance to farmers as how they should adjust fertiliser use to seasonal rainfall (see Piha, 1993, for an outstanding, practical, profitable – and totally ignored – example of how to match fertiliser to rainfall patterns to improve fertiliser use efficiency and profitability).

Fertiliser efficiency in smallholder cropping systems can be improved through the addition of small amounts of high quality organic matter to tropical soils (Snapp, 1995). This practice increases soil microbial activity and nutrient cycling, and reduces nutrient losses (Snapp, 1995). The organic matter may come from a range of sources – options include legume rotations and green manures, animal manures, intercropping, strip cropping, relay cropping, and agro-forestry.

Legume-based agriculture led the agricultural revolution in Britain and has been the focus of well-meaning efforts to transform smallholder African agriculture since the turn of the last century. The contribution of legumes is usually to add nitrogen[1] to the soil, together with some organic matter from the decay of their roots after harvest. Nitrogen is an important (but not the sole) plant nutrient limiting crop yields in many African soils. But despite many years of effort, legumes remain marginal in many of the maize-based systems of the region. The most suitable legumes, from the soil fertility perspective, are often the hardest for the farmer to adopt. Broadly speaking, those that have the greatest impact on soil fertility are also those that need the most initial investment in labour and land, and provide fewer short-term food benefits. The family may not be able to release land from food crops because of the need to meet today's food supply. But this is at the cost of building up the long-term fertility of the soil to meet tomorrow's food needs.

Legumes, like other crops, are sensitive to the availability of nutrients[2] in the soil. In southern and eastern Africa, low phosphorus levels in the soils can make legumes unproductive – so the farmer cannot obtain the nitrogen benefit from their use unless he or she applies a phosphorus fertiliser to the legume. That fertiliser – necessary to 'kick start' the system – may be too costly or unavailable. Good quality legume seed is often expensive because leguminous plants often do not yield heavily and thus bulking up seed for sale is often a slow and expensive process. Traditionally, many farmers intercrop their main food crop with legumes which can provide a useful complement to the family diet. But getting increased legume yields in an intercrop is difficult. Either a modest legume crop is grown (which adds little to soil fertility or food security) or else a more aggressive productive one is planted which may compete strongly with the main food crop and depress the yields of that crop if not well managed.

Grain legumes – groundnuts, pigeonpea, cowpeas – are widely grown by farmers in southern and eastern Africa; mainly for home consumption of the seed and sometimes for the leaves. But the more productive, higher yielding grain legumes offer relatively little organic matter and nitrogen to the soil since almost all the nitrogen is removed from the field in the grain (Giller *et al.*, 1997).[3] There are important exceptions. Carr (1994) reported that, on severely depleted soils in Malawi, the self-nodulating (promiscuous) soyabean variety *Magoye* produced more calories per unit of land than unfertilised maize, in addition to fixing nitrogen from the atmosphere. Promiscuous soyabeans are attractive to smallholders because not only do they produce a valued grain but they also have good root and above ground biomass. The *Magoye* soyabean is grown very widely in Zambia, but for reasons that had little to do with improving smallholder livelihoods, the Malawi Government forbade the promotion of this variety. Farmers living near the Zambian border took matters into their own hands, crossed the border, and brought the seed back for themselves.

Agroforestry technologies offer promise. The use of tree fallows avoids the competition effect between trees and crops (Kwesiga and Coe, 1994). But where land is limiting, the feasibility of fallow systems is yet to be proved. *Faidherbia albida* is a vigorous leguminous tree, long used by African farmers for improving crop yields in many habitats where the tree is naturally abundant. This species has the unique characteristic of retaining its leaves in the dry season and shedding them at the onset of the rains. The resultant fine mulch of leaf litter undergoes rapid decomposition enriching the topsoil with plant nutrients and organic matter. Saka *et al.* (1994) have described how natural stands of the tree have been used in maize production systems in Malawi. Although the value of *F. Albida* is recognised by farmers, the tree has not been integrated systematically into maize-growing areas.

Malawi, soil fertility, agricultural policy and famine

In Chapter 5, we saw through an analysis of Malawi's recent agricultural history, how the failure to face up to the underlying problems of smallholder agriculture had led to disastrous outcomes for the poor. Even when Malawi was producing a maize surplus (until the mid-

1980s), household food security was poor – as indicated by widespread and pervasive malnutrition and one of the highest levels of child mortality in the world. Growth across the agricultural sector was inconsistent and was affected by agricultural export growth in which smallholders played a minor role. Agricultural liberalisation policies introduced from the mid-1990s undermined the illusion of price stability, and put an end to the input subsidies and credit programmes which had helped shore up maize production at an increasingly high cost.

As the fields of Malawi's smallholders became less productive and their land holdings grew smaller, maize became increasingly dominant in the cropping system. Rotation crops and intercrops had declined in importance, or in many cases, disappeared altogether. Because of pressure on land, most farmers grew maize in continuous cultivation rather than under the traditional long fallow rotation which restored soil fertility and reduced the build-up of pests and diseases. As the soil resource base degraded, crop yields fell.

External influences further damaged Malawi's food security. In the late 1980s and the early 1990s, a number of severe droughts affected Malawi's agriculture. The demand for food was increased by the influx of refugees from the civil war in neighbouring Mozambique. Two imported pests – the cassava mealy bug from the Democratic Republic of Congo (then Zaire) in 1973, and the cassava green mite from Uganda – threatened cassava production, an important alternative staple food crop (Herren and Neuenschwander, 1991).

Input subsidies for seed and fertiliser spiralled out of control and had to be abandoned. Those farmers that had been receiving subsidised inputs of improved seed and fertiliser no longer did so – and they consequently stopped buying these inputs. But as farmers reduced their use of improved seed and fertiliser, maize production fell precipitously. By early 1998, it was evident there was a severe food crisis. An active high-level Food Security Committee chaired by the Ministry of Finance was established. The Minister of Agriculture, Aleke Banda, who had earlier been Minister of Finance, made it a national priority to produce sufficient quantities of the national staple food in order to foster economic stability.

In response, a group of individuals in Malawi – scientists, economists and policy makers – decided, with some modest financial and technical support from The Rockefeller Foundation, to develop a programme to support the Minister's emphasis through making full use of local knowledge, skills, and resources. They pooled their skills in a coordinated effort to address the country's increasingly severe food shortages through what became known as the Maize Productivity Task Force (MPTF). The Minister asked the MPTF to provide a set of radical and innovative recommendations to deal with the emerging crisis. This powerful signal from government gave the MPTF the opportunity to upgrade 'good technical recommendations' directly into a national policy.

A comprehensive smallholder strategy

The Starter Pack

In response to Malawi's serious food crises of the late 1980, in a remarkably few years the International Maize and Wheat Improvement Centre (acronym from the Spanish) (CIMMYT) and Malawian scientists managed to produce new varieties of flinty,[4] high-yielding hybrid maize well-suited to Malawi's needs. Companion agronomic research promised to reduce the need for commercial fertiliser and improve soil fertility. It identified crop rotations and complementary agro-forestry cultures that economised on purchased inputs (especially fertilisers) as well as improving household nutrition. Once new hybrids were developed and complementary crops identified, the Rockefeller Foundation inspired institutional innovation, the MPTF, organised 5 years of extensive farmer trials, nearly 2000 per year, to identify for each of Malawi's major agro-climatic zones the most economically efficient package of practices, the 'Best Bet'[5] for that region. By 1998, the MPTF could recommend with confidence these improved systems to farmers.

However, with 60 percent of the population surviving on less than one dollar per day, few Malawians could purchase the new seeds and fertilisers that could help them break the cycle of poverty. This gave rise to the concept of giving to all farmers a Starter Pack of the new inputs. The Universal Starter Pack was designed using the 'Best Bet' technology to jump-start maize production for all smallholders. This would simultaneously improve the food security of all food-deficit smallholder households, and increase the marketed surplus available to urban consumers hence, bringing food prices and inflation down sharply.

All smallholders in Malawi were given a package containing 2.5 kg packets of hybrid seed and the economically viable recommended quantity and type of fertiliser sufficient to plant 0.1 hectare of land. Each household would have sufficient extra maize to feed itself for a month in the food shortage season. During this season, market value in 1998 was estimated at a minimum of MK500, which was more cash income than a poor family would earn in a year. At the national level,

2.8 million households producing 100 kg more per household would provide an incremental national production of 280,000 tons. The cost of a representative pack was estimated at US$18 per household, making a total direct annual program cost of $32.4 million. If the value of the incremental maize was more than $180 per tonne, the program would more than offset its cost.

All inputs generated incremental production. It was more robust than a credit programme for the poor and reinforced the national policy of moving towards a liberalised market. The vast majority of smallholders were so short of cash, that at that time, they represented no market for hybrid seed or fertiliser. Therefore, giving them a starter pack would not displace any commercial purchases. Since the package was small, it would stimulate, not diminish the incentive to purchase more inputs. There were evident rewards to good husbandry – especially with regard to timeliness of planting, fertilising and weeding. This provided a strong incentive and reward for using the inputs well. It was, in effect, a nationally implemented, but individually operated, technology testing and demonstration programme for a small part of each farm. The effort had the potential, therefore, to be developed, refined, and adapted in future years to 'fast track' further technology choices in the smallholder sector and thus diversify farming systems and increase smallholder incomes.

The 'Best Bet' inputs and practices were incorporated into the Starter Packs distributed to 2.8 million smallholder farmers in 1998 and 1999.[6] Evaluation data showed that the starter packs raised maize production on average by about 125–150kg per household, which was significantly more than was estimated in the project design. Production in each of those two years was approximately 2.5 million tons – 500,000 tonnes higher than ever before or since (67 percent higher than the 20-year average).

Since most rural households in Malawi run out of maize well before the next harvest, in poor harvest years, such as during 2001–2002, those households who have cash compete for the small amounts of available maize, prices rise sharply, and poorer households are driven out of the market. The result is a sudden food crisis. The Starter Pack programme was remarkably successful in keeping prices low during the food shortage period. In terms of cost-effectiveness, the Starter Pack programme performed extremely well compared to alternative food crisis prevention measures, such as general fertiliser price subsidies and relief interventions, such as subsidised commercial food imports and food aid.[7]

Three critical elements formed the core of the MPTF recommendations. Fundamental to improving productivity were two new varieties of semi-flint hybrid maize, developed expressly for Malawi's conditions MH17 and MH18. These embodied the hard endosperm of the traditional varieties, important to protect maize in on-farm storage from weevils and also to produce good flour from hand-pounding in villages. But, as importantly, they used whatever fertility was available much more efficiently than traditional varieties. Traditional varieties produced only 8–12 kg of maize per kg of nitrogen, while the improved hybrids produced 20–25 kg.

Secondly, the recommendations recognised the importance for all farmers (especially the poorest) of maximising the use of locally available fertility sources. This meant growing leguminous crops in combination with maize and other food crops as well as using farm manures such as composts, as these provide organic sources of nitrogen, enhance soil structure and reduce soil erosion. Implementing nitrogen-rich rotations not only reduces the need for expensive commercial fertilisers but also improves diets by adding protein and energy-rich foods such as soyabeans and groundnuts.

Finally, the 'Best Bet' recommendations reflected economically-viable fertiliser doses tailored to local soil conditions and took advantage of nitrogen available from the recommended leguminous crops. The revised fertiliser recommendations were significantly more affordable for smallholders. The amounts of fertiliser recommended were much lower than existing (and totally uneconomic) national recommendations, thus requiring a much smaller cash investment for their purchase.

As the Starter Pack's objective was to bring about long-term change in farming practices, the programme, along with its important complementary measures (an extensive radio extension campaign, packaging commercial fertiliser in small bags, a 'fertiliser for work' programme, efforts to expand savings and credit), was designed to run for five to ten years. It was not conceived as an emergency 'one-shot' increase in food production. The programme recognised that it takes time to effect changes in farming systems.

The Starter Pack also provided incentives which are very different from those generated by a food aid intervention. Food aid generally is distributed without regard to how much or how little effort was expended to produce food. It does not provide any incentive for a farmer to work hard. In contrast, a free but good quality input intervention rewards initiative and good husbandry, especially timeliness of planting, fertilising, and weeding. Yields can be three to four times higher with good husbandry than without.

Complementary measures

The MPTF also proposed a series of other interlinked and complementary elements:

- Ensuring that supplies of small bags of hybrid seed and fertiliser (1–3 kg) were readily available for purchase in all rural markets at a price comparable to those of existing large bags (50 kg).
- Supporting the drive to improve productivity with both traditional extension work and an extensive radio campaign reinforcing the 'Best Bet' extension messages included in the Starter Packs. (Subsequently the European Union provided thousands of wind-up radios to ensure that farmers everywhere could listen to the messages.)
- Providing opportunities for able-bodied individuals to increase their purchasing power for seed and fertiliser through a structured 'fertiliser (and seed) for work' programme to be implemented during the dry season.
- Building an effective savings club movement tied to the purchase of agricultural inputs along the lines of that which had proved so successful in Zimbabwe.

In summary, the programme represented a comprehensive strategy to provide all smallholders the means to test for themselves improved maize seed and fertiliser technology with a complementary legume rotation under their own conditions, without the risk inherent in purchasing the necessary inputs.

Dr Elias Ngalande, Principal Secretary in the Ministry of Finance, commissioned the MPTF to develop its Starter Pack proposal into a formal strategy for the government, with donor support, to actively encourage and empower farmers to implement the 'Best Bet' technologies. The support of Dr Ngalande and Minister Banda was crucial to including the Starter Pack proposal into Malawi's national policies. Mr Banda even locked key Ministry of Agriculture and Irrigation officials and senior representatives of the major fertiliser companies into the Ministry Conference Room and told them not to come out until the programme was designed properly. Demonstrating support at the highest level of Government, President Bakili Muluzi participated in the development of a training video for field staff involved in the programme.

In summary, the Starter Pack programme was a focused technology transfer programme, intended to be long-term, aimed at enabling the poorest to access the improved technologies they needed to break out of the vicious poverty cycle in which they were trapped. It provided a unique opportunity to build on the best of local knowledge and expertise (both at farmer and researcher/policy-maker level) and was a practical working example of how to link research, extension and national policies.

A return to free inputs

Unfortunately the essential complementary measures recommended by the MPTF were lost in the protracted debates about whether the programme should be universal or targeted, and whether it unreasonably reinforced a maize-dominated agricultural economy. Some members of the donor community were sceptical that a large-scale populist agricultural programme would be fairly implemented in a pre-election year, and considered that the programme would be used to promote the interests of the governing party.

In fact, as noted earlier, the Starter Pack programme proved more successful than the MPTF had dared to estimate. National food security was achieved, maize prices were stabilised and there was no food crisis. Ironically, as a direct result of pressure from the donor community, the programme was changed and scaled down to form part of a targeted 'safety nets' programme. It no longer had a role in addressing household or national-level food security; instead it provided targeted income support to the most vulnerable households. In 2000–2001, 1.5 million smallholders were targeted and the pack size and composition was altered significantly. Importantly, the 'best bets' link was lost and the seed and fertiliser used in the packs became those administratively convenient to provide rather than those which produced the best results for farmers. The inputs were delivered late and as a result, the targeted inputs programme (TIP) contributed only 75,000 tonnes of maize to a total maize harvest of 1.49 million tonnes. Despite evidence of a further impending food crisis, the starter pack was scaled down in 2001–2002 to one million beneficiaries and the TIP contributed only 40,000 tonnes to a total maize production of 1.3 million tonnes.

As a direct result of donor reluctance to support a 'free inputs' programme, the TIP became just that – a free inputs system without a clear development objective to enable those receiving the inputs to break out of dependency. The implementation of the TIP was an annual struggle between donors and the Malawi Government as to the size of the pack and the size of the distribution. The contents of the pack lost all relation to evidence-based decision making. They did not reinforce the productivity focus of the initial concept and, indeed, served to undermine serious attempts to transform smallholder agriculture in Malawi. The protracted discussions on the size and distribution of the packs mean that the packs were delivered late (so their effectiveness is even further reduced), they did not reach farming leaders (and thus had minimal impact in creating needed change), and the effort actively disrupted the national market for seed and fertiliser as the demand for packs was not known by suppliers in time for them to place orders in advance.

The food crises of 2001–2002 and 2002–2003

It is impossible to say whether, had the Starter Pack programme been in place, the dreadful famine of 2001–2002 and 2002–2003 could have been avoided. However, it is evident to even the least informed observer that change is desperately needed in Malawi smallholder agriculture. Poverty remains pervasive, there has been some modest agricultural diversification – but the sustainability of these efforts in the face of such desperate poverty is questionable. The data show that the direct cost of importing enough maize to ensure national food security – either in the form of commercial imports or food aid – is between three and a half and five times the cost of growing the maize at home using starter packs.

The failure to build on the potential opened up by the MPTF was a serious error. Malawi relied on an agricultural economy that was fiscally unsustainable. The restructuring and liberalisation of markets that followed the drought-related food crises in the late 1980s were necessary. They broke up a system of political patronage that condemned most of Malawians to a life of inevitable poverty. The development of a more representative democracy with the fall of the Banda government was widely welcomed, both inside Malawi and by outsiders. The MPTF provided evidence-based technical support to much needed political change.

As has been shown clearly throughout this book, Malawi faces an unenviable complexity of problems with limited resources of human skills, capital, and income-generating potential. Opening markets to allow for choice is an important step, but when those affected are too poor to make use of the new options, more is needed. There is significant capacity which can be built upon at all levels in Malawi – from farming communities through to national policy makers. The MPTF was a unique exercise in capitalising on this capacity through sensitive and careful networking.

It was also a harbinger of future opportunities. In the 2001 and 2002 growing seasons, Malawi suffered two very poor food production years. In 2002–2003 the situation was so bad that it was not a food crisis but a famine. Yet, as following sections will show, Malawians at all levels pulled together to create a response to the famine that was remarkably effective. It is our hypothesis that, with the correct policy signals and encouragement, the same powerful collaboration could be harnessed to break out of the poverty trap – not just in Malawi, but in Africa as a whole. Malawians have shown that, even with limited resources and under considerable pressure, sensible, productive and equitable policies can be developed and implemented with flair and success.

The programme developed to deal with the food crises of 2002–2003 was massive and comprehensive. It dealt, not only with the immediate problems of alleviating a humanitarian disaster, but also with the wider issues of protecting the vulnerable and putting together longer-term efforts to recover from the famine. It involved close and effective collaboration between the government, donors, the private sector, civil society and a range of interest groups. It required that all involved develop new ways of working and of doing business. That these challenging objectives were largely achieved is a clear indication of the potential that can be released if the correct signals and priorities are developed and followed through in a coordinated and collaborative fashion.

The National Food Crisis Recovery Programme

Severe food shortages became apparent in Malawi in late 2001 and intensified at the beginning of 2002.[8] But, at the same time (as we saw in Chapter 7), the donor community were locked in discussions regarding the perceived poor management of the Strategic Grain Reserve. There was also a widespread belief (based on hope rather than fact) that increased production of alternative food staples would compensate for the decline in maize production (see Chapter 7). Many thought that there was extensive hoarding of maize and, as a result, there was a maize pricing, rather than a maize availability, problem.

The Malawi Government and its development partners were simply talking past each other. There were real reasons for concern about aspects of macro-economic management, poor governance and corruption. This led to an increased level of cynicism that appeared to preclude the dispassionate analysis of available evidence. The initial leadership and direction to break out of this impasse came from outside the Malawi Government and the major donors. The NGOs collected evidence from detailed field studies, while civil society and the churches raised the alarm. It was this work, combined with clear signs of an imminent serious food crisis that led to the President declaring a State of Disaster in late February 2002. But by then six vital months had been allowed to elapse.

The President told the world that 'Malawi is facing a catastrophic situation with up to 78 percent of farm families being without food.' The Vice President presented the Appeal of the National Food Crisis Task Force to the donor community on 20th March 2002. He emphasised that: 'Coping mechanisms including casual labour and distress sales of household assets have been stretched and eroded, while people are dying from hunger-related diseases. Although the next harvest will offer some temporary relief, the food crisis will deepen during the next hungry season.' (Malewezi, 2002).

The Appeal outlined the need to provide humanitarian assistance to a population without food – estimated at the time to be 2.2 million people. It also intended to expand cash for work, food for work and supplementary feeding for malnourished children, pregnant women, lactating mothers and under-five children and to expand the school-feeding programme.

But the Appeal was more than just a plea for emergency food. It had a vision for addressing the longer-term food security issues raised by the food crisis. It noted the health problems related to waterborne diseases and poor hygiene, and commented that 'hunger exacerbates chronic malnutrition and reduces immunity to all diseases. 23 districts are experiencing a cholera outbreak with a total of 18,026 cases and 506 deaths' (Malewezi, 2002). The need for appropriate institutional arrangements to address the key components of the response to the food crisis was identified and the framework for close collaboration between the government, civil society organisations and cooperating partners to address comprehensively the issues emanating from the food crisis was established.

Providing emergency food to the vulnerable

A Humanitarian Response Sub-Committee of the Joint Food Crisis Task Force was established to 'monitor and assess the situation requiring humanitarian aid in the country' (Ministry of Agriculture and Irrigation, 2004). The key responsibility for the Sub-Committee was to coordinate the food relief and humanitarian operations for the vulnerable population (which peaked at 2.8 million people in February 2003). The immediate need was to develop institutional mechanisms to deliver this quantity of food to targeted beneficiaries at the community level. In April 2002, a 'town meeting' (convened by the United States Agency for International Development) proposed an NGO Consortium[9] to deliver food aid. The Joint Emergency Food Action Programme (JEFAP)[10] was established.

JEFAP was an innovative new partnership that strengthened collaboration between the Malawi Government, all cooperating partners, the World Food Programme (WFP), NGOs operating at the district levels and the district authorities. It proved crucial to the success of the humanitarian relief programme. Typically in the past, NGOs involved in humanitarian interventions tended to work outside Government structures and it was difficult to put together a nationally coordinated programme. By contrast, under JEFAP, all participating NGOs worked within a common structure using formal, agreed guidelines.

Two key mechanisms were introduced that were central to the success of the humanitarian relief operation. Firstly, the targeting of districts and households for the humanitarian relief operations was done through JEFAP on the basis of objective criteria and in a fully transparent manner. Secondly, there were regular reviews of the programme with representation from Government Departments, WFP, collaborating partners, participating NGOs and CISANET (the Civil Society Agriculture Network). In addition, a Parliamentary Committee was appointed to monitor the implementation of JEFAP in the field. The Department of Poverty and Disaster Management Affairs appointed field emergency monitors in every district with the support of UNDP. The WFP also placed food aid monitors at distribution points. Where problems arose and were referred to the political level, these were immediately investigated by the Chair of the NGO Consortium in collaboration with government officials. They reported back to the National Food Crisis Task Force and action was taken to address problems or to improve communication at the district levels.

This was no small exercise. In July 2002, just over 600,000 beneficiaries received food rations. By February 2003, the numbers had swelled to 3.1 million. Each beneficiary family received a food ration of 50 kgs of maize grain, 5 kgs of soya flour, 5 kgs of legumes (mainly beans and peas), and 2 litres of cooking oil every month.[11] The general food distribution was conducted in a professional manner. While there were inevitable problems, there was excellent collaboration between Government and the private sector transporters, combined with competent logistical support from the World Food Programme. Phiri (2004) noted:

> The major positive attribute that should be learned, and if possible replicated in future programmes, is the high level of commitment and dedication from all the stakeholders that were involved at various levels. Government officials, NGOs and donors worked together tirelessly to ensure success of the programme. Against all odds and immense challenges, the programme still managed to achieve remarkable success in averting what would have been a major humanitarian crisis. The JEFAP experience in Malawi is generally regarded as the most successful response to the food crisis in the southern African region.

Problems arose around targeting[12] – a difficult challenge where 65 percent of the population live below the poverty level even in normal years. There were isolated instances where targeting criteria were not applied universally. Inevitably also there were some breakdowns in communication at the district levels. These are to be expected in any emergency situation. However there were effective institutional mechanisms in place to deal with problems as they arose.

The JEFAP built on existing supplementary feeding programmes (supported by the government, the donor community and individual NGOs) and served to widen access to them. The programme focused on under-five severely malnourished children admitted to Therapeutic Feeding Centres (TFCs) and their carers. The programme also supported moderately malnourished children and at-risk pregnant and lactating mothers attending Maternal and Child Health (MCH) Clinics. A school feeding programme – which complemented an on-going effort reaching 50,000 pupils – helped 110,000 pupils in five districts. Each child in the participating 145 primary schools received a food ration of 600 calories per day. To the credit of all involved, the rate of acute malnutrition declined from an average of 12 percent at the outset of the food crisis to less than 5 percent at the end of the emergency operation (Ministry of Agriculture and Irrigation, 2004).

Lessons for the future

The humanitarian response

The humanitarian response to the 2001–2002 and 2002–2003 food crises show that where there is political will and commitment from all stakeholders, programmes will be implemented successfully. At the outset, all stakeholders recognised that Malawi was facing a serious and urgent emergency that needed action on a broad scale. Government, donors and stakeholders collectively addressed the issue of how to implement a relief operation for 2 to 3 million Malawians. The government and donors explored options to work with leading NGOs in each District and the NGO Consortium was established. Then a thorough and careful analysis was undertaken constructively to determine how to make the programme work within a realistic evaluation of capacity constraints.

This is in marked contrast to the ultra-cautious approach typical of the fight against AIDS and poverty alleviation in general where excessive requirements for accountability tend to block initiative. Accountability in the use of public resources is necessary, but not sufficient for effective problem-solving. Too often, action is stalled until complex financial accountability mechanisms are developed. Three factors contributed to the remarkable success of the humanitarian response:

- An exceptional degree of collaboration between all implementing partners – the government, NGOs, district authorities and community leaders. Everyone involved worked in a dedicated manner to respond to the humanitarian emergency.
- Decisions were taken on the basis of objective criteria – both in terms of targeting the most vulnerable areas and targeting households at the community level.
- Strong mechanisms for monitoring, transparency and accountability from the Food Crisis Joint Task Force, civil society and from Parliament.

The humanitarian relief programme was viewed as a national programme that everyone contributed to. It demonstrated that it is possible to 'build a virtuous cycle' when there is genuine collaboration and all actors involved have a common goal. This was a remarkable achievement that has laid the foundation for more effective collaboration between all partners to address problems of national and household-level food insecurity in future provided that the principles of transparency and accountability are maintained.

A Malawi Green Revolution

Interventions to provide access to inputs and markets

The lessons from the response to the food crisis can also be used to create a Malawi Green Revolution. A Malawi Green Revolution Strategy will require a concerted effort to build a productive, commercialised and profitable agricultural sector based on broad-based participation in the development of the sector, especially by the poor and vulnerable. The strategy would be based on a clear recognition that lack of cash dominates the choices available to the typical Malawi farmer. Many Malawian farm families face a dreadful series of choices. The technologies which they are recommended to use are incomplete, often uneconomic, and do not provide a reliable and effective road to escape poverty. Only an investment in the right inputs, used in the right way, can rescue them. The strategy would create a broad-based opportunity for all Malawi smallholders to benefit directly from new opportunities through **effective interventions to provide access** to improved seeds, fertilisers and other critical inputs that are the foundation for essential growth in productivity.

Key principles for programme implementation

- Sufficiently comprehensive enough to address the problem of hunger in rural and urban households without building debts.
- Sustained for the medium term (10 to 15-year financing framework of guaranteed funding).
- Benefit all smallholder households.
- Incorporate the 'Best-Bet' technologies – high quality seed designed for the specific agro-ecological conditions, early maturing varieties to reduce vulnerability to drought, economically efficient fertiliser recommendations, and correct husbandry practices: early planting, on-time fertiliser application, correct weeding practices.
- Address effectively soil fertility depletion and environmental sustainability through a focus on profitable and economically viable legumes and other biological technologies to promote soil restoration.
- Promote crop and livelihood diversification.
- Active private sector partnership and collaboration with district assemblies and NGOs

One option, which mirrors the situation in the early 1980s (described in Chapter 5) is a blanket subsidy. In this case, resources are programmed to reduce the price of all inputs (such as fertilisers) to all purchasers at the point-of-sale. This has the advantage of being simple to implement, at least appears not to discriminate between different groups (although the reality may be different), and is highly visible to the electorate. The disadvantages are that the policy actually excludes poor households (the majority) who cannot afford to buy the inputs even at subsidised rates. The consequent impact on poverty is negligible as the principal beneficiaries are those already able to purchase those inputs. Costs can quickly spiral out of control since the government does not control the international price of inputs, the exchange rate or the demand. Uncertainties regarding government intentions directly and seriously disrupt trade as importers and farmers wait to see the size of the subsidy before placing commercial orders – no one is going to pay cash for an item that might be provided free.

Another option might be termed an 'area-based subsidy' – which is what the original universal starter pack was. This is a subsidy that will provide inputs sufficient to purchase 'best bet' inputs for priority national crops (maize in the first instance) for a specific area of land. The intention is to provide all farmers with the resources they need to start the long haul out of poverty. With increasing food security, the subsidy can be varied to promote crop diversification through changing the mix of inputs that are subsidised. For example, in the first year of such a programme, the focus might be on the inputs needed to produce the staple food (typically maize). By the third year, the maize component might be stepped down and other important food/cash crops (groundnuts, beans, pigeonpea) might form the bulk of the pack (and can be adjusted according to agro-ecological area and market conditions).

This type of subsidy has the advantage that it reaches all farmers. Farming leaders can be actively involved in the promotion and improvement of new technologies. There are clear rewards to good husbandry and effective use of inputs, and direct impacts on poverty through improving food security and nutrition. It provides a mechanism for driving the nation out of poverty and into profitable agriculture and other associated businesses, and can be adjusted to changing national priorities by changing subsidised input mix. The costs are known largely in advance, it complements and does not disrupt trade (provided it is properly planned and implemented with sufficient lead time).

However it does need adequate lead time for proper implementation, and a commitment to the programme for 10–15 years. There is little international experience in the implementation of this type of subsidy. Importantly, it relies on the availability of proven and reliable improved technologies suitable for the poor as well as for the better-resourced farmers. To have a reliable and significant poverty reduction impact, inputs will need to reach all smallholders, be made available on time (before the planting rains), be based on high productivity and reliable technology, and be supported by radio messages and a focused extension effort.

Such a programme in Malawi could be an expanded version of the original universal Starter Pack initiative. For example, in the first year of the programme, all rural households in Malawi (3.1 million) would receive sufficient improved maize seed and fertilisers to plant 0.4 ha of land based on the specific recommendations for maize production in their area. The recommendations of Action Group 1 of the 1999 Maize Productivity Task Force will be revisited and updated in the light of current market prices for maize and fertilisers. This would bring food prices down sharply. Pesources could then be made available for schools and hospitals to buy up additional food for supplementary feeding programmes for vulnerable groups (following the successful practices developed during the 2002–2003 famine).

A big change from the original Starter Pack will be the evaluation, in a highly participatory manner with farmers, of various crop diversification options. This would be introduced from the second year and would form a corner-stone of the effort. The aim would be to create ownership amongst farmers, policy makers, and agricultural specialists of common goals and objectives. Priority options would be developed for different regions of the country and the packs made available to farmers will be adjusted accordingly. But the packs would not be stand alone – the programme would be implemented alongside a comprehensive but enhanced exercise to improve market access to smallholders. On the inputs side, this will involve, together with the rural stockists' development programme currently being implemented by a number of agencies, a comprehensive effort to empower farmers to make informed choices on the most appropriate inputs according to their needs. This will follow the well-established approach developed by Farm Input Promotions Africa (FIPS-Africa) in Kenya and Tanzania. On the output side, marketing arrangements developed by NASFAM and other national agencies will be expanded and developed to improve market development.

Careful research protocols, which can be understood by farmers and extension workers, will be developed (based on FIPS methodology) to:

- Identify the constraints limiting crop productivity in any one area.
- Raise awareness of the potential from using improved inputs amongst local farmers.
- Ensure that stockists have the correct inputs for the area.

Farmers will be encouraged to experiment with inputs for themselves through the promotion of 'minipacks' (such as small packages of 100g or 200g of the appropriate fertiliser). These can be made available for sale at all stockists. An associated Raising Awareness Programme targeted at schools, churches and church groups will provide a further source of support and information for the experimental use of such minipacks.

The focus will be broadened beyond fertilisers to encompass other constraining factors on crop productivity. New varieties of higher-yielding, drought-tolerant or disease- or pest-resistant maize and other crops (beans, cowpeas, for example) need to be made available to farmers and sufficient information be given to them to enable them make the best choice of seed. Herbicides, a valuable labour-saving intervention, are not accessible to poor farmers, especially women who carry the main burden of household and farming activities. A central focus will be building partnerships with farmers. Farmer Field Schools (FFS), using proven experimental protocols will be introduced to allow farmers to investigate a range of technologies (such as crop responses to different fertiliser formulations). This will empower farmers with the information they need to select the best technology combinations for their needs.

The programme will be carefully coordinated with the on-going food and inputs for work activities and will be carefully designed to complement them. The evidence from these programmes showed that nearly 90 percent of beneficiaries use all their inputs. They are evidently popular and effective. A recent review showed that 95 percent of farmers wanted inputs and not cash and that most beneficiaries belonged to the poorest segments of their community.

Concluding comments

The removal of fertiliser subsidies and donor conditionalities against subsidies on agricultural production has been a major issue of contention between the Malawi Government and donors for well over a decade. Fertiliser subsidy removal was a conditionality under the Structural Adjustment Programme of the 1980s when the focus was on increasing smallholder production of cash crops rather than on promoting food crop production. As Harrigan (2003) notes:

> The ensuing clash between the Ministry of Agriculture and World Bank staff was the beginning of a protracted and as yet unresolved

debate on the most appropriate food security policies for Malawi. The Bank's policy prescriptions were influenced by the Washington Consensus's faith in the market mechanism including international markets, and its antithesis to state interventionism, including subsidies and controlled prices.

The agricultural dimensions of poverty in sub-Saharan Africa are poorly understood by many policy makers – amongst development agencies as well as by the governments of developing countries. It is incontrovertible that African smallholders have to move beyond subsistence. While improving maize productivity is an important part of the answer, much more needs to be done. An obvious solution, which has already been alluded to, is to open up new potential income streams that poor families can link into. The encouragement of cash cropping is one such stream. But the practice is often more difficult in practice in than theory. The Malawi case illustrates just how difficult the successful implementation of a smallholder based cash cropping strategy can be in a resource-poor economy.

Policy linkages   A common problem throughout sub-Saharan Africa is the poor linkages among farmers, NGOs, extension services, policy makers, and the private sector. The Malawi Maize Productivity Task Force, which developed the Starter Pack concept, was a multi-agency, multi-disciplinary team that worked systematically and with strong national leadership to develop solutions to a pressing national problem. It provided a model through which a coordinated, cost-effective, and efficient technology transfer process can evolve, using the best of national and international expertise in a focused, problem-solving effort. The best of local knowledge and expertise, both at farmer and researcher/policy maker levels, was used to develop a practical example of how to link research, extension and national policy to improve living standards for rural people reliant on agriculture. The fiscal cost was predictable in advance, and there were benefits to good husbandry (as opposed to blanket subsidies). Provided the effort is properly agreed to and planned in advance, the quantities of improved seed and fertilisers used in the packs are known and the normal commercial market need not be disturbed. In fact, the programme will add to, rather than displace, normal commercial demand.

Explicit consideration of scale   The Starter Pack program was a focused programme, intended to be long-term, aimed at enabling the poorest to access the improved technologies they needed to break out of the vicious cycle of poverty in which they were trapped. It provided all smallholders with a highly cost-effective means of testing improved maize seed and fertiliser technology with a complementary legume rotation under specific conditions, without the risk inherent in purchasing the necessary inputs. It directly facilitated farmer experimentation with promising technologies. Small packs were seen by the fertiliser industry as the key to protecting (indeed promoting) their commercial sales.[13] The poverty reduction impact of the effort was to put improved technology into the hands of **all** smallholders. The increased national production came initially from the multiplier effect of using good quality seed with the right fertiliser for the area in which the crop is grown. The essential element was timeliness. The effect is only sufficient it goes to all smallholders, if it goes out on time (before the planting rains), if is based on high productivity and reliable technology, and is supported by radio messages and a focused extension effort.

Safety nets or development? The Starter Pack, as originally designed, was seen as part of a process through which all smallholders could diversify their livelihoods and move from subsistence agriculture into commercially viable production (not necessarily in agriculture). The major constraint in achieving this was persistent and widespread food insecurity which forced many of the poor into distress sales of food and other assets, took them off their farms at critical times of the year, and which was driving the price of food higher year by year. The initial components of the Starter Pack were, therefore, focused on the main staple food, maize. After 2 years of implementing the Universal Starter Pack Programme, the donors decided to shift the focus to a Targeted Inputs Programme (TIP) intended to provide a safety net for the poorest rural households. This targeting of only some smallholders within communities proved disastrous.[14] The robust and widely verified technologies that formed the components of the original Starter Pack were changed and the link with science (and to economically viable improved technologies) was lost.

In 2005, as the result of widespread dissatisfaction with the TIP experience, the original Starter Pack evidence was reviewed. An international collaboration involving Malawian and overseas scientists and policy makers developed a revised Starter Pack proposal aimed at creating a Green Revolution in Malawi. Various crop diversification options will be evaluated by farmers and priority options be developed for different regions of the country. The pack will not be stand alone – it will be implemented alongside a comprehensive but enhanced exercise to improve market access to smallholders, and farmers will be empowered to make informed choices on the most appropriate inputs for their needs.[15]

The proposed programme provides the opportunity for the poor of Malawi to lift themselves out of poverty. It has a defined subsidy element which allows all to use the best of modern agricultural technology to reduce (and ideally eliminate) the chronic food insecurity that dominates all aspects of Malawi life. But, having learned how to use these resources, a variety of inputs are made available through the private sector in a manner which helps farmers to choose in an informed (but not prescriptive) manner to develop and expand their rural enterprises. The concept will be developed further through close interaction and discussion amongst many concerned individuals and institutions. But the principles of providing the poor with access to the best of available options and allowing them to make informed choices according to their circumstances is fundamental to the exercise.

As the MPTF showed, even a poor country like Malawi has a body of competent technicians who need to be brought into the policy formulation process for the benefit of all. It is almost unbelievable that the careful analyses of the MPTF in Malawi have been allowed to disappear almost in their entirety, especially given the disastrous outcomes of external advice to national and household food security in that country. Policy needs to be based on evidence and not on theory. The MPTF had a solid foundation of scientific expertise upon which to base its recommendations. The results from implementing these recommendations are, on unbiased examination of the evidence, impressive. If this foundation had been developed and enhanced, Malawi could today be starting its long haul out of poverty into a more prosperous future. Instead, local skills and knowledge were deeply discounted and instead 'universal solutions' plugged in which better fitted powerful external perceptions. The outcome for too many Malawians has been tragic – and fatal.

The Malawi Green Revolution initiative has shown how quickly and effectively local talent, linked to wider networks, can be used to address critical problems with imagination and flair. In less than 4 weeks, the Malawi Green Revolution grew from a tentative exchange of e-mails to a major policy document developed for the Malawi Government. Contributing to this were Malawian scientists and policy makers, supported by informal networks of experienced practitioners in Africa and overseas.

Notes

1   Most (not all) legumes form symbiotic associations with soil bacteria. The bacteria form nodules in the roots of the legumes and fix nitrogen from the air. This nitrogen is available for the legume to use (and thus produce high protein grain) and some is left in the soil with the legume roots after the crop is harvested which a subsequent crop can use.

2   The major nutrients required to feed a crop are nitrogen (N), phosphorus (P) and potassium (K). Other minor nutrients are also required.

3   Species that combine some grain with high root biomass and shoot-leaf biomass (such as pigeonpea, *Cajanus cajan*, and dolichos bean, *Dolichos lablab*) offer a useful compromise of promoting farmer adoption and improving soil fertility (Giller personal comm.).

4   Flint (or hard endosperm) maize is well-suited to the storage and processing methods employed by most Malawian farmers. Previously all improved maize varieties were dent or soft endosperm types which suffer high losses during storage and processing at household level.

5   These are technologies which are deemed to have particular value for identified farming environments or groups. Screening criteria used include:
    - the ability to raise profit and productivity in the short term (1–3 years),
    - application across a number of agro-ecologies,
    - modest costs in terms of cash and labour,
    - minimal competition for arable land, and,
    - more than one end-use for the farmer.

6   For the Task Force report, see The Rockefeller Foundation, *Malawi: Soil Fertility Issues and Options*, Lilongwe, May 1998. (Malcolm Blackie, Task Force Leader). The original Starter Pack proposal is described in: Charles Mann, *Higher Yields for All Smallholders Through 'Best Bet' Technology: The Surest Way to Restart Economic Growth in Malawi*, CIMMYT Network Research Results Working Paper No. 3, Harare, Zimbabwe; March 1998.

7   See: *Starter Packs: A Strategy to Fight Hunger in Developing Countries?*, (Ed.) Sarah Levy. CABI Publications.

8   The Malawi Government, in early 2002, estimated the food gap at around 600,000 tonnes.

9   The NGO Consortium was chaired by Care International: each district had a leading NGO and district assisting Partners. The following NGOs were to lead in the different districts: *Africare* operated in Mzimba, Nhhata Bay, Likoma and Ntcheu; *Care Malawi* operated in Lilongwe and Dowa; *Save the Children US* operated in Balaka and Mangochi, *Save the Children UK* operated in Mchinji and Salima, *World Vision Malawi* operated in Chikwawa, Nsanje, Mwanza and Thyolo, *Catholic Relief Services* operated in Kasungu and Zomba, *Oxfam* operated in Mulanje, *Emanuel International* operated in Machinga, *Concern Universal* operated in Dedza, *Goal* operated in Blantyre and Chiradzulu while the *Salvation Army* operated in Phalombe (Alexander Phiri, Assessment of the Malawi Government strategy used to address the *2001–2002* Food Crisis. First Draft Report, Emergency Drought Recovery Programme, Lilongwe, Malawi.)

10 JEFAP's objectives were to prevent severe food shortages that could lead to starvation at the household level, safeguard the nutritional status of vulnerable groups, preserve productive and human assets from liquidation and

distress selling, and prevent distress migration from affected areas to urban centres.

11 The ration was intended to meet the consumption requirements of an average family of 5.5 individuals. Although this was the agreed nutritionally balanced ration, it was not always possible to provide it.

12 Eventually agreed as the poorest third of the population.

13 Interview excerpts with *Victoria Keelan, Managing Director, Norsk Hydro Malawi*, in *Starter Pack: From Best Bets to Safety Net*, Film by Charles Mann, Development Communications Workshop, 2005. Forthcoming with supplemental material on DVD from www.devcomworkshop.org.

14 For the evidence and conclusions of these comprehensive multi-year evaluations, see: *Starter Packs: A Strategy to Fight Hunger in Developing Countries?*, (Ed.) Sarah Levy. CABI Publications.

15 This will follow the well-established approach developed by Farm Input Promotions Africa (FIPS-Africa) in Kenya and Tanzania. On the output side, marketing arrangements developed by farmers associations and other national agencies will be expanded and developed to improve market development.

Bibliography

Blackie M., Benson T., Conroy A., Gilbert R., Kanyama-Phiri G., Kumwenda J., Mann C., Mughogho S., Phiri A. and Waddington S. (1998) 'Malawi Soil Fertility Issues and Options: A Discussion Paper', Maize Productivity Task Force, Paper Commissioned by the Secretary to the Treasury for the National Food Security Task Force.

Blackie M. and Woomer P. (2005) 'Challenges and Opportunities of the Regional Universities Forum for Capacity Building in Agriculture in Kenya, Malawi, Mozambique, Uganda and Zimbabwe', report to the Board of the Regional Forum for Capacity Building in Agriculture, September 2005.

Carr S. (1994) 'The unique challenge of Malawi's smallholder agricultural sector', mimeo.

Economist Intelligence Unit (2004) 'Malawi Country Report', London: EIU

Giller K., Cadish G., Ehaliotis C., Adams E., W. Sakala W., and Mafongoya P. (1997) 'Building soil capital in Africa' in: Buresh R., Sanchez P. and Calhoun F. (eds). 'Replenishing soil fertility in Africa', SSSA special pub. no. 51, Soil Science Society of America, Madison, Wisconsin.

Harrigan J. (2003) 'U Turns and Full Circles: Two Decades of Agricultural Reform in Malawi: 1981–2001', *World Development* 31 (5): 847–63.

Herren H. and Neuenschwander P. (1991) 'Biological Control of Cassava Pests in Africa', *Annual Review of Entomology* 36: 257–83.

Esser K., Øygard R., Chibwana C. and Blackie M. (2005) 'Opportunities for Norwegian Support to Agricultural Development in Malawi', Department of International Environment and Development Studies, NORAGRIC: As, Norway.

Kwesiga F. and Coe R. (1994) 'The effect of short rotation *Sesbania sesban* planted fallows on maize yield', *Forest Ecology and Management* 64, 199–208.

Levy S. (2005) ed. 'Starter Packs: A Strategy to Fight Hunger in Developing Countries?', Oxford: CABI Publishing.

Malewezi J. (2002) 'Briefing Note to Donors/Cooperating Partners: National Food Crisis Recovery Programme: Addressing Medium Term Food Security Issues', Office of the Vice President, Lilongwe, Malawi.

Mann C.K. (1998) 'Higher yields for all smallholders through "Best Bet" technologies: the surest way to restart economic growth in Malawi', CIMMYT Working Group, No. 3, Harare, Zimbabwe.

Ministry of Agriculture and Irrigation (2004) 'Evaluation of the Joint Food Crisis Task Force', Lilongwe, Malawi.

Phiri A. (2004) 'Assessment of the Malawi Government Strategy used to address the 2001–2002 Food Crisis: First Draft Report, Emergency Drought Recovery Programme', Lilongwe, Malawi.

Piha M. (1993) 'Optimising fertiliser use and practical rainfall capture in a semi-arid environment with variable rainfall', *Experimental Agriculture 29*, 405–15.

Saka A., Bunderson W., Itimu O., Phombeya H. and Mbekeani Y. (1994) 'The effects of *Acacia albida* on soils and maize grain yields under smallholder farm conditions in Malawi', *Forest Ecology and Management 64*, 217–30.

Sesman B., Wood G., Anselme M. and Avery A. (2004) 'Skills training for youth', *Forced Migration Review 20*, Brighton, Sussex: Institute for Development Studies.

Snapp S. (1995) 'Improving fertiliser efficiency with small additions of high quality organic inputs', In: Waddington S.R. (ed.) *Report on the First Meeting of the Network Working Group. Soil Fertility Research Network for Maize-Based Farming Systems in Selected Countries of Southern Africa*, The Rockefeller Foundation Southern Africa Agricultural Sciences Program, Lilongwe, Malawi and CIMMYT Maize Program, Harare, Zimbabwe. pp. 60–5.

10

Breaking Out of Economic Isolation and the Poverty Trap

Anne Conroy and Malcolm Blackie

Introduction

Previously, in Chapter 6 we saw that most Malawians live below the poverty line, subsisting in rural villages or urban shanty towns which lack even the most basic amenities. A significant minority do not have access to clean water or sanitation. Economic isolation is made worse by poor roads and limited market access. In these circumstances, many households find it difficult to meet basic subsistence requirements, much less generating a surplus for the market. High transport costs push up prices of essential imports of fertilisers and fuel is costly making it difficult for Malawi to compete in international trade, thus reducing prospects for export-led growth. This unhappy picture is compounded by a poor investment climate, the absence of foreign direct investments and constraints on the local private sector in increasing investment, employment and growth.

Bringing about change will be tough. The villages and urban slums of Malawi are populated by malnourished children and by under-employed or unemployed young adults. Forty-seven percent of the total population are aged less than 15 years old and Malawi's fertility rate is 6.1 (UNDP, 2005). Lifting people out of poverty means, at a very minimum, raising household living standards significantly above subsistence. But, at the time of writing, Malawi faces yet another devastating food crisis with probably close to 5 million people needing humanitarian assistance in between late September 2005 and the anticipated April 2006 harvest.

While challenging, the situation is not hopeless. A recurrent theme throughout this book has been the opportunities for change that can be released through well-implemented consultation and collaboration between the public and private sectors in the national interest.

Importantly, the potential of drawing on the energy and enthusiasm of the young has yet adequately to be explored. Young Africans are showing considerable initiative in expanding into new entrepreneurial activities. It is important that the voices of the new generation of Africans be brought into the consultation process.

A new generation is emerging in Africa anxious for change and concerned to alter the present, rather than re-living the glories of past liberation wars. Most of these young Africans want to be better educated and earn a living. Formal training courses, even if accessible and affordable, are often too long and inflexible. They are typically less useful for girls who may not be able leave home or take the same risks as boys. The young need a system of education which allows them to learn new opportunities in places such as drop-in centres where they can follow courses, hold meetings, share resources and feel at home. Such opportunities help them onto the first step of the economic ladder. They learn from each other and form unions or associations to learn skills. They gain confidence through peer interaction. They set standards and become proud of their knowledge and services; they learn leadership, management and business skills.

The growth in the mobile phone industry (where the young have led the way in phone repairs) provides an example of the power of this approach. No older 'experts' set the agenda; no school yet offers a course. Repairers, always young, teach each other. The person with knowledge gains respect as he passes on a particular skill, even though it may reduce his own business. In the eastern Democratic Republic of Congo, ravaged by war, young people have set up FM radio stations using old walkie-talkies and cassette players. In Bunia, Radio Canal Revelation provides what the audience wants with the tiny income they earned from passing on greeting messages. It has also become an informal journalism school, where students critique each other's programmes (Sesman *et al.*, 2004).

Efforts to break out of economic isolation and poverty need explicitly to exploit this energy to create opportunities for the brightest youths, who may have been deprived of formal education in their earliest years, to move upwards through the post-secondary education system. The AIDS pandemic makes this change even more urgent. As we have already seen, too many children are orphaned, or have had to drop out of school, due to the ravages of HIV/AIDS on family circumstances. Secondary (and even primary) education is becoming a luxury rather than the norm for increasing numbers of young people in Africa.

So the scene shifts to investments – and the structures to be put in place to release the skills and the energies, especially of the young, to create a real momentum for change. In this chapter we focus on five critical investments needed for Malawi to break out of the poverty trap:

- Education.
- Building environmental sustainability, including sustainable access to safe water.
- Creating basic infrastructure (roads, power and regional integration).
- Addressing constraints to private sector development.
- Transforming the world's trading system to allow poor countries to compete in world markets.

Education in Malawi

Not only is education positively associated with better agricultural productivity, higher incomes, lower fertility rates and improved nutrition and health, it is also a pre-requisite for attaining these outcomes. Basic education was, quite rightly, accorded the highest priority in Malawi's first Poverty Reduction and Growth Strategy. Prior to the advent of multi-party democracy in 1994, less than 50 percent of the school-age population (1.9 million children) had access to primary education. Free primary education was introduced in 1994 and enrolment increased to 3.2 million almost overnight. But a modern, progressive nation needs quickly to build yet greater skills into its work force. Sustainable national development also requires the development of secondary, tertiary and vocational education, as well as an explicit focus on enhancing civic education (Malawi Government, 2002). A broader approach to education is needed which increases access to all levels of education, progressively eliminates inequalities in enrolment, and contributes to building a solid economic base within society.

Primary education

The national ambition is for all children to complete primary education (Standards 1 through 8). While budgetary allocations to the Ministry of Education have increased, the extra funds have not been sufficient to meet the needs imposed by an increasing school enrolment (as a result of universal free primary education). Quality has suffered and there is a high drop-out rate. The proportion of children starting Standard 1 who reach Standard 5 has fallen from 38 percent in

2000 to 34 percent in 2005 (Malawi Government, 2005). The official view is that this is caused by household food insecurity, poverty, lack of access to basic equipment and trained teachers, and cultural practices. This has some truth but does not explain the fall adequately. Girls are particularly unlikely to complete primary school due to early marriage and/or pregnancy, the poor school environment and poor school sanitary facilities[1] (Malawi Government, 2005). The poor quality of education is a serious problem. Teaching and learning materials (such as text books) are scarce and costly. The pupil to *qualified* teacher ratio is 118:1 and, on average 95 pupils are squeezed into a class. This contrasts with the national target (hardly ideal) ratio of 60:1 for both (Malawi Government, 2002).

Secondary education

The scenario at the secondary school level is even less promising. Only 18 percent of Malawian children go on to secondary education. Children from low-income families and girls are especially unlikely to proceed beyond primary school – the latter account for only 37 percent of total enrolment. Total secondary school enrolment in 1999 was 236,000 pupils, who were taught by 5269 teachers. There are three major categories of secondary schools – Conventional Secondary Schools (CSSs) Community Day Secondary Schools (CDSSs) and private secondary schools. In 2004, there were 97 CSSs, 553 CDSSs and 401 private secondary schools. CSSs are government-funded secondary schools where access is restricted to qualified candidates who have passed the Malawi Junior School Certificate of Education (JCE). Most teachers in these schools are secondary-trained and educational standards have broadly been maintained. However, it is in the other two categories of schools that most of the increase in secondary school enrolment has occurred. But these often employ untrained teachers and have sub-standard facilities. Examination results are poor.

Overall, the quality of secondary education is compromised by inadequate learning materials, deteriorating infrastructure and untrained teachers (Ministry of Economic Planning and Development, 2004). Government policy is to improve the quality of secondary education through instituting an updated, relevant and rigorous programme of teacher education, combined with revising the curriculum to equip students with life, technical and entrepreneurial skills. But, as with primary schools, the resources needed to achieve these ambitions have yet to be adequately put in place.

Tertiary education

The investments in tertiary education are small within Malawi (although overseas training does provide additional support in this important area). In 2002, there were 4000 places available for tertiary level students. Females occupy less than 30 percent of the places. Boarding facilities, funding levels, physical infrastructure and human resources are all over stretched. Just over 1000 students graduate from tertiary institutions annually – far too few to build the needed capacity within the public and private sectors, especially when so many of Malawi's professionals are dying due to the HIV/AIDS pandemic.

Investments in education

The initial focus on primary education (in line with Government policy and the Millennium Development Goals) has been at the expense of essential investments in secondary, tertiary and vocational education. To an extent, this is now being (at least partially) addressed. For example, the World Bank granted Malawi US$32 million for an education sector programme in April 2005. The principal component of the programme is US$15.5 million for teacher capacity development, with the aim of making teaching methodology more effective and to improve teaching conditions.

But there is a continuing drain of the best teachers to other jobs, or even to other countries. Radical thinking is needed to attract qualified teachers back into Malawi's education system and to design an attractive and substantially scaled-up programme to accelerate teacher training. This should be combined with efforts to attract qualified teachers back into the sector. This could involve, for example, bringing back qualified, retired teachers through a programme of retooling and updating their skills and knowledge.

There are severe capacity constraints in all areas of the economy, including science, technology, health care, engineering, and within the public sector and judiciary. This contributes to a deterioration in the quality of basic public services to support economic growth and poverty reduction. These constraints cannot be addressed without a comprehensive programme to improve the quality of education at all levels. Experience from the agriculture sector provides an example of how they might be addressed. There are significant shortages of appropriately trained development specialists (particularly at the MSc level). University professors have heavy teaching and administrative responsibilities which make field research almost impossible to undertake meaningfully. Most university research until recently was, therefore, confined to on-station laboratories and field stations, with little direct interaction with farmers. Furthermore, most graduate training opportunities relied on overseas universities and the limited number of scholarships available to national universities rarely provided more than student tuition and living costs. In the absence of research grants, it was difficult to involve students in on-farm studies.

Where these problems have been addressed (both The Rockefeller Foundation and the Norwegian Government have provided innovative support for tertiary agricultural education in Malawi), the response of the universities has exceeded all expectations (Blackie and Woomer, 2005). University departments are now venturing into challenging new fields, and are able to compete internationally to attract resources. Most importantly they are also retaining staff and university engagement with communities has been stimulated. But much more is needed – under the New Partnership for African Development (NEPAD) guidelines, the agriculture sector is expected to provide 6 percent growth. Unless the sector, and especially its training institutions, are provided with substantially greater resources, there simply will not be enough skilled technicians around to develop and promote the innovations required to pull Malawi out of poverty.

Civic education

Malawi is a fascinating and compelling case study in the transition from one-party rule to democratic politics. We saw in Chapter 1 the human rights and other abuses that took place under colonialism and one-party rule. The outcome was widespread behavioural destruction throughout every social, cultural and economic stratum. One-party rule continues to cast a long shadow, which is manifested in the many ways:

- 'Big men' and paternalistic leadership structures prevail.
- Helplessness is the norm. Power is seen as highly centralised (which it was) so there is little point (in fact, it can be positively harmful) in engaging in self-help and building local initiatives.
- An absence of accountability. Local political structures are seen as belonging to the person in power. When reasonably free elections are subsequently held, parliamentarians cheerfully change party allegiance without consulting the electorate.

The outcome is that political parties disintegrate and politicians switch allegiance at a mesmerising pace. Politicians increasingly appear to focus on personal interests rather than national priorities. The electorate becomes disillusioned with democratic politics and voting levels fall. The core principles of democracy must be learnt. Democracy can only survive if all accept it as a way of life and identify with its values, concepts and institutions.

Traditional authorities play an important role in building a democratic ethos and in promoting development activities. They are the custodians of culture and traditional values, perform quasi-judicial functions, and provide an essential link between the state and the community. Traditional authorities need to be helped to understand the concepts and implications of democracy and how they complement traditional systems of rule. Then the community as a whole needs to be brought on board to foster a spirit of national development, accountability and transparency. The lack of political commitment to civic education and neglect of some of the successful institutions to promote civic education (such as the Public Affairs Committee[2]) has increased the scope for abuse of power in Malawi's recent history. This undermines efforts to promote economic development and poverty reduction.

The radio is an important resource for national civic education programmes. Such programmes are needed to help people, long accustomed to central, autocratic rule, to understand the basic elements of democratic government, including accountability by public officials, freedom, the importance of a democratic opposition, minority rights and conditions for change in power. Typical components of a civic education programme would include:

- The institutions of a democratic state, including how elections work, the rule of law, the means of accessing institutions of justice and the limits to the power of the police and the army.
- Understanding the concept of human rights as enshrined both by the United Nations and Malawi's Constitution.
- Building community participation in new decentralised local democratic structures.
- How to protect and manage common resources within a democratic environment.
- Learning to build community action programmes to address pressing problems such as food insecurity and HIV/AIDS.

(Office of the Vice President, 1999)

Building environmental sustainability

Environmental sustainability impacts on many areas of concern to the poor. For example, there has been progress in expanding access to potable water since 1990. In 1990, 62 percent of the population had access to safe drinking water, whereas today this had grown to 67 percent – a steady, but not overwhelming progress. However, this achievement will be quickly undermined unless the overall problem of rapid environmental decline is halted and reversed. As we have seen in earlier chapters, this environmental degradation is driven by poverty, high population growth, and an absence of options for the poor to do otherwise than mine their environment. The issue of deforestation is particularly urgent. As we have seen in Chapter 6, fuel wood provides 91 percent of Malawi's energy demand and the rate of deforestation is estimated at 40,000 hectares per annum (EIU, 2004). There is an urgent need for civic education on the potential consequences if deforestation continues at such a pace and to prioritise and fund programmes for re-afforestation and to reinstate Tree Planting Week. There is also the need to strengthen capacity in the area of environmental impact assessment and in dispute resolution (Government of Malawi, 2005).

With its natural resource endowment, Malawi could feed its people (Esser *et al.*, 2005). The majority of the Malawian people have settled in the highlands to benefit from the relatively high rainfall and pleasant temperatures. Low crop production per unit area requires that large parts of the landscape must be cultivated to feed the people. In consequence, farmers open up steep land that is not suitable for cultivation without careful protection. With a focused effort in productive technology promotion (as evidenced by the initial Starter Pack initiative), croplands could yield several times more than at present, thus allowing protection of sensitive watersheds, forest areas and springs without compromising household food security or national food production. Large investments will be needed to create a sustainable and productive agricultural sector. But the alternative is a continuation of widespread soil erosion and consequent increased siltation of rivers, dams and lakes – and the recurring costs of humanitarian assistance to the starving who will face ever more frequent food crises. The economic justification of making such investments appears compelling.

Today, environmental degradation is severe and, without a solution to the pervasive poverty in the country, further catastrophic decline of natural resources is inevitable. By improving the productivity of agriculture and improving the livelihood options of smallholders (thus releasing them from the tyranny of resource exploitation as a survival mechanism), the destruction of ecosystems and landscapes can be halted and reversed. It is undeniable that Malawi smallholders have to move beyond subsistence. While improving food productivity is an important part of the answer, much more needs to be done. An obvious solution is to open up new potential income streams that poor families can link into. The encouragement of cash-cropping is one such stream. But, as we have also seen in other chapters, this option is held back by the logistical problems faced by Malawian farmers in reaching international markets. Tobacco, sugar and cotton are all cash crops which grow well in Malawi but, by the time the goods from Malawi reach the market, they are already too expensive.

There are options which, with imagination, can be pursued. The Malawi Economic Growth Strategy focuses on growth in production of traditional export crops as a strategy for economic development. It should be remembered, however, that there is still considerable scope for import substitution. In most years Malawi imports several hundred thousand tonnes of maize. Half of the milk consumed is imported, as is almost all of livestock feed. All these are opportunities for import substitution. Malawi used to be a major producer and exporter of quality groundnuts but the market for chalimbana groundnuts (Malawi's principal conventional variety) has declined. International Centre for Research in the Semi-Arid Tropics (ICRISAT) are promoting increased production of new varieties of quality groundnuts and other grain legumes (especially pigeon peas) for which there are reasonable market prospects internationally. Increased production of all pulses would make a major contribution to food security as they improve household diets and are an especially important weaning food for infants. Firstly however, seed supply constraints must be overcome. Recently, smallholder farmers have started to diversify successfully into paprika production and export with the support of NASFAM. Total export value was just over US$150,000 in 2003 (Ministry of Economic Planning and Development, 2004).

Investments in economic infrastructure

The state of Africa's infrastructure is so poor that a recent meeting of African Finance Ministers identified infrastructure as the top priority for growth.[3] Economic infrastructure is expensive (in terms of time, capital and human resources) to develop; yet it is essential to progress. Difficult decisions with respect to determining priorities (which roads, hospitals, schools should be built this year), quality (what standards should these be built to), and function (to build a few well-equipped central hospitals or focus on district clinics) have to be made. Even in the wealthiest nations, there is rarely, if ever, sufficient resources to develop and maintain the desired national infrastructure. In a desperately poor country, the exercise in setting priorities can be extremely challenging. In Malawi, at the present time for example, there is a good case for emphasising the maintenance of rural roads over the construction of new roads in the short term. One justification is that deferring investment in road maintenance results in the need for three times the investment later on. Another is that, under the Road Maintenance Initiative of the National Roads Authority, labour-intensive maintenance efforts linked to 'food for work' and 'fertiliser for work' programmes can stimulate much needed agricultural production and address poverty.

The donor community have long been enthusiastic supporters of infrastructural development and public works. They produce discrete, visible outputs that can be handed over intact for the recipient country to run and maintain. In Malawi, as elsewhere, this can lead to a multiplicity of efforts which may leave the country with a set of infrastructural developments that individually can be justified but do not add up to a coherent whole. These investment programmes need to be brought into a coordinated national programme, based on national priorities and implemented through a Sector Wide Approach:

> Programmes that were implemented in isolation with no sustainable methodology for continuity seem to have been less effective. This could be due to the lack of coherent policy in the programmes that could provide direction   (Tera International, 2004).

Public works programmes may be implemented in response to emergencies – such as food crises – when jobs and food are scarce. But there is a cost to be paid. People may be severely malnourished and the most vulnerable may be unable to take up the employment opportunities provided. Moreover, their participation may divert energy from agricultural production during critical periods. Some of these problems can be avoided through bringing all such initiatives under a single national programme with long-term, consistent funding. Then priorities can be properly established with local authorities and communities, and the needed capacity for proper supervision and implementation of contracts put in place (Tera International, 2004). This allows local communities to become familiar with the potential services available to assist with planning and implementation. The needed local balance between maintenance as opposed to expansion of infrastructure can be struck, design standards appropriate to local needs developed and local expertise enhanced.

Not all infrastructural investments will fit this locally focused, decentralised model. The absence of a reliable national electricity supply is a drag on development. Malawi has innovative plans to link up to the Mozambican grid rather than pursue expensive options for building an independent national capacity. Although most Malawians will continue to rely on traditional sources of energy in the foreseeable future, and thus will only indirectly be affected by improved electricity supply, health centres, schools, private businesses and government offices will all function better as access to this important resource is expanded. So also with telecommunications – access to good telecommunications is not a luxury but a necessity for effective participation in the global economy. The expansion of mobile telephones throughout Africa is testimony to the importance of this technology to businesses, governments and private individuals alike.

As in the linkage to the Mozambique electricity supply, there are real opportunities to enhance infrastructure through regional efforts – especially road and rail systems, ports and air freight capacity, energy and communications. Anyone travelling in Africa quickly learns the barriers and costs created through the multiplicity of regulatory regimes, types of red tape, border controls and tariffs through which goods, services, money and people have to pass to do business in Africa (Commission for Africa, 2005). So linking to regional efforts to develop infrastructure will be a crucial component of Malawi's break out of economic isolation. The Nacala Transport Corridor offers considerable potential for reducing external transport costs. Nacala is the best deep water port closest to Malawi. It is accessible by rail but the track is in poor condition and the port itself operates inefficiently. A regional effort to rehabilitate the poor sections of track, reduce seasonal flooding of the line, and bring the port and the rail operators in Malawi and Mozambique into a coordinated whole would transform Malawi's trading potential.[4]

Addressing constraints to private sector development

The major constraints to private sector development have been outlined previously. They include poor macro-economic conditions, a badly developed (and enforced) legal and regulatory system, inadequate economic infrastructure, and poor cooperation between the private and public sectors.

There are two dominating problems. The first is Malawi's indebtedness which drives the macro-economic instability and stops coherent national investment programmes. Malawi's external debt is US$3.23 billion compared with a national GDP of US$1.5 billion. Domestic debt is at the unsustainable level of MK60 billion, which includes arrears to the private sector of MK10 billion (Ministry of Finance, 2005). The second is the recurring theme of this book – food crises. Food crises derail long-term efforts and push national priorities into dealing with short-term problems. Debt builds up and the development investments needed to break out of food crises (and poverty) simply cannot be made. Rather the reverse happens – the country slides ever deeper into poverty. In recognition of this widespread phenomenon across Africa, the *Commission for Africa* recommended that all external debts should be cancelled – which was apparently endorsed at the Gleneagles Summit in July 2005. However, despite this, the debts of most of Africa's highly indebted poor countries – including Malawi – have to be paid.

Nevertheless, there are options for 'self help' that can be productively explored to improve the investment climate. Taxes can be made more 'business friendly'. The Malawi Government, in close consultation with the private sector, undertook a comprehensive review of the tax legislation in 2004–2005 and subsequently, the tax policy was amended in the 2005 Budget. Changes included the removal of ministerial powers to grant tax waivers (an area of abuse in the past). New commercial courts, funded by the European Commission, were introduced and tax levels and thresholds adjusted to encourage entrepreneurship. As importantly, government spending has to be carefully brought under control. To help achieve this, the Malawi Government is introducing an enhanced public-accounting computer system. In addition, it will reduce its debts to the private sector by MK2 billion (20 percent of the outstanding amount) and will attempt to convert some of the balance (mainly Treasury Bills) to longer-term debt stock (Ministry of Finance, 2005). This should relieve some of the pressure on financial markets and allow the private sector more access to finance.

The performance of the donor community has also been unimpressive, with inconsistent and often faulty advice and support. During the last two to three decades, African economies have been subjected to a set of policies that have not transformed the economy or led to sustained economic growth. In the 1980s, in response to a request by African governors at the World Bank for advice on how they could raise their rates of economic growth to Asian levels, the World Bank responded with the Berg report whose central message was to 'get your prices right'. Malawi has for many years been a good pupil. Between 1979 and 1999 the country earned a place among what the IMF characterised as 'very prolonged users' of its facilities. Malawi had six programmes with the IMF. In 17 years out of this 20-year period, Malawi was under one IMF programme or another. In the IMF/World Bank documents evaluating the policy performance of African economies between 1981–1998, Malawi tops the list with seven appearances among 'Good adjusters', followed by Uganda and Kenya with five each (Mkandawire, 2005).

> The major funders now admit to a whole range of errors they have made. They now talk of Comprehensive Policy Frameworks, PRSPs, Post-Washington Consensus, Institutional reforms etc. What they do not seem to recognise is that the accretion of errors has produced economies that are maladjusted and caught in a 'low growth equilibrium' trap. What may be required is a massive aid to correct some of the huge mistakes visited on the continent. Quite remarkably, there was no such reflection in the final documents of the G8 meeting. What seems likely is that the same folks who brought maladjustment to Africa may emerge strengthened from all of this. If the additional funding serves to strengthen the hand of the Washington institutions and to re-enforce their grip on African economies, then aid will be doing more harm than good. If, on the other, aid is given to correct some of the gross maladjustment caused by the policies of the 1990s – if it is aimed at allowing Africans more room for manoeuvre by relaxing both financial and geographical constraints, and if it is built on a genuine sense of solidarity and mutual trust – then aid will contribute to placing African economies on durable developmental paths that goes beyond ending hunger.' (Mkandawire, 2005).

Government interventions in the fertiliser market: a case study of unhelpful government/private sector relations

Fertiliser is one of the most strategic inputs since access to fertiliser directly affects the productivity of agriculture. We have already seen how land-locked Malawi faces high freight and handling costs for both

imports and exports.[5] Fertiliser importing and marketing was liberalised in the early 1990s to facilitate private sector participation in
these functions. The response has been spectacular – the private sector,
comprising six major importers, accounted for 97 percent of the fertiliser imports in Malawi during 2004–2005. The publicly-funded
Smallholder Farmer Fertiliser Revolving Fund of Malawi (SFFRFM[6])
accounted for the remaining 3 percent (Ministry of Agriculture and
Food Security, 2005). Three of these importers have established retail
market networks comprising some 300 stores in the major agricultural
areas, mainly servicing the estate crop sector. Today, the fertiliser
industry is competitive and efficient, employs thousands of Malawians,
and generates substantial tax revenue.

But, in 2005, with a food crisis looming, the government once again
entered the fertiliser procurement arena. The decision was made to
provide a universal subsidy to fertiliser sales for the 2005/2006 growing
season; a policy which had more to do with the national politics of
Malawi than a rational analysis of what was needed to stimulate agricultural growth. A tender was launched by the SFFRFM in early March
2005. The local private sector was unhappy with the lack of transparency and professionalism of the tender process – a concern which
sadly was borne out by events. For example SFFRFM awarded the
tender for the supply of urea[7] fertilisers to an entity whose tender price
was US$50 per tonne less than the world market price. Despite assur-
ances that the fertiliser had been shipped,[8] in mid-October 2005 the
tender had to be cancelled when the supply company was alleged to
have terrorist links. The outcome was a desperate scramble by all concerned to find an alternative source of supply.

The decision to exclude the local private sector from the tender and
from discussions surrounding strategies to increase fertiliser use by
smallholder farmers will have damaging consequences for the whole
economy. The decision to implement the eventual strategy (a universal
fertiliser subsidy) meant that farmers, quite rightly held back on purchases from the private sector until they knew how much subsidised
fertilisers they would be able to buy. The private sector being short of
orders, delayed placing their imports. The outcome, tragically, will be
that this essential commodity will arrive late and will inevitably be
used inefficiently.

Transforming trading rules

Trade is a key driver of economic growth. Developing countries, particularly in Asia, have used trade to break into new markets and transform

their economies. However, Africa in the last three decades experienced a collapse in their share of world trade from around 6 percent in 1980 to 2 percent in 2002. This has been caused partly, by the fact that the composition of African exports has remained essentially unchanged (CFA, 2005). While trade barriers imposed by the rich nations are 'politically antiquated, economically illiterate, environmentally destructive and ethically indefensible',[9] Africa simply does not produce enough goods of the right quality and the right price. This situation will only change with improving transport infrastructure, reducing Africa's internal barriers to trade and diversifying African economies away from current levels of dependency on primary commodities.

We have already seen the limitations to growth options imposed by the high transport costs in Africa. Malawi illustrates this clearly, as it is unable to realise the natural comparative advantages of production because of the heavy comparative disadvantage in transport costs. But transport costs are exacerbated by the numerous internal barriers to trade, which hinder its ability to grow. These include excessive bureaucracy, cumbersome customs procedures, and corruption by public servants who use bribes to supplement their meagre wages at roadblocks. Africa suffers from the highest customs delays in the world, adding as much as 10 percent to the cost of exports (CFA, 2005). The following excerpt is takes from recent diary notes on a visit to Uganda:

Then off to Kampala. We go fine until we get to the border – where the trucks are backed up for several miles. Jackson Kabeye drives right past the trucks up to the gate. There is a discussion with a rather scruffy young man, some documents are handed over, the out gate is opened and in we go. We clear customs and immigration in about an hour – mainly using the out route. Our guide is with us each step of the way and seems to do the paperwork. Later Jackson tells me that this is the only way to get through. The guides share what they earn with the officials. If you try and do it yourself, there is always something wrong and the process takes forever. Is this colluding with corruption or just facing reality??? A cheery Uganda immigration officer approves my visa and gives me a four week stay – so I can remain on and enjoy Uganda after my business. They think that a real joke but nice to have a pleasant face after all the indifferent officials so far. The Ugandan at the final check asks for a large soda – I miss the point but Jackson hands over few small coins and we leave. That is corruption. Our guide unsuccessfully tries to renegotiate his fee.

(Blackie, 2005)

It is not surprising that under these circumstances, trade between African countries is pitiful – a mere 12 percent of all African goods go to other African countries. This is caused not only by the fact that many are producing similar commodities, but also by self-inflicted problems such as complex tariff and regulatory barriers, and restrictions on the operations of foreign transport operators.

But looming over all this is the monster of protectionism in the developed world. The trading relationship between the developed and developing world has long been dominated by a complex web of rules, taxes, tariffs and quotas which favour the rich. Rich countries spend around US$350 billion a year on agricultural protection and subsidies – about 16 times their aid to Africa (CFA, 2005). Taxpayers and consumers in the developed world pay heavily to subsidise their farmers. Seventy-five percent of agricultural subsidies go to the wealthiest 25 percent of farmers – landowners and agribusiness (CFA, 2005). When commodities are grown that are uneconomic in the absence of subsidies – sugar beet in Europe, and cotton in the United States – African countries that have comparative advantage in these crops are unable to compete in the market. The on-going Doha Trade Round launched in November 2001 is committed – on paper at least – to improving market access for poor countries. Progress is glacial which is a scandal.

However, although trade is important, the popular slogan of 'trade not aid' is wrong. Poor countries need 'trade plus aid' since trade reforms alone are insufficient to enable the poorest countries to escape poverty. Sachs (2005) argues that even if trade reforms would raise the incomes of the poorest countries by billions of dollars per year, only a small fraction of that would be available for funding the vitally important public investments needed to escape the poverty trap. In fact, the most immediate gains from trade accrue to the richest and middle-income countries who are already engaged to an extent in international trade and who have the potential to gear up as opportunities emerge. Trade alone will not enable the people in isolated villages in Africa to break out of poverty.

Conclusion

African countries face many daunting challenges. Many are locked into a cycle of crises from which even the most gifted policy makers would find it difficult to escape. At the heart of the problem is a critical lack of investments – especially in education and in infrastructure. They are not helpless – as we have seen, there are actions well within their capacity that could be taken which would help reduce some of the many constraints that they face. But it is both inequitable and unrealistic to expect the poor to buy their way out of poverty. Even if they do try and buy their way out, they are forced to pay excessive prices (due to protectionism in the rich world), making it seem like usury. In the twenty-first century, the world can do better than this.

Notes

1 For a searing indictment of female education in Africa (with a focus on Malawi) see the documentary 'These Girls are Missing' filmed by Michael Camerini and Shari Robertson, Camerini/Robertson Films, New York.
2 The Public Affairs Committee (PAC) is an inter-faith committee set up by the major faith communities in Malawi initially to spearhead informed opposition to one-party rule. It has continued as a powerful voice to ensure that communities are informed about the actions of the government and to promote peaceful community discussion on matters of national concern.
3 January 2004 African Finance Ministers Meeting in Cape Town hosted by Trevor Manuel. The Commission for Africa has recommended that Africa needs an additional US$10 billion a year in infrastructure investment.
4 There are also a number of other factors that affect trade in general which are beyond the control of the Malawi Government, individual importers or exporters. One is the worldwide shortage of containers due to the increase in demand for shipping services to India and China (Tera International, 2004). There is a need to improve operating conditions along the corridor to make it more attractive and for Malawi to ensure that it takes full advantage of its investment share of this important transport corridor.
5 Freight and handling accounted for 35 percent of delivered costs of fertiliser in 2004–2005 and 48 percent in 2003–2004 (when international fob prices were approximately half those of the previous year).
6 The parastatal fertiliser importers established SFFRM in the 1980s to manage fertiliser imports on behalf of the Malawi Government. SFFRFM also managed the Fertiliser Buffer Stock that was established by the European Commission to provide insurance for Malawi's fertiliser supply when external transport routes through Mozambique were closed during the civil war.
7 Urea is a top dressing fertiliser for maize containing 46 percent Nitrogen.
8 The government, struggling to manage a volatile political environment, delayed putting out the bad news that the fertiliser was not going to arrive. While understandable, this meant that contingency measures to identify alternative sources of supply were delayed.
9 Commission for Africa (2005), pg. 49.

Bibliography

Blackie M. (2005) 'Personal Communication,'
Blackie M. and Woomer P. (2005) *Regional University Forum for Capacity Building in Agriculture – programme development*: a report for the RUFORUM Board Meeting, December 2005 (mimeo).

Esser K., Oygard R., Chibwana C. and Blackie M. (2005) 'Opportunities for Norwegian support to agricultural development in Malawi', *Noragric report No. 27*, Aas: Norwegian University of Life Sciences.

Malawi Government, Office of the Vice President (1999) 'Sectoral Report on Civic Education', Report prepared for the Vice President's Office by Dr Volker Monikes, Technical Advisor to the National Initiative for Civic Education (NICE), Lilongwe, Malawi.

Malawi Government (2002) 'Malawi: Poverty Reduction Strategy Paper', Lilongwe, Malawi.

Malawi Government (2005) 'Malawi Millennium Development Goals: Progress Report to the United Nations Millennium Summit', Lilongwe, Malawi and Malawi Resident Mission to the United Nations, New York.

Mkandawire T. (2005), 'Malawi After Gleneagles: A Commission for Africa Case Study', Text of the Keynote Address at the Scotland Malawi Forum, Scottish Parliament, November 2005.

Ministry of Agriculture and Food Security (2005) 'A Comprehensive Programme for Breaking out of Hunger: Component One: Inputs Vouchers', Lilongwe, Malawi.

Ministry of Economic Planning and Development (2004) 'Economic Report', Lilongwe, Malawi.

Ministry of Finance (2005) 'Budget Statement', Presented to the National Assembly, Lilongwe, Malawi.

National Statistics Office (2005) 'Flash Results of the 2004 Demographic and Health Survey', Lilongwe, Malawi.

Sachs J. (2005) 'The End of Poverty: How we can make it happen in our lifetime', U.K.: Penguin.

Tera International Group Inc. (2004) 'Malawi Transport Cost Study, Policy Review Report', Report prepared in collaboration with the Ministry of Transport and Public Works, the International Bank for Reconstruction and Development and the Road Maintenance and Rehabilitation Project, Lilongwe, Malawi.

The Commission for Africa (2005) 'Our Common Interest: Report of the Commission for Africa', London. [available on-line: http://www.commissionforafricaorg/English/11-03-05_cr_report.pdf]

United Nations Development Report (2005) 'International Cooperation at a Crossroads: Aid, Trade and Security in an Unequal World', New York.

11
Changing Mindsets

Anne Conroy and Malcolm Blackie

Introduction

The Malawi case has illustrated the complex interactions between issues of governance, macro-economic management, economic policy, health, HIV/AIDS, agricultural collapse and hunger. Poor governance and macro-economic stability deter investments and undermine growth, while the AIDS pandemic undermines the capacity to implement programmes in poverty alleviation. Food crises exacerbate malnutrition and fuel the AIDS pandemic as people are forced into high-risk sexual behaviour as a survival strategy. The threat of food shortages creates macro-economic difficulties as scarce foreign exchange is diverted to purchase and import food reserves, diverting resources from investment in development programmes. External and internal debts rise inexorably.

African governments face a challenging, but not impossible, situation. As any visitor to Africa knows, that while there is desperate poverty, there is also a powerful urge to succeed. Throughout our analysis, we have actively sought to discover those practices that lead to success. Many are overlooked in the bleak landscape of failure which is so often perceived as the African reality. In this chapter we bring together the issues that need to be addressed in confronting poverty and realising the Millennium Development Goals in sub-Saharan Africa.

The G8 Summit at Gleneagles in July 2005 agreed to substantial increases in aid for all developing countries, with a particular emphasis on Africa. The G8 (and the African leaders who attended the Summit[1]) set out an ambitious agenda:

- Double the size of Africa's economy and trade by 2015.
- Deliver increased domestic and foreign investment.

- Lift tens of millions of people out of poverty every year.
- Save millions of lives a year.
- Get all children into primary schools.
- Deliver free basic health and primary education for all.
- Provide as close as possible to universal access to treatment for AIDS by 2010.
- Generate employment and other opportunities for young people.
- Bring about an end to conflict in Africa.

While there are concerns as to whether Africa has the capacity to absorb additional funds, we have seen clearly in earlier chapters how devastating resource constraints prevent African Governments from scaling up successful interventions for poverty reduction and reaching these goals.

Ensuring that the G8 delivers on its promises will require sustained advocacy by churches, civil society and the international scientific community. Stephen Lewis comments gloomily that 'between principle and delivery lies an unblemished record of failure'.[2] Fergal Keane (2005) writes:

> The poor and down-trodden will stay poor and down-trodden; they will always be unseen, people who are talked about rather than talked to, until they do something terrible. Then we pay attention.

This observation is haunting because it highlights uncomfortable truths. It challenges our attitudes to the poor. Do we see poor people as equal to us? If we are honest, we very often we do not. How else can the rich world live with the scandal that thousands of people die every day for the lack of food and basic medicines?

It is possible to lose sight of humanity in the tragic statistics. Behind every statistic of death is a unique human being. Jonathan Dimbleby, the Head of Voluntary Services Overseas, writing recently in the *Observer*, was shell-shocked by a recent visit to Malawi. Dimbleby witnessed an 18-year old girl die painfully of meningitis in a district hospital with virtually no drugs. He noted that if the world leaders had witnessed her death and the grief of her family, they would have shared the dismay of the medical team that could do nothing to prevent her becoming another statistic in a country where life expectancy has already fallen to 37 years (Dimbleby, 2005).

Such scenes are an everyday occurrence in Malawi. Last month, Anne attended the funeral of a 5-month-old girl who had died of malaria. Malaria kills infants quickly, efficiently – and needlessly. The funeral scene was all too familiar. The men were sitting outside the house quietly mourning with her father; the women were sitting inside the house praying and singing. The mother was inconsolable beside the tiny coffin in the front room. This tragedy is repeated over and over again behind the headlines. Worldwide, a child dies every 3 seconds from a preventable, treatable illness. But to those of us on the ground, we sense that the world leaders (and too many of those from Africa) are remote from this reality – the suffering and death of ordinary human beings; the funerals of the poor, the marginalised and the dispossessed. Working with patients in hospitals you see their sufferings, moving in and out of consciousness often in beds without clean bed linen, in hospitals without drugs. We see the fear and grief of their relatives who know that their lives cannot be saved. We see exhaustion of health workers trying to cope with impossible demands. We see malnourished children in nutritional rehabilitation centres and recognise that they may never fully recover. Working with farmers on the land, we see the awful struggle they face just to feed their families, much less building a cash reserve for school fees, or visits to a clinic.

Addressing poverty in Africa is about saving the lives of our fellow human beings. This can be lost in the discussions of 'targeting aid to the best-governed countries'. Corruption is a blight on too much of the developing world and there is little logic on pouring cash down rat holes. But with good will, ingenuity, and the use of trustworthy local information, corrupt officials can be brought down, while still providing support to the poor and the vulnerable. Corruption is a challenge to all. It should not be an excuse for the wealthy to duck helping poor countries struggling to address famine, build health systems, meet IMF conditionality and win the war against corruption.

At the centre of it all, is learning to trust the people in developing countries. When politicians seek to abuse their powers, the people, churches and civil society will oppose them. The history of mankind is a history of abuses of power and struggles for freedom. The most effective checks on abuse of power come from the people within the countries themselves as only they have the long-term commitment to the development of their nation. Where governance or macro-economic management is weak, increased support should be targeted through faith communities and locally-based agencies such as selected NGOs, CSOs and CBOs. This includes helping build institutions that promote good governance and the defence of human rights, as well as national

Parliaments, CSOs, the faith communities and press organisations so that they can hold the Executive to account.

The focus on corruption by political leaders overshadows the struggle of ordinary people against appalling odds to improve the quality of their lives. Children dying of malaria and other communicable diseases, and children orphaned by AIDS, need support now. They cannot wait for a gradual build-up of development assistance over five years.

In this chapter, we address the need to put human rights and human development at the centre of development policy. This responsibility applies equally to all African governments and to the international community. The commitment to realise human rights in Africa must be met with a commitment to improve governance (everywhere) and to provide additional finance. The chapter is also a personal reflection on the journey out of poverty. Despite the Gleneagles Summit, in poor countries like Malawi, little has yet changed for the lives of the poor and little looks to change in the future. We examine the achievements of recent years and take the most useful lessons from these. This includes exploiting the best of national talents and skills, information sharing, communication and collaboration. We show how, through such a focus, real change could be brought about through a change in mindsets and a commitment to public service, integrity and dedication.

Human rights and human development

All human beings are born free and equal in human rights (United Nations, 2000).

Every nation on earth has signed up to the Millennium Development Goals and the Universal Charter of Human Rights.[3] Sadly, there are too many exceptions to the implementation of these worthy goals. There have been worthy commissions who have made recommendations to address failures in meeting the objectives of the Charter. In 2001, the Macro-economic Commission on Health outlined the linkages between health, poverty reduction and long-term economic growth. It noted that the AIDS pandemic represented a unique challenge of unprecedented urgency. It offered a new strategy for investing in health for economic development and called on the international community to begin the process of dramatically scaling-up the access of the world's poor to essential health services. The resources required for implementation needed an increase in official development assistance for health of

0.1 percent of the GNP of wealthy nations (World Health Organisation, 2001). Unfortunately, nothing much has happened.

The Millennium Commission reported:

> A special aspect of the project is the rare and powerful opportunity to give voice to the hopes, aspirations, and vital needs of the world's poorest and most voiceless people. We have met countless heroes and heroines of development in the last three years of our work – in the villages and slums of Africa, Asia, Latin America and other parts of the developing world. We have seen people preserving their spirit, integrity and hope for the future even when they have little else, when tragic circumstances have left them bereft of health, education, possessions and a means of livelihood. The human spirit is, we have seen in innumerable occasions is truly indomitable. (UN Millennium Commission Project, 2005).

Ideas are plentiful and there is new commitment from the G8 but what is needed is to break the 'non-implementation syndrome'. However, there is a common thread to all the recent efforts. World poverty need not persist and could be halved within the coming decade. Billions more people could enjoy the fruits of the global economy. Tens of millions of lives can be saved. Practical solutions exist, the framework is established, and the cost is affordable. What is needed is action (UN Millennium Commission Project, 2005) – and this requires a transformation in values to put human dignity and human rights at the centre of development policies.

At one level, this involves some serious evaluation of the purpose and direction of aid from rich to poor countries. Aid, especially during the Cold War, was used extensively to promote perceived interests of the powerful. Dr Banda in Malawi was able to finance his draconian and exploitative policies by posing as an anti-communist. This stance brought in substantial resources from the Western hemisphere desperate to find a friend in black Africa. Jonas Savimbi in Angola was able to finance a dreadful war of attrition against his compatriots using a similar strategy. The evidence is surely incontrovertible that this is a spectacularly bad way to promote change for the better in the developing world. Sub-Saharan Africa, with its young and weak national government structures, has been particularly badly affected by the vagaries of so-called aid programmes targeted at creating allies at the international level. Furthermore, the outcome has been too many murderous regimes – some deliberately destructive such as Samuel Doe in Liberia, some who have simply served to impoverish their peoples and drive them further into poverty such as Daniel arap Moi in Kenya.

An international development assistance regime which has human rights as its primary goal avoids propping up the 'arap Mois' and 'Samuel Does' of this world. It provides an opportunity for the many talented and concerned Africans, who are too often sidelined at present, to begin to influence development policies (as they so ably did during the 2002 famine in Malawi) for the benefit of all. Rich countries can show that their aid investments are, indeed, creating change for the better. Poor countries will no longer stagger from crisis to crisis, but will be able to put in place thoughtful, long-term strategies for development. The only losers will be the tyrants, people-smugglers and war-mongers of rich and poor countries alike.

Issues that have to be addressed at the national level

Improving governance

Our primary emphasis is the need to put human rights at the centre of all development policies and to improve governance. Unless governments take the need to protect and nurture (rather than exploit and rob) their citizens seriously, it is difficult to see how benevolence from outside can help. This is not difficult – it involves ensuring that politicians do not steal too much, that the bills can be paid without unnecessary borrowing (or resorting to printing banknotes), and that the country is open to ideas, to debate, to information, to trade, to business.

Governance provides the framework for the implementation of all policies. Key elements of good governance include commitment to the rule of law including security in property and tenure rights, safety from intimidation and violence, transparency in government functions and predictability in government behaviour according to the law.

As aid has most impact in well-governed countries, it makes sense to target aid at such countries. That is the easy job. The difficult one is to deliver aid effectively in poor countries where macro-economic management and governance is weak. Typically in such countries, economic development stalls when governments do not uphold the rule of law, pursue sound economic policy, make appropriate public investments, manage a public administration well, protect basic human rights and support civil society organisations – including those representing poor people – in national decision making (UN Millennium Commission Project, 2005). The people of these countries should not be punished for the failures of their leaders. Moreover, poverty and despair generated by poor governance in one country will inevitably spill over national boundaries and destabilise others. Delivering aid in this second, more difficult, group of countries where there is poor governance will require substantial investments in capacity development for civil society organisations, the faith communities and community-based organisations to enable them to provide essential services for the poor.

Strong civil society engagement and participation are crucial to effective governance because they guarantee oversight, represent the views of the poor and the marginalised. At times it is only the civil society organisations and churches that truly represent the poor. They provide an external and well-grounded perspective on programmes. Civil society organisations can help improve the value of public investments and serve as watchdogs for the development and implementation of government policies. For them to flourish, they need decentralised government structures. We have seen how poor countries struggle to implement development programmes as the tiny national resource of skilled manpower either departs for better opportunities in countries where their talents are recognised, or is cut down by disease and death (or arrested by the authorities). Decentralisation simply cannot happen in any meaningful way without a major effort to build additional capacity to implement consequent activities at the local level.

Sound economic policies involve a rational balance of responsibilities between the private and public sectors to secure sustained and widespread economic progress. In most well-governed countries, the government provides an enabling environment for private sector investments and growth. The public sector provides infrastructure (roads, utilities etc.) and public services (education, health, water and sanitation) throughout the country to promote private sector growth and poverty alleviation. This requires accountability and transparency in the use of public funds and adherence to the budget. There is a strong consultative process surrounding the budget design to ensure that the most effective programmes are included and to ensure popular participation in budgetary implementation. Within the public sector, there is strong and effective financial management. Instances of mismanagement are identified and dealt with promptly to prevent the build up of unnecessary debts.

None of this is impossible, even for poor nations, to achieve. The rules are well known. It means that development projects should not be politicised or targeted to areas of support for those in power. An independent civil service is needed to provide accurate information to help decision makers, analyse options, make recommendations impartially, and implement agreed policies. This requires good technical skills, the ability to communicate effectively across ministries and a well-informed institutional memory. Where Africans have been given the chance to vote for change after years (and even decades) of oppression, they have stated their views clearly and unequivocally. In Kenya, Rhodesia (and later in Zimbabwe), South Africa and Mozambique, they have, as other peoples in other lands, voted for a clean government even at the cost of short-term pain. That wish may be over-ruled by those with vested interests (as for so long in Kenya and more recently in Zimbabwe). Providing corrupt governments with aid simply prolongs the agony. The alternative is to provide governments with advice (which they can ignore or use as they will) and their peoples with support through increased support to NGOs, civil society institutions and the churches.

This has worked well in the past. During Ian Smith's time in Rhodesia (and also during apartheid in South Africa) aid was diverted into building capacity. Those governments were entirely resistant to the kind of change that could be engendered by an aid programme. The resources were not stopped, instead they were diverted elsewhere. When the fall came (and even Malawi's Kamuzu Banda was only president-for-life, not president-for-ever) as it inevitably did, there was a critical mass of young enthusiasts desperate to return home and create change. But this, as Zimbabwe so amply demonstrates, is not sufficient. The investment in capacity then has to be followed up strongly by civic education to inform people of their rights and responsibilities, and programmes to undertake important tasks such as strengthening the independence of the legislature and providing support to Parliamentary Committees to learn to analyse issues independently and hold the Executive to account. It is in this crucial follow-up phase, when a new administration is learning the difficult arts of government that so many aid programmes have failed. They have simply transferred their allegiance from the old, oppressive regime to the new. In such circumstances, the new regime quickly learns the bad habits of its predecessor and the return of bad governance is almost inevitable.

Donor relationships

The planning and implementation of development programmes needs radical improvement. All have a role to play. Donors have to discover more productive ways of interacting and building relationships, with national governments and their citizens. Central governments need to learn how to exploit the wealth of information that they have amongst their own people. Instead of dominating and instructing (and then wondering why their orders are resented or ignored), they should help and assist. Finally, information needs to be used impartially for informed decision making. An environment can be created in which all can collaborate in the interest of development.

Where donor aid accounts for 20 percent or more of GDP, the external debt is greater than national GDP, and the country will typically be on a strictly monitored programme with the International Monetary Fund. The two major international financial institutions (the World Bank and the IMF) will have the stronger voices in determining development policies, and most bilateral donors will coordinate their programmes with the Bank and the IMF. If the country is deemed 'off-track' with the IMF, budget support will be suspended, leaving the government with little more resources than those needed to pay statutory expenditure, debt services, wages and salaries. This typically leaves little room for the implementation of development programmes, and may lead to a significant increase in domestic debts.

National policies are then determined by the Ministry of Finance in consultation with the IMF and World Bank. The budget and even the content of bills presented to Parliament have to be agreed in advance by the IMF. The time required for the complex discussions involved eats into that available for necessary national consultation across sectors and with parliamentarians.[4] If the government is weak, the budget (or bills) agreed with the IMF may well be defeated in Parliament. Then negotiations have to begin again, funding is delayed, and there is an inevitable impact on the delivery of essential services.

This lack of time also prevents adequate dialogue within the government across sectors. Institutions responsible for implementing programmes have to be consulted about issues that fall under their responsibilities if reforms are to be properly and efficiently implemented. But time constraints may prevent this. Key government officials may become very exposed in this process. A Treasury Secretary delaying a response to the IMF in order to consult colleagues in sectoral ministries risks being accused of being obstructive and may lose his job.

Both donors and recipient governments have a vested interest in releasing funds against future targets for change. The data underpinning these targets may well underestimate constraints and will almost certainly be obtained without proper detailed analysis and scrutiny.

Targets may underestimate the effects of delays in tendering, approval or procurement of essential equipment. Many proposals underplay difficulties inherent in expanding successful projects to scale and rarely build in adequate contingencies for failure. The effects of an advanced AIDS pandemic on programme implementation are usually ignored. James (2004) has argued that:

> The recent head office demands for greater focus on results and tighter budgets appear increasingly detached from reality on the HIV-affected ground. Donors appear surprised when the indicators in their log frames are not achieved.

The drive to demonstrate rapid results and meet unrealistic targets also provides an incentive to either hide errors or fail to learn from them (or to blame someone else). Effective development does not take place in an environment of fear. All implementing partners need to learn how to work together towards a common goal. This means understanding the causes of problems. If the data underlying a programme are unreliable, it makes little sense to obscure the fact – but this, sadly, is often what happens. In a top-down approach to addressing perceived failure (even if the original objectives and targets were unrealistic), external consultants are brought in to manage the programme rather than build local capacity. The short-term problems may be alleviated but the long-term issues remain unaddressed.

The donor community can play a unique and constructive role in promoting change. They and their advisors, have information, resources and the final say in virtually all negotiations. National specialists bring local knowledge, cultural understanding, and (if these skills are exploited properly) a sense of ownership and commitment. This contrasts with the manner in which national capacity can be undermined when programmes and policy conditionality are imposed by donors without proper consideration of local constraints and needs. At worst, some donors act in an arrogant and cynical manner; at times even showing contempt for their national counterparts. This reinforces dependency and inferiority, creates resentment (and a consequent lack of ownership and commitment), and serves to drive the best locals out of the public service. There is a need for the representatives of donor agencies to have more humility, to recognise that there are no magic bullets, and to be aware that development challenges are long-term and complex.

Senior management time is one of the most binding constraints to planning and implementation of development programmes in countries trapped in poverty. Yet key ministries and national agencies (such as the AIDS Commissions) can be swamped by visiting missions who all compete for access to senior managers. This is counter-productive for all concerned and directly inhibits the evolution of a decentralised system in which change takes place from the bottom up – not by orders from the power brokers at central government and donor levels. Too often, the solution at present is to provide technical assistance to help relieve pressure on top management. Again, this is a short-term patch which hinders a long-term solution of the problem. Frequently, technical assistance is seen to drive the agenda of donors thus again destroying the needed sense of ownership of change. Rather, the government and donor community need jointly to identify the need for technical assistance or consultancy support. This can then be provided through a common pool.

Exploiting national talents and skills

Many senior government policymakers have a serious vested interest in the control of development programmes. The benefits, for those who manage the flow of funds, can be considerable. The World Bank supported an Agricultural Services Project in Malawi to promote smallholder development in that country. After over a decade of substantial funding through the Ministry of Agriculture, a review indicated that 70 percent of the resources had never left the Ministry headquarters. Less than a quarter of the funds could be linked to perceivable activities in smallholder areas. The impact on poverty and on creating change for the poor in Malawi was invisible. Ironically, the World Bank was the dominant donor to the agriculture sector over this period.

This example serves to illustrate how, in a top-down culture, those in positions of power can choose to ignore the opportunities for national, as opposed to personal, development. Decisions are taken at the central level and implemented in the periphery. Those at the local level, with in-depth knowledge that can be used constructively to adapt programme design and implementation, are not engaged in the process. Field-level expertise is often subject to a very cursory analysis, with meetings called (at headquarters, of course) at short notice. It may be impossible for local experts to change their plans or even to afford the travel and costs involved. These consultations may be postponed or cancelled (again without adequate notice). Where they do take place, dialogue is unequal and there is little real consultation. Programmes and policies are thus developed by headquarters with very limited understanding of field-level constraints.

Information sharing, communication and collaboration

Knowledge is power. In an ideal world, information is used impartially to inform decision making. This information is accurate and is accessible and comprehensible to decision makers. It is shared across constituencies to promote understanding and build momentum for change. There is an open and non-judgemental dialogue to identify the key obstacles to implementation so that these can be addressed.

The reality, sadly, is very different. A politicised civil service has little reason to give accurate or impartial advice in an environment where influential interest groups dominate long-term national interests. Where the need to meet external conditionalities for structural adjustment lending or budget support is critical, there is a real temptation to adjust the data to get government and donor approval.

Monitoring and evaluation data are often inadequate, and policy information is not provided in high quality, accurate, briefing documents that highlight issues and that identify and cost different options accurately. Importantly, because of weaknesses in sectoral ministries, cross-sectoral analyses are either inadequate or missing. In 2005, for example, in Malawi, the key Ministry of Agriculture had limited policy analysis capacity – and the Ministry of Agriculture was bypassed completely on key issues including the debate on fertiliser policy. Agricultural policies are developed in last-minute consultations surrounding the national budget with little detailed understanding of the realities of smallholder agriculture in that country.

Already twelve years into the democratic transition, we have yet to learn that policies cannot be determined only by technocrats working for the government and the donor communities. We should not be surprised if parliamentarians do not understand the full intricacies of different policy options during the debates in Parliament. We have consistently failed to provide essential information to Members of Parliament to allow them to debate issues constructively.

Collaboration between all parties – government ministries, donors, civil society and Parliament – is essential to progress. If one influential group refuses to collaborate, development is held back. We have seen how, in the Malawian food emergencies, effective and powerful collaboration was quickly put in place to deal with an immediate humanitarian crisis. It does not seem impossible that these same skills and efforts can be harnessed for the equally important problems of development – improving the productivity of food crops and diversifying export crops, enhancing primary health care and disease prevention, treating and mitigating on-going health problems. This puts collaboration at the centre of development, rather than as a response to emergency situations, and provides the momentum needed to meet the Millennium Development Goals. Collaboration is essential for development and requires the ability to work together constructively, to listen and to address problems jointly.

Chapter 9 on 'Breaking out of Food Insecurity' outlined the elements for successful development. The experience of the highly successful Maize Productivity Task Force and the successful Starter Pack Programme demonstrated the importance of careful analysis of key constraints in a specific environment. It was led by the Malawi Government and by a cross-sectoral team of scientists, policy makers, civil society organisations and the private sector all working in partnership under national leadership.

The government determined its own priorities with regard to national food security and asked a team of national leaders for advice. The advice given to the National Food Security Task Force was grounded in science and evidence given by the national authorities. There was also high-level political leadership and commitment because the programme met national priorities rather than priorities imposed by donors or donor conditionality. There was detailed follow-up and people were held accountable for their actions by a dynamic Minister of Agriculture – Aleke Banda. The Minister did not accept failure as an option, he expected everyone concerned to work to make the programme a success.

The second example of the importance of collaboration is found in the exemplary response to the food crisis of 2002–2003. Once the scale of the food crisis was acknowledged by the government, donors and all stakeholders, everyone worked together to address the crisis. The process was inclusive – everyone was prepared to make the compromises that are necessary if there is to be a national response. Everyone worked under the national leadership of the National Food Crisis Task Force. Decisions were taken on the basis of objective criteria. Information was circulated to all stakeholders and strong mechanisms for monitoring, transparency and accountability were put in place. This ensured the success of the humanitarian response.

Changing mindsets

Core values

This chapter is about changing mindsets, it is also about changing values. All development activities are supposed to promote human development and human dignity. This requires dedication and the recognition that all human beings are equal. If we put the values of equality and human dignity at the centre of development policies, the many obstacles will resolve themselves. Core obstacles include arrogance, the failure to listen, the failure to collaborate and the failure to focus on action rather than words. The core values for promoting human development are public service, integrity, dedication, a commitment to justice, a belief in the future and hope.

Arrogance and ego is arguably as great an obstacle to successful development as the lack of resources. We see it in all spheres of national and donor politics. Arrogance blinds people because they are so certain that they are right. It prevents people from reviewing evidence or from basing decision making on objective criteria. It undermines the potential for compromise or collaboration and almost inevitably puts people on a path of confrontation – which is never in the interests of the poor.

Arrogance is closely related to ego – the belief that the individual is more important than the issue, and it leads to ruthless competition and the certainty that one is always right. The most vicious debates concerning development rarely relate to issues of substance or policy; they are about influence, power and reputation. The development professionals are sadly not immune from the destructive influence of arrogance and ego. Because heads of donor missions control resources, they have considerable power and limited accountability. This allows them to advocate policies or force through conditionalities with limited scrutiny or review. Policies change but the certainties with which they are advocated rarely do.

An early casualty is collaboration and team working. If someone believes that they are right, then there is no need to listen to alternative suggestions. The absence of a genuine dialogue with people operating at the ground level undermines local ownership – leading to activities that are externally driven, externally controlled and destined to fail. This is particularly destructive in the political arena and undermines the process of democratic transition as politicians prioritise their personal rather than the national interests. The first 10 years of democratic politics in Malawi (1994–2004) focused on 'Poverty Alleviation'. People soon spoke of 'personal poverty alleviation' as the President and Cabinet acquired prestige cars, property, wealth and an insatiable appetite for first-class airfares and five-star hotels. Parties fragmented because of power struggles for the top positions (virtually every political party has broken up or been in and out of alliances with the ruling party). With new parties being registered only to be disbanded within months, it is becoming virtually impossible to understand what any political party stands for in Malawi's new democratic dispensation.

All this undermine people's confidence in democracy and allows religious and regional differences to be exacerbated and exploited – which is potentially very destructive. Malawi has always been a very poor, but peaceful country. This peace is threatened when politicians are not prepared to put aside their personal rivalries and work together in the national interest, especially during the current crisis.

Power becomes increasing concentrated as those people in power draw their information from a declining (and small) clique of advisors. Representatives of donor missions mainly listen to their head offices or fellow heads of mission. Decision makers are chained to the desks and computers in capital cities, only occasionally venturing out into areas of deprivation (and even then typically under very controlled circumstances). The voices of the poor or those of people implementing field programmes are excluded, resulting in decisions being taken which do not reflect the reality of a desperate, grinding poverty.

Actions not just words

Development and poverty alleviation needs action – warm words are not enough. There is a veritable industry of International AIDS conferences, attracting the most senior officials from the National AIDS Commissions and Ministries of Health. While the decision makers are away, programme implementation stalls. Thoughtful analysis of problems is an essential component of successful problem solving – but analysis needs to be firmly rooted in a context of implementation and accountability. As an illustration, we will look at the UN Secretary General's Task Force on Women and Girls in southern Africa. This Task Force was established following the visit of Stephen Lewis and James Morris to southern Africa in 2002. These two special Envoys identified gender inequality and the AIDS pandemic as major drivers of the food crisis. They recommended that these issues should be addressed immediately. In response, the United Nations appointed consultants to compile immediate reports so as to 'be seen to do something' than actually taking action. In the rush, national authorities were almost completely side-lined, and meaningful consultation, listening or understanding the cultural context were largely overlooked.

A report was compiled and representatives from affected countries were summoned to Johannesburg, when again time constraints precluded any meaningful discussion of the issues or recommendations. A glossy (but largely competent) report was produced and disseminated on time – and the initiative foundered in the critical area of follow-up. The Task Force was disbanded and the Ministry of Gender left to 'implement the recommendations' without any additional financial or technical support. The flurry of activity and words has contributed little to addressing one of the most fundamental drivers of the AIDS pandemic.

Realising the Millennium Development Goals will require a commitment to public service, integrity and dedication. The commitment to public service is fundamental in both the political and development spheres. Expenditures evaluated in terms of their opportunity costs and public funds would not support the unjustified consumption of the elite. Luxury cars would not be bought using Drought Relief funds and delegations to external conferences would consist only of those essential to the agenda of the meeting. Politicians would serve and represent the interests of the people who elected them. This requires consultation and the ability to place national interests above personal, party or regional interests. Sadly this is rarely the case. During the last food crisis, Malawi's politicians focused on the unnecessary distraction of a Presidential Third Term. As what appears to be an even more devastating famine emerges in 2005–2006, politicians are changing allegiances at a mesmerising pace. At a time when the country desperately needs stability in order to consolidate the gains in macro-economic management and address the food crisis, the opposition is focusing on the threat to impeach the president, while the government is trying to consolidate the power-base of the newly established Democratic Progressive Party.

Integrity or 'adherence to moral principles' is also fundamental for progress. It means that people should tell the truth and act in a trustworthy manner. Where people consistently fail to honour agreements – especially with people they judge as less important or less influential than them – it creates suspicion and mistrust, which in turn undermine potential for collaboration. Establishing relationships of trust is a pre-requisite for collaboration which in turn is a pre-requisite for progress. It is virtually impossible to make progress where people do not adhere to agreements or share information openly.

There is an unfortunate, but perhaps understandable incentive to conceal information when things are going wrong. In such a situation, people often seek to assure their colleagues or superiors that 'they should not worry because everything is under control'. This is probably the most dangerous statement in development because it postpones remedial action, sometimes with devastating consequences. It is not possible to plan or to address problems that emerge inevitably in any programme unless you have accurate information on where the bottlenecks and constraints are. It is impossible to focus limited resources and energy on key constraints when you do not know what they are. Once any member of a team starts obscuring the truth, it is necessary to continue to do so. For example, once you have said that the fertiliser is at the port, it is difficult to admit that the contract with the fertiliser supplier has in fact fallen through. The tendency to obscure facts and withhold essential information inevitably makes a bad situation far worse. It also damages relationships, often irreparably, when the rest of the team repeat inaccurate information in good faith and subsequently find their own reputation for honesty undermined as the programme fails and the poor suffer.

There is a need for dedication by everyone involved in both public life and public service. The vast majority of Malawians demonstrate this dedication every day of their lives – the doctors, nurses and clinical officers working night and day in under-staffed, under-resourced hospitals and health centres, the teachers struggling to educate children in poorly-resourced classrooms with very poor wages. The vast majority of people working at the periphery, directly with the people are outstanding in their dedication. Senior officials in Malawi's ministries labour long hours attempting to balance multiple priorities and to make progress. There is a need to extend such dedication to everyone involved in public service – in politics and in the donor community. There is a need to instil the sense that everyone is personally responsible for and accountable for their actions.

Finally, there is a need for a commitment to justice, a belief in the future and hope. A commitment to justice is driven by a belief in the equality and the dignity of all human beings. All nations have signed the Universal Declaration on Human Rights. Where governments act to defend human rights, they are working towards human development. Throughout the world, people are struggling for justice with courage and conviction, even though their actions are rarely recognised. But we believe that a commitment to justice is the only way of overcoming poverty, hunger and disease in Malawi and elsewhere.

Poverty, hunger and disease present formidable challenges, and in the face of the suffering surrounding the AIDS pandemic, inevitably there are moments of despair. But there is a need for hope in the future and to recognise that the formidable challenges can be overcome. In the words of our friend Joseph Mpingangira 'the greatest challenge is despair, not the disease.'

External observers and even some Malawians focus on problems as though they are insurmountable or even worse, lapse into cynicism. Speaking at the Scotland/Malawi Forum in a moving and impassioned statement, Bishop James Tenga Tenga said:

> Malawi is our country; there are so many things about Malawi that are good. We are proud of our country. We are proud to be African. We face major challenges but we are struggling to overcome these. When you only focus on the negative and do not acknowledge the efforts made by ordinary people to create change, you destroy their spirit. We are making progress, we will overcome these obstacles.

Notes

1   These included the Presidents of Algeria, Ethiopia, Ghana, Nigeria, Senegal, South Africa and Tanzania and the heads of the Africa Union Commission, International Monetary Fund, United Nations and World Bank.
2   Statement at the Opening of the 3rd International AIDS Society Conference, Rio de Janeiro, Brazil.
3   The Universal Declaration of Human Rights enshrines the right to life and liberty, equality before the law, privacy, freedom of thought, conscience and religion, peaceful assembly and association. It establishes the right to work, to a standard of living adequate to the health and well-being of the family, to free primary education, to education that is directed to the full development of the human personality and to strengthening of respect for human rights and fundamental freedoms (United Nations, 2000).
4   The final negotiations for structural adjustment programmes with the World Bank or IMF always take place in Washington which makes local consultation even more problematic.

Bibliography

Commission for Africa (2005) 'Our Common Interest', Report of the Commission for Africa, London.

Dimbleby D. (2005) 'Our Last Chance', The Observer Newspaper, 11th September 2005.

Food and Agriculture Organization and the World Food Programme (2005) 'Crop and Food Supply Assessment Mission to Malawi', June 2005.

James R. (2004) 'Dodging the Fists? The Crushing Blows of HIV/AIDS on leaders in Malawi', INTRAC, Blantyre, Malawi.

Keane F. (2005) 'Of all of these people: A memoir', Hammersmith: Harper Collins Publisher.

Lewis S. (2005a) ' Statement at the Opening of the 3rd International AIDS Society Conference, Rio de Janeiro, Brazil', Office of the UN Special Envoy for AIDS in Africa, New York.

Lewis S. (2005b) 'Statement at the University of Pennsylvania's Summit on Global Issues in Women's Health, Philadelphia', Office of the UN Special Envoy for AIDS in Africa, New York.

UN Millennium Commission Project (2005) 'Investing in Development: A Practical Plan to Achieve the Millennium Development Goals: Overview', Millennium Project, United Nations, New York.

United Nations (2000) 'Human Development Report' (The Universal Declaration of Human Rights, pp. 14–15.

World Health Organization (2001) 'Macroeconomics and health: Investing in health for economic development', World Health Organization, Geneva, Switzerland.

12
Ending Extreme Poverty in Malawi

Anne Conroy and Jeffrey Sachs

Introduction

Ending extreme poverty in Malawi is an ambitious, but not impossible, objective. We owe the children of Malawi nothing less. It will require a transformation in values surrounding international aid, debt, trade and security. The excellent 2005 Human Development Report on 'International Cooperation at the Crossroads focusing on Aid, Trade and Security in an Unequal World' should be compulsory reading for everyone involved in development. It reminds us that 'the promise to the world's poor is being broken' (United Nations, 2005).

> What begins with the failure to uphold the dignity of one life, all too often ends with calamity for whole nations. (UN Secretary General Kofi Annan, Human Development Report p. 150).

The report highlights many unnecessary scandals. Current annual spending on HIV/AIDS, a disease that claims 3 million lives a year, represents only 3-days worth of military spending. For every US$1 invested in development assistance, another US$10 is spent on military budgets. Total development assistance from the Organisation for Economic Cooperation and Development (OECD) countries was US$69 billion in 2003. These same countries spent US$642 billion on the military. Three children die every minute as a result of malaria in Africa alone. Many of these deaths happen for the lack of a simple insecticide-treated bed net at a cost of US$3. Rich countries spend around **US$1 billion per day** subsidising their farmers and hand out support to the agriculture of developing countries of just **under US$1 billion per year**. This costs developing countries about

US$24 billion a year in agricultural income – not counting the dynamic and spill-over effects.[1]

The Millennium Development Goals **can** be met, but only if all countries involved break with business as usual and **scale up action now**. Ending extreme poverty in Malawi and elsewhere will need more than the continuing practice adopted by too many in the international aid community of recycling the same pledges for decades. Gleneagles in 2005 drearily repeated the promises of Monterrey in 2002:[2]

> No country genuinely committed to poverty reduction, good governance and economic reform will be denied the chance to achieve the MDGs through lack of finance. (*Commission for Africa* 2005, p. 302).

This is not just nonsense, it is criminal. At the time of writing (late October 2005), there is a real danger that many of the poor in Malawi will die of famine – unnecessary deaths which could have been prevented as we have shown in earlier chapters. At the same time, people are dying in Pakistan because food and shelter cannot be delivered. The needed helicopters exist – they are deployed in a controversial war in Iraq which soaks up men and treasure. Surely, in the name of humanity, 3 weeks did not need to pass before the first helicopters arrived. That expensive military machine should be able to operate to a higher standard with all the resources it soaks up. Total military expenditure approaches 1 trillion dollars (Lewis, 2005). The international community did not lack the knowledge, resources or military hardware to deliver enough food, aid, medicine and tents to Pakistan. What the world lacked was a credible political will to mount a response commensurate with the needs.

Television crews are filming people who have lost their limbs due to the lack of medical supplies and who are close to death from exposure in Pakistan. We can anticipate that in a few short months, these same journalists will be taking footage of those dying of hunger in Malawi. It is a real scandal to witness people dying on television from preventable and predictable causes – reflecting indifference to our fellow human beings on a scale that is unforgivable. In the words of Stephen Lewis 'there will be no excuses to hide behind, only the graves of the betrayed'.

What is needed

The numbers cannot be disputed. The cost of ending poverty – the amount required to lift 1 billion people above the US$1 per day poverty line – is estimated at US$300 billion per annum (UNDP, 2005). But ending extreme poverty, of the kind we have explored in Malawi, will need much more. The Millennium Commission Project (2005) notes:

> We have the opportunity in the coming decade to cut poverty in half. Billions more people could enjoy the fruits of the global economy. Millions more lives could be saved. The practical solutions exist. The political framework is established. And for the first time, the cost is utterly affordable. Whatever one's motivation for attacking extreme poverty – human rights, religious values, security, fiscal prudence, ideology – the solutions are the same. All that is needed is action. (Introduction to the Millennium Development Project Overview, p. 1).

The Millennium Commission Project has identified the Quick Wins – these are the interventions that could bring breath-taking gains within the first few years. They include:

- Eliminating school fees to ensure that all children are in school.
- Providing impoverished farmers in sub-Saharan Africa with affordable replenishment of soil nitrogen and other nutrients.
- Providing free school meals for all children using locally produced food with take-home rations.
- Designing community nutrition programmes that support breastfeeding.
- Providing access to complementary foods and where necessary provide micro-nutrient supplementation.
- Provide regular annual de-worming to all school children in affected areas to improve health and educational outcomes.
- Train large numbers of village workers in health, farming and infrastructure (one-year programmes).
- Distribute free, long-lasting insecticide-treated bed nets to all children in malaria endemic zones to cut decisively the burden of malaria.
- Expand access to sexual and reproductive health information services, family planning and contraceptive information and services.
- Expand the use of proven drug combinations for AIDS, tuberculosis and malaria. For AIDS, this includes successfully completing the 3*5 initiative to bring anti-retrovirals to 3 million people by 2005.

- Set up and fund community-based slum upgrading and earmark idle public land for low cost housing.
- Provide access to electricity, water, sanitation and the internet for all hospitals, schools and other social institutions using off-grid diesel generators, solar panels and other appropriate technologies.
- Reform and enforce legislation guaranteeing women and girls property and inheritance rights.
- Launch national campaigns to reduce violence to women.
- Establish in each country in the Office of the President or Prime Minister a scientific advisor to consolidate the role of science in national policy making.
- Empower women to play a central role in formulating and monitoring MDG-based poverty reduction strategies and other critical policy reform processes, particularly at the level of local government.
- Provide community-level support to plant trees to provide soil nutrients, fuel wood, shade, fodder, watershed protection, windbreaks and timber.

All the above will have to be paid for but the costs are not overwhelming. The developed world can look to meeting these goals by increasing overall aid flows to a modest 0.5 percent of GDP by 2010 and 0.7 percent by 2015. Much is being lavished on excessive military costs in the world overall; the costly toys and manpower are (fortunately) often never actually put into use. In comparison, using data from the Millennium Commission Project (2005), the costs of meeting the Millennium Development Goals in Malawi for a population of approximately 12 million people is estimated at US$1.452 billion in 2006 scaling up to US$2.268 billion in 2015.[3] These numbers are not impossible to achieve.

The *Commission for Africa* Report (2005) argues, as we have, for increasing investments in vital areas such as education, health and infrastructure. They estimate, for sub-Saharan Africa, a need of an additional US$75 billion per year. Half of this should be made by 2010 and one-third should be financed by the African governments themselves. Thus the international community should increase annual aid flows to Africa by US$25 billion.

There is therefore no doubt about the magnitude of resources that are needed to make a difference in Africa. The *Commission for Africa* (2005) addresses the question of whether there are options other than an increase in official development assistance to finance the development requirements. It discounts the role of foreign direct investment

(FDI) in kick-starting growth. FDI flows to Africa are insignificant in per capita terms and have not generally been associated with broad-based growth. Most FDI is in the extractive industries (oil and mineral) and is focused on just three countries – Nigeria, South Africa and Angola together represent 59 percent. There are some opportunities for FDI especially in the areas of infrastructure such as telecommunications. The politically more tricky areas of electricity and water are not attractive, with a few notable (and controversial) exceptions.

While in the developing world generally remittances are a key source of finance – growing from US$20 billion in 1983 to nearly US$200 billion in 2003 (far more than international development assistance) – they are modest in Africa (*Commission for Africa*, 2005). The cost of making remittances is relatively high, and deposits in African banks have high risks. Many migrants hold their funds abroad and support relatives as they try to gain education and other opportunities outside the continent. Capital flees from situations where inflation and corruption is problematic – probably cancelling out the effects of remittances. The *Commission for Africa* suggests that throughout Africa, the reversal of capital flight is likely to follow rather than to lead development.

Sub-Saharan Africa has one of the lowest savings rates in the world (16 percent). Malawi, with its extreme poverty, has one of the lowest savings rate in Africa. There is little scope for savings in public investment or consumption:

> The simple reality is straightforward; let me set the context. It is Official Development Assistance that goes to the social sectors, health and education in particular, giving governments the chance, the opportunity, the hope of overcoming poverty and the burden of disease. There is no other source of funds that goes so directly to the sectors on which the most vulnerable citizens of Africa depend. (Lewis, 2005, p. 26).

A perspective on what can be done

At the end of the Second World War, the international financial institutions, the World Bank and International Monetary Fund, were set up at Bretton Woods. Their mandate was reconstruction and development. The need was clear:

> the truth of the matter is that Europe's requirements are so much greater than her present ability to pay that she must have substan-

tial additional help or face economic, social and political deterioration of a very grave character. (George C. Marshall[4])

In three years, the United States transferred US$13 billion in aid to Europe, equivalent to 1 percent of GDP. The transfers were driven by moral conviction and by the recognition that prosperity and security in the United States depended on European recovery (UNDP, 2005). At the end of the 1960s, the Commission on International Development convened by the World Bank under the auspices of the former Canadian Prime Minister Lester Pearson revived the spirit of the Marshall Plan. It argued for donors to provide 0.7 percent of GDP in development assistance by 1975. The case for the target was partly moral and partly enlightened self-interest:

> The fullest possible utilization of the world's resources, human and physical which can be brought about only by international cooperation helps not only countries that are now economically weak, but those that are strong and healthy. (UNDP, 2005)

The pledge to commit 0.7 percent of GDP to aid was revived in 1992 at the Earth Summit in Rio de Janeiro and reaffirmed at Monterrey in 2002. Donor nations agreed collectively to undertake 'efforts to reach' the 0.7 percent target – words that stop short of a commitment. Then the European Finance Ministers agreed to move towards 0.5 percent of GDP in June 2005, while at the 'historic' Gleneagles Summit, some of the G8 countries made non-binding commitments to reach the 0.7 percent target: Britain by 2013, France by 2012. Both Germany and Italy have placed conditions on meeting even the 0.5 percent of GDP pledge by 2010. Japan, currently spending 0.18 percent of GDP on aid, pledged to double aid to Africa. The United States with its miserly 0.15 percent of GDP on international aid will almost certainly duck the 0.7 percent target by 2015 especially as Congress keeps failing to approve money for the Millennium Challenge Account. Canada, presently contributing around 0.25 percent of GDP on overseas aid, has not set a target for future levels.

It is the small nations of Norway, Luxembourg. Denmark, Sweden and the Netherlands that have already spent more than 0.7 percent of GDP on overseas aid, while Portugal is close to the target (UNDP, 2005). A cynic might notice an inverse relationship between the amount of noise that surrounded commitments to 'move towards' targets that were agreed upon 36 years ago (the Gleneagles Summit) and their achievement. In contrast, it is the 'quiet' Scandinavian countries and the Netherlands who deliver on their pledges in quality aid programmes.

Some thoughts on debts

The G8 Summit at Gleneagles did not break any new ground on aid, but it made the following pledge on debts:

> The G8 has also agreed that all of the debts owed by eligible highly indebted poor countries to the IDA, the International Monetary Fund and the African Development Bank should be cancelled, as set out in our Finance Ministers agreement of June 11th. We also welcomed the Paris Club decision to write off around US$17 billion of Nigeria's debt. (Gleneagles, 2005; Chairman's Summary)

This indeed appeared historic – a decision that could give hope for millions of Africans. However, we soon learned that the most important word was 'eligible'. Eligibility was defined as those countries that had reached the 'decision point' of the Highly Indebted Poor Country (HIPC) criteria – those who had met the IMF criteria. But, as Mkandawire (2005) observes the 'good policy' regimes imposed on African countries were largely designed for stabilisation and debt management. They did not allow them to catch up economically with more developed countries and, in fact, were the polar opposite of those known to be associated with past successes in Asia and elsewhere. The contemporary experience of China stands as an indictment to the policy regime imposed on Africa today.

The major funders, including the IMF, admit to some of the errors they have made. They do not seem to recognise is that the accretion of errors has produced economies that are maladjusted and caught in a 'low-growth equilibrium' trap. It is only the survivors of this dreadful policy advice that are being provided with debt relief. Those too weak or poor to overcome the difficulties imposed on them have to wait. This is more than unfair. Quite remarkably, there was no such reflection in the final documents of the G8 meeting. What seems likely is that the same folks who brought maladjustment to Africa may emerge strengthened from all of this. If the additional funding serves to strengthen the hand of the Washington institutions and to re-enforce their grip on African economies, then aid will be doing more harm than good. If, on the other, aid is given to correct some of the gross maladjustment caused by the policies of the 1990s – if it is aimed at allowing Africans more room for manoeuvre by relaxing both financial and geographical constraints, and if it is built on a genuine sense of solidarity and mutual trust – then aid will contribute to placing African economies on durable developmental paths that goes beyond ending hunger (Mkandawire, 2005).

Between 1970 and 2002, Africa acquired US\$294 billion of external debt, little of which benefited the poor. Over the same period, it paid back US\$260 billion, mainly in interest payments. In 2002, Africa still owed more than US\$230 billion in debt. Following the G8 Summit, US\$40 billion in external debt was written off for 18 countries (14 in Africa). The annual saving on debt service payments is approximately US\$1 billion. Africa remains shackled with a debt of US\$200 billion in debt – but oil-rich Iraq's US\$31 billion external debt with the Paris Club was cancelled. Something does not smell right (Lewis, 2005).

Twenty years ago President Julius Nyerere asked the governments of the West 'Should we really starve our children to pay our debts?' He did not get a direct answer but, in practice, it was 'Yes'. 'The heaviest burden of a decade of reckless borrowing is falling not on the military or on those who conceived the years of waste, but on the poor who have to do without necessities'.[5]

Malawi owes some US\$3.1 billion, of which 82 percent is owed to multi-lateral creditors (the World Bank, the International Monetary Fund, and the African Development Bank), 17.5 percent to bilateral creditors and 0.5 percent to commercial creditors. Debt service totalled US\$112 million in 2004. Yet 5 million Malawians were in need of humanitarian assistance at the end of 2005 and the beginning of 2006. The most recent food crisis has pushed people deeper into poverty. Many have had to rely on the most destructive coping mechanisms: taking children out of school, selling assets and high-risk sexual behaviour simply to survive. The cost of servicing Malawi's external debts will be malnutrition and famine in 2005 – and a possible repeat in 2006 as the harvest will be compromised unless someone mobilises the resources to provide smallholder households with sufficient seed and fertilisers to increase productivity. Little wonder that Africa is still 'the hopeless continent'!

Malawi has been excluded from debt cancellation because it is not at the HIPC completion point. This is not something the poor created – fiscal discipline went off-track in the last years of President Muluzi's administration as he tried to cling to power. The poor have to pay of the debts of the rich. The new government has made commendable efforts to restore fiscal discipline, but have inherited MK60 billion in domestic debts – some 37 percent of GDP (Zamba, 2005). It has also inherited MK10 billion in arrears to the private sector. This is an impossible situation – over two-thirds of the budget is debt repayment and statutory expenditure, leaving less than one-third for the provision of services (Whitworth, 2005).

There is a real sense of injustice that the G8 is only cancelling the debts of 'eligible' countries – the good performers with the International Monetary Fund – including many of the countries represented on the *Commission for Africa*. Africans feel strongly that the poor will pay for the debt with their lives for this unwarranted 'favouritism'. Maybe it is not so – but that is how it looks to the poor and dispossessed in Africa.

Concluding comments

Ending poverty in Malawi, as elsewhere, will require a coherent and comprehensive programme of debt relief. It will also require an honest delivery of the commitments made at the many high-level meetings – Rio, Monterey, and Gleneagles – of new funding. This needs to be provided in a sustained, predictable, and flexible manner, according to the needs of the countries themselves rather than to drive the multiple conflicting agendas of different donors. We endorse the arguments put forward by Hilary Benn that development cannot be imposed. It can only be facilitated. It requires ownership, participation and empowerment, not harangues and dictates. (Department for International Development, 2005).

Thandike Mkandwire is even more forthright:

....by the mid-1990s, 'institutional reforms' – or 'good governance', as this was popularly known in donor circles – became the new mantra in the policy world. A wave of institutional reforms swept across the African continent. Already by the beginning of the millennium, there were increasing doubts about the 'institutional fix' and the institutionalists began to lose ground. While many countries had, under the aegis of the international financial institutions, introduced major institutional reforms, the economic recovery remained elusive. This prompted the new question, 'Why is it that even when countries adopt the recommended polices and the right institutions, economic growth does not take place?' One response to this new question is that 'institutions do rule', but the institutions peddled by the international financial institutions were the wrong ones, partly because of 'monocropping' through the one-size-fits-all institutional design, and 'monotasking' that insisted that all institutions should be harnessed to the protection of property rights.

These institutions differed radically from not only those behind the East Asia miracle and China but also from those of any successful case of development in modern times. Indeed, in the successful 'late industrializers' many of the institutions being pushed as prerequisites for development never served the functions attributed to them and they were assiduously avoided in all strategies of 'catching up'.

(Mkandawire, 2005)

Mkandawire is right. National ownership and leadership are fundamental to coherent progress in development and poverty reduction. Malawi is not on-track for meeting the Millennium Development Goals except for universal primary education. It is noteworthy that Malawi was the first country to introduce free compulsory primary education in 1994 – long before it received debt relief or was exhorted to do so by the international community. Enlightened political leadership at the national and international levels is needed now more than ever before. While some progress has been made in reducing infant and child mortality, life expectancy is low and falling due to one of the worst AIDS pandemics in the world. Maternal mortality increases inexorably and tragically. Malawi has the highest population density in Africa for a country with a single rainy season. Land distribution is highly unequal with smallholder land-access diminishing; nearly half of all smallholders are functionally landless with land holdings of less than 0.5 hectares of land (Frankenberger *et al.*, 2003). Not surprisingly, the vast majority of smallholders are unable to purchase improved seed and fertilisers that is so critical to food security. Environmental degradation is proceeding at an alarming rate. Without a major change, the future is bleak. Business as usual will result in falling per capita incomes and growing poverty. Malawi's National Economic Council predicted in 1998 that per capita GDP would decline to US$130 (in constant dollar terms) by 2020 if there is a continuation of present levels of growth (National Economic Council, 1998).

Developing capacity to implement the 'Best Bets' identified by the Millennium Commission probably represents the greatest challenge and opportunity for progress. The process has to be led by the nationals of the country – the experience of Malawi demonstrates that the faith communities, civil society and the technocrats have done a remarkable job in representing the needs and priorities of the poor. By contrast, high-level development specialists and national leaders talk above the heads of poor people. This is disempowering, insulting, hurtful and very counter-productive. The Commission for Africa highlighted the importance of appreciating the local cultural context and working with the faith communities that have structures and credibility at the local level. This will require a paradigm shift in the way in which we think about development and poverty reduction. With imagination, effort, and hard work, change can come about. What is needed is for Africans to be given the opportunity to express themselves as equals and not as supplicants. This will only happen when we transform values to genuinely respect the dignity and equality of all human beings.

Notes

1 Every dollar lost through unfair agricultural trade costs more than a dollar to the communities affected because lost purchasing power means less income for investment and employment. The spill-over effects are great. Research in Africa suggests that for every dollar increase in income, the rural economy generates another three dollars through local markets. This would suggest that the real costs for developing countries of rich country agricultural support may be as high as US$72 billion per year – an amount equivalent to all official aid in 2002 (UNDP Human Development Report, 2005).
2 The International Conference for Financing for Development in Monterrey, Mexico which intended to make a global partnership for poverty reduction.
3 The Millennium Commission Project conducted detailed fieldwork in five countries to calculate the cost of the annual public investments required to meet the MDGs. For Ghana, the required annual public investments for reaching the goals add up to US$80 per capita in 2006, scaling up to US$124 per capita in 2015. Needs assessments for other developing countries show similar levels of required investment. This figure does not include the cost of technical cooperation for capacity building and other purposes including emergency assistance or other development assistance that does not directly finance the capital or operating costs of MDG interventions. When the added costs at the national and international level – in capacity building expenditures of bi-lateral and multi-lateral agencies, outlays for science and technology, enhanced debt relief and other areas are added, the full costs of meeting the MDGs in all countries are US$121 per capita in 2006, rising to US$189 per capita in 2015.
4 Quoted in Delong B. and Eichengreen B. (1991) 'The Marshall Plan: History's most successful structural adjustment programme' Centre for Economic Performance, the Anglo-German Foundation and Landeszetralbank, Hamburg.
5 Peter Adamson quoted in Stephen Lewis (2005).

Bibliography

Commission for Africa (2005) 'Our Common Interest: Report of the Commission for Africa', London (http://commissionforafrica.org/english/report/thereport/finalreport.pdf) accessed May 2005.

Delong B. and Eichengreen B. (1991) 'The Marshall Plan: History's most successful structural adjustment programme', Centre for Economic Performance, the Anglo-German Foundation and Landeszetralbank, Hamburg.

Department for International Development (2005) 'Partnerships for Poverty Reduction: Rethinking Conditionality', DFID, London.

Frankenberger T., Luther K., Fox K. and Mazzeo J. (2003) 'Livelihood Erosion Through Time: Macro and Micro Factors that Influenced Livelihood Trends in Malawi Over the Last 30 Years', Care Southern and Western Africa Regional Management Unit (SWARMU).

Lewis S. (2005) 'Race against Time', Anansi Canada.

Mkandawire T. (2005) 'Malawi after Gleneagles: A Commission for Africa Case Study: Text of the Keynote Address at the Scotland Malawi Forum', Scottish Parliament, November 2005.

National Economic Council (1998) 'Vision 2020, National Long Term Perspective Study', Lilongwe, Malawi.

United Nations Millennium Project (2005) 'Investing in Development: A Practical Plan to Meet the Millennium Development Goals', Report to the UN Secretary General, London: Earthscan.

United Nations (2005) 'Human Development Report 2005: International co-operation at the crossroads: Aid, trade and security in an unequal world', United Nations, New York.

Whitworth A. (2005) 'Malawi's recent fiscal performance and prospects', Unpublished paper, Department for International Development, Lilongwe, Malawi.

Zamba C. (2005) 'Debt', Unpublished paper presented to the Scotland-Malawi Forum Meeting, The Scottish Parliament, Holyrood, Edinburgh.

Afterword

Tom Arnold, CEO, Concern Worldwide

Karen Blixen started her wonderful book 'Out of Africa' with the simple sentence 'I had a farm in Africa, at the foot of the Ngong Hills'. I didn't have a farm, but I lived in Africa, in Malawi, in 1979 and for part of 1980. I left with a deep affection for the country and for its people. For me, the expression 'Malawi – the Warm Heart of Africa' is a true statement and not just a slogan for use in a tourism marketing campaign.

I returned 22 years later, in May 2002. I had started as CEO of Concern Worldwide in late 2001. Concern had been examining the option of starting work in Malawi to do long-term development work to address the needs of a very poor country. But in the early months of 2002, it became clear that Malawi was facing a major food emergency. With the encouragement of the government, Concern started operations immediately, distributing food and cash to mission stations and community groups who could get help to people who had no food or money.

Malawi's 2002 Hunger Crisis

With the reduced harvest in 2002, it was clear that the country would face serious food shortages for the coming year. This meant that additional food would have to be imported – a combination of food aid and commercial imports – and that a big effort had to be put into increasing winter cropping in Malawi for harvest in late 2002. On my visit in May, I saw that work was underway to get the necessary seeds and inputs to farmers and community groups who had access to low-lying land suitable for winter cropping.

I returned to Malawi in September 2002. The winter cropping had been successful. Short-term rains meant that the maize planted a few months earlier looked very good. When harvested in a few weeks time, it would certainly ease some of the food shortages. But one afternoon as we examined this sign of hope, we came across three funerals – one in a small town, two more in the countryside. I was told that the number of people sick and dying from AIDS was impacting on the society and the economy in many ways – and one major impact was on the capacity of the farming sector to produce enough food for the country's needs.

The Book's Cast of Characters

I had met Anne Conroy on my visit in May. She was working for Vice President Justin Malewezi. Her commitment to Malawi was obvious. She was clear about what needed to be done to improve the lives of ordinary Malawians. She had an ability to connect big policy issues, whether for the government or donors, to realities on the ground. And she seemed to operate as an efficient spider at the centre of an intricate web, which was being woven for the sole purpose of helping Malawi escape from its deep poverty trap.

Anne was particularly passionate about what HIV/AIDS was doing to her adopted country. She had played a key role in preparing Malawi's submission to the Global Fund. The submission had been regarded as being of a very high standard but she was angry that decisions had not been taken quickly enough and resources deployed to start tackling the problems so eloquently described in the submission.

She wanted, she told me, to write a book about what HIV/AIDS was doing to Malawi and asked me whether Concern would help finance it. She told me the cast of characters she had co-opted to her enterprise. The combination of the purpose, and the cast, made for an easy decision.

I had got to know Jeff Sachs in his capacity as Chairman of the Millennium Project, which UN Secretary General Kofi Annan had established to chart the policy road map through which the Millennium Development Goals could be achieved. The Project consisted of ten Task Forces looking at what needed to be done to achieve particular goals. I had been delighted to be asked to serve on the Task Force for Hunger. I had seen the passion and expertise Jeff had brought to his role. It went beyond being a chairman; he was a driver, an inspirer, an encouraging cajoler, an impatient taskmaster. I was reminded of the famous line from the great Irish poet Yeats: 'The best lack all conviction while the worst are full of passionate intensity'. Except that, in Jeff's case, he had both the conviction and the passionate intensity.

Jeff and Bono were friends. Everybody knew Bono. Along with fellow Irishman, Bob Geldof, he was the most prominent global campaigner for action against poverty. Many people did not know where this commitment could be traced back to. He had certainly been influenced by the six weeks he spent in Ethiopia, along with his wife Ali, during the famine in the 1980s. It was there he first came across Concern's work and had become friends with one of the legendary Concern characters, Fr Jack Finucane. He has been a supporter of our organisation ever since. Along with Jeff, he had visited Malawi in 2001. He witnessed the devastating effects of AIDS and it had left a deep impression on him.

Anne had introduced me to Justin Malewezi. He had a reputation of being a talented and honest political leader, with a special commitment to dealing with the AIDS crisis facing his country. Alan Whiteside had co-authored, with Tony Barnett, a great book – Aids in the 21st Century – which I had read. The first time I heard him speak, he had reduced many of his audience to tears with a story of a grandmother who carried a dying child on her back so that the child would have some human comfort as she slipped from her short life.

I did not know Malcolm Blackie, but, from what Anne told me about him, I knew the book would benefit enormously from his contribution. I knew of Stephen Lewis of the UN – he has a reputation of being a passionate advocate for serious action to deal with the AIDS pandemic.

My Hope for this Book

The book which has emerged as a result of the co-operation from these talented and committed people is significant. As far as I am aware, it is the first attempt to document the impact HIV/AIDS has on an entire country. The facts and the analyses presented are grounded in a deep understanding of the realities of life in Malawi. It documents the nature of the poverty trap which Malawi is trapped in. But it also points to what needs to be done, by Malawians and by outside agencies, if the country is to escape from this poverty trap.

Concern is deeply committed to working in Malawi for the foreseeable future. I am proud of what we have achieved since starting our programme there in 2002. We have partnered effectively with Malawian government ministries and with civil society groups. We have pioneered a new approach to dealing with malnutrition, called Community Therapeutic Care (CTC), which the Ministry of Health will introduce into the public health system. We are researching how better nutrition can improve the life prospects of people infected by HIV and AIDS.

Our support for this book is part of our commitment to Malawi's future. I want this book to be more than a work of scholarship. I would like its publication, and the discussion of the issues which this will give rise to, to be a catalyst for action. There are many players who must act, ideally, in a coordinated way.

The Malawian government is obviously a key actor. It has made progress in improving governance and in bringing order to the public finances – but more needs to be done. The leaders of faith communities have a critical leadership role to play if some of the deep-rooted cultural practices which help spread HIV infection are to be tackled. Improving access of girls to education and increasing the status of women is crucial. External donors must provide sustained and appropriate aid programmes.

If these things happen, there is hope. Ultimately, this book is about helping to devise a practical agenda to turn hope into positive action – and build a better future for Malawi and its people.

Index

acute respiratory infections, 34
adjustment, structural, 30, 94–5, 98,
    113, 122, 135, 178, 214, 220n4,
    232n4
    policies in 1980s, 18–20
ADMARC (Agricultural Development
    and Marketing Corporation), 18,
    95–6, 102n5, 122–3
    cash flow problems of, 97
    policy elements, 96
adolescence period, HIV prevalence,
    during, 58–60
adult deaths, impact, 145
agriculture
    Agricultural Development and
        Marketing Corporation,
        see ADMARC
    Agricultural Productivity
        Investment Programme, 98
    Agricultural Sector Adjustment
        Credit (ASAC), 18
    agricultural sector, investments
        needed for, 192
    AIDS impact on, 71
    collapse of, see under collapse of
        agriculture
    constraints in, 4–5
    contribution to foreign exchange
        earnings, 24
    crop substitution, 18
    decline in, 23
    development strategy between
        independence and the late
        1970s, 17
    dualistic nature, 24
    in the early twenty-first century, 88
    post-independence strategy, 17
    productivity issues, 90
    reorientation policy in 1980s, 18
    soil fertility, lack of, 1
agro-forestry, 161–2, 164
AIDS and disease crisis, breaking out
    of, 138–58

care of orphans, 144–5
health sector response, 150–4
health sector, 146–54
impact mitigation, 144–5
Information, Education and
    Communication (IEC), 139–41
mother to child transmission, 151
prevention strategies, 141–3
reducing the spread of the virus,
    141–2
scaling up best-practices from the
    community level, 149–50
traditional measures, 138
treatment strategies, 152–4
voluntary counselling and testing
    (VCT), 139–40
AIDS pandemic, see also HIV/AIDS
    pandemic
age and sex distribution of, 53
AIDS Control Plan, 139
AIDS crisis, 49–68, see also
    HIV/AIDS pandemic
blood safety and waste disposal,
    150–1
and disease crisis, breaking out of,
    138–58, see also separate entry
gender inequality fueling, 29
health sector response, 150–4
impact on adult mortality, 64
impact on children and the elderly,
    75–7
impact on the National economy
    and development, 70–83, see
    also individual entry
impacts, 144
key drivers of, 49
life expectancy with and without,
    65
on programme implementation,
    212
post-screening counselling for, 151
Alliance for Democracy (Aford), 131
anemia, 34

Angola, 31n8
animal manures, 161
antenatal clinic data, 42, 50, 128,
    150–1
Anti Retroviral Therapy (ARV)
    therapy, 148–9, 152, 154, 158n9
April Youth Week, 105
area-based subsidy, 176
arrogance, 216
    as an obstacle to development, 216

Balaka, 136n14
Banda Aleke, 131, 163, 167, 215
Banda Hastings Kamuzu, 14, 16–18,
    20–1, 30, 93–4, 96, 98, 105,
    118–19, 131, 139, 157n1, 169,
    207, 210
Barnett T., 61
Beira, 110
Benn, Hilary, 9
'Best Bet' technology, 135n1, 164–7
bicycles, 106
Blackie M.J., 6–7, 12n1, 87, 90,
    182n6, 190, 199
Blantyre, 62, 67n4, 74, 117n6,
    136n14
Botswana, 76
Bretton Woods Institutions, 226
British Government, in Malawi, 16
    British Department for
        International Development
        (DFID), 149
    British Overseas Military
        Administration, 116n1
Buddenhagen I., 88
burley tobacco production, 24,
    102n12
    in 1994, 96
    liberalisation of, 96
business, AIDS impact on, 73
Byerlee D., 90

Canadian International Development
    Agency (CIDA), 149
Canadian Public Health Association
    (CPHA), 157–8n6
Carr S., 162
cash crops, 24
cash-cropping, 193

cassava, 24, 183
    cassava yields 1994–2002, 124
    Mealy bug, 95, 163
Centre for International Health (CIH),
    74
Chagunda, 116n3
Chakwamba Gwanda, 131, 136n10
changing mindsets, 203–20
    actions not just words, need of the
        hour, 217–20
    core values, 215–17
    donor relationships, 210–13
    exploiting national talents and
        skills, 213
    human rights and human
        development, 206–8
    information sharing,
        communication and
        collaboration, 214–15
    issues to be addressed at the
        national level, 208–20
Chikwawa, 136n14
children's condition in Malawi
    Child Labour-Statistical
        Information Monitoring
        Programme on Child Labour
        (ILO/IPEC-SIMPOC), 83n7
    diseases of, 28
    early marriage, 29
    educational status, 11, 29
    malnutrition, 4, 39–41
    poverty, 29
    transactional sex in, 29
Chilembwe Uprising of 1915, 16
Chipoka, 106
Chiradzulu, 136n14
chitemene slash-and-burn system, 88
Chokolo, 55
Cholera, 34
Christian Health Association of
    Malawi, 38, 43, 146, 153
CISANET (the Civil Society
    Agriculture Network), 172
civic education programme,
    components of, 191
civil society engagement and
    participation, 209
civil society organizations (CSOs), AIDS
    undermining the capacity of, 75

cohesion, 67n2
Cold War effect on Malawi's
   development, 20
collaboration, 6, 47, 111, 170–5, 214–15
collapse of agriculture, 87–102
   fertiliser subsidies, 98–100
   from the perspective of the
      household, 92
   land, agricultural productivity and
      land policy, 92–4
   macro-economic policy reform,
      94–100
   Malawi case study of disaster,
      94–100
   market and crop pricing reform,
      96–8
   tradition and African smallholder
      cropping stems, 87–92
colonial economy, 16
   labour reserve economy, 16
   peasant cash cropping, 16
   plantations, 16
commercial legal system, 111
Commission for Africa report, 4, 9–10,
   196, 201nn3, 9, 225–6, 230, 232
communication, 25, 138, 140–1, 154,
   172, 214–15
Community Day Secondary Schools
   (CDSSs), 116–17n5, 188
community home-based care, 144,
   157n3
community participation, lack of, 39
compost, 91–2, 166
condom use, 58, 60–1, 141
   condom social-marketing, 141
   factors militating against, 61
   women inability to insist on, 61
Conroy A., 7, 11–12, 12n1, 204
Conventional Secondary Schools
   (CSSs), 188
coping mechanisms, 171
corruption, 205
   by political leaders, 206
cotton, 24
cowpeas, 162
credit system, 98
   collapse of, 99
crop production increase using
   fertilizers, 160–2

debts, 228–30
   debt cancellation, 25, 229
   debt service, 211, 229
   domestic debt, 25–7, 116, 118–19,
      130, 196, 211, 230
   external debt, 23, 25, 27, 30, 114,
      135, 196, 211, 229
   HIPC process, 25, 228–9
dedication, 143, 156, 173–4, 206,
   215–16, 218–19
Dedza, 136n14, 157–8n6
deforestation, 92, 109, 192
Democratic Progressive Party (DPP),
   131, 218
Demographic and Health Surveys
   (DHSs), 50, 57
   1992 and 2000, 40
demographic indicators, 71
   life expectancy, 22–3, 31n7, 34, 49,
      65–7, 70–1, 204, 231
Department of International
   Development (DFID), 133–4
development programmes, 210
DeVries J., 89
diarrhoea, 1–2, 28, 34
Directly Observed Therapy Supervised
   (DOTS) programmes, 37, 153
disease, *see also under individual disease
   names*
   affecting crop husbandry, 2
   anguish of, 33
   outcome of, 1, 33
District and Village Relief
   Committees, 127
domestic debt, 25
   constraining private sector
      development, 196
   increase in, 130
domestic road transport, 106–7
donor community, in promoting
   change, 210–13
drought, 95
   drought-related food crises in the
      late 1980s, 169
   drought-resistant grains, 24

economic isolation, 104–17, *see also*
   transportation
   critical investments needed for, 187

energy sector, 109–10, *see also separate entry*
  infrastructure failure leading to, 104–6
  and the poverty trap, breaking out of, 185–201
  of villagers' lives, 105
economy
  AIDS pandemic impact on, 70–83, *see also separate entry*
  in the early 1960s, 94
  economic infrastructure, investments in, 193–5
  economic isolation, 104–17, *see also separate entry*
  by the end of the 1980s, 18
  foreign exchange earnings, 24, 107
  gross domestic product (GDP), 17–18, 22, 25–7, 71–3, 82n4, 107, 113–14, 130, 196, 211, 225, 227, 230–1
  inflation, 21, 26, 82n3, 99–100, 111–14, 120, 125, 164, 226
  interest rates, 21, 26, 82n3, 99, 111, 113, 122, 125
  Savings rate, 226
economy, AIDS pandemic impact on, 70–83
  1993–2003 GDP, 72
  and private sector, 73–4
  costs of, 1995–1996, 74
  illness during the peak agricultural season affecting, 79–80
  labour affected by, 80
  long-run economic costs of, 73
  macro-economy, 72–5
  Malawi and African economies, 71
  Malawi case study, 70–2
  public sector and the development process, 74–5
  social and demographic indicators, 71
'edge of survival', farmers in, 89
education in Malawi, 187–91
  civic education, 190–1
  investment needs in, 187
  investments, 189–90
  primary education, 187–8
  secondary education, 188

teaching and learning materials, 188
  tertiary education, 189
  untrained teachers, 188
  vocational education, 110, 117n5, 187, 189
ego, as an obstacle to development, 216
2004 election, 130
electricity
  Electricity Supply Corporation of Malawi (ESCOM), 110
  hydro-electric power stations, 110
  infrastructure, 104
  supply status, 110
energy sector, 109–10, 195, *see also individual entries*
  charcoal, 109
  coal, national demand for, 110
  electricity supply status, 110
  firewood, 109
  fuel wood demand, 109
environmental degradation, 192
environmental sustainability, investment needs in, 187, 192–3
Episcopal Conference of Malawi, 20
Essential Health Care Package (EHP), 44, 138, 146–8, 152
  design and implementation, 47n6
  services delivered, 147
European Union, to rescue food crisis, 133
Expanded Targeted Inputs Programme, 132
export tax, 18, 31, 109
external debt, 229
  constraining private sector development, 196

Faidherbia albida leguminous tree, 162
Faith Community, 143
Fallows, 79–80, 87–8, 162–3, 183
famine
  2002 famine budget disruption, 125–6
  Famine Early Warning System Network/World Food Programme (FEWSNET/WFP), 134

famine – *continued*
in 1998, 99
lessons from, 125–30
Farm Input Promotions Africa
(FIPS-Africa), 177, 182n15
Farmer Field Schools (FFS), 178
feeding
supplementary, 127, 171, 173, 177
therapeutic, 127, 173
fertility/fertilisers
fertiliser market, 132
fertiliser market, government
interventions in, 197–8
fertility rates, 35
interaction with rainfall, 87–8, 161
interaction with weeding, 90–1,
165, 167, 175
organic sources of, 92
prices increase, between May and
October 2004, 132
recommendations, 92, 160–1, 166,
175
subsidies, 19, 95, 98–100, 131–5,
178, 198
for work programme, 166–7, 194
fisheries sector, 24
Fisi, 55
Flint (or hard endosperm) maize,
182n4
Food and Agricultural
Organisation/World Food
Programme (FAO/WFP), 133
food crises, 41
constraining private sector
development, 196
emergency food to the vulnerable,
171–3
Food Crisis Task Force, 126, 133
importance of collaboration in, 215
in 1987, 18
in 1992, 20
National Food Crisis Recovery
Programme, 170–1
of 2001–2002 and 2002–2003,
169–73, *see also* 2002 food
crises
2002 food crisis
anaemia increase, 129
as humanitarian emergency, 128

coping strategies, 128
from food insecurity to famine,
119–25
gender-based violence during, 129
haemorrhage increase, 129
health sector position during, 130
impact on young men, 129
impact on young women, 129
international press and high-profile
visitors, attention to, 127
malnutrition increase, 129
sexually transmitted infections
increase, 129
teenage pregnancies increase, 129
UN survey on, 128
food insecurity
breaking out of, 160–83
causes of, 95
explicit consideration of scale,
179–80
humanitarian response, 173–4
lessons for the future, 173–8
making fertilisers profitable, 160–2
policy linkages, 179
safety nets or development, 180–1
success of, factors contributing, 174
food security
external influences damaging, 163
a key theme in 2004 election
campaign, 131
situation in 1998, 99
food staple, 7, 18, 87, 95, 124, 163,
170, 176, 180
Foreign Direct Investment (FDI), 23,
225
formal training courses, 186
'Free inputs', 98, 120, 168
freight charges, 107–8
international freight routes, 108
fuel imports, 110

G8 Summit, 203, 204, 207, 228
ganyu labour (off-farm casual work),
79–80
reduced opportunities for, 97
gender inequality
and AIDS pandemic in Malawi, 56
of HIV/AIDS, 53–4
gender-based violence, 29

geography, 14
    geographical isolation, 115
Ghana, 232n3
Gillespie S., 40
Gini index, 23, 31n8, 67n3
Gleneagles Summit, 196, 206, 227
Global Fund Programme, 155
gonorrhoea, 142
governance
    2003–2004 government budget,
        26–7
    civic education, 190, 202
    constitution, 17, 21, 30, 118, 146,
        191
    corruption, 205
    government faith community
        consultation on HIV/AIDS, 143
    government/private sector relations,
        197–8
    rule of law, 191, 208
    third term debate, 131, 218
Grain legumes, 162
    management, 121
Green Evolution approach, 5–6
green manures, 161
Green Revolution, 5, 174–8
    interventions to provide access to
        inputs and markets, 174–5
    policy linkages, 179
    programme implementation,
        principles, 175–8
groundnuts, 24, 162
GTZ (the German Aid Agency), 106

Haddad L., 40, 144
Harrigan J., 178
health issues
    and disease, 33–47
    financing limitations, 44–5
    health indicators, 34–5
    Health Plan (1999–2004), 146
    human resources limitations, 43–4
    key challenges to, 43–5
    Life expectancy, 34
    mortality and morbidity in major
        causes of, 34
    and poverty, 33–4, 155
health policy
    basic health care, 45

Essential Health Care Package,
    44–6, 47n6, 138, 146, 148, 152
Sector Wide Approach, 45, 137,
    146–7, 194
health systems
    for AIDS and disease crisis, 146–54
    essential laboratory services, 147
    human resources, 43
    referral systems, 144
    position during food crisis, 130
herbicides, 178
high risk sexual behaviour, 60–1
Highly Indebted Poor Country
    (HIPC), 228
HIV transmission, drivers of
    adolescents, 40, 49, 57–60, 66
    high-risk sexual behaviour, 49, 60,
        128, 156, 203, 229
    impact mitigation, 144
    married women, 35, 55, 61
    orphans, 55, 63, 66, 70, 76, 80–2,
        145
    palliative care, 144
    sexual abuse, 57, 59–60, 63, 141
    sexual violence, 55
    susceptibility, 2, 42, 45, 55, 76
    unequal power relations, 55, 60
    vulnerable groups for HIV
        transmission, 6, 18, 24, 29, 39,
        53–60, 63, 66, 75–7, 80, 89, 97,
        126–7, 135, 143, 145, 153, 168,
        170–3, 194, 205, 226
    young women, 55, 57, 59–60, 62,
        66, 129
HIV transmission, *see also* condom
    use
    awareness creation, challenges, 156
    homosexual transmission, 54
    infected blood, 54
    mother to child transmission, 151
    prevention strategies, 141–3
    sexual transmission, 34, 42, 46, 69
    traditional healers in, 143
    vulnerability of young people, 57–8
HIV/AIDS pandemic
    adolescence, HIV transmission risk
        in, 58
    among sex workers, 61
    Blantyre, 51

HIV/AIDS pandemic – *continued*
  children orphaned by, 63
  cultural and socioeconomic
      context, 55, 59
  demographic consequences of, 63
  drivers of the pandemic, 54–63
  first survey, in 1987, 50
  gender inequality causing, 54–7
  gender inequality causing, 55–6
  HIV-infected population of, 52
  HIV-positive employees, 74
  HIV-positive women, 50
  impact on agricultural production
      systems and rural livelihoods,
      79–81
  impact on agriculture and
      livelihoods, 77–81
  impact on private sector
      development, 25
  impact on the health sector, 43
  in 1985, 50
  in children, 57
  in primary schools, 57
  infected blood, 54
  influential groups in the fight
      against, 142–3
  Kamboni, 51
  Kasina, 51
  Lilongwe, 51
  Malawi's responses, 139–45
  Mbalachanda, 52
  Mchingi, 51
  microbicides, 156, 161
  Nkhotakota, 51
  Nsanje, 51
  Ntcheu, 51
  nutritional stress, 78
  observed and projected, 52
  peri-natal transmission, 54
  poverty causing, 55
  prevalence and migration, 62
  safe blood, 150
  sentinel surveillance data, 50–1
  sexual abuse causing, 55, 59–60
  social and behavioural factors
      causing, 54
  Thonje, 51
  transmission modes of, 54
  treatment, 153
  unsafe medical practices, 54

  vaccine development, 156
  voluntary counselling and testing,
      139–40
  vulnerable groups for HIV
      transmission, 53
  women's vulnerability to, 55–6
hope, 8, 11, 12, 57, 118, 143, 170,
    207, 216, 219, 226, 228, 235,
    236–7
household coping mechanisms,
    disruption to, 128–30
Human Development Index (HDI),
    31nn7–8
human resource
  constraints, 39, 43–4
  investment in, 148–9
human rights
  abuses, 20
  equality and dignity, 10
  and human development, 206–8
  human rights record, 20
humanitarian crisis, increased
    vulnerability to HIV/AIDS, 129
humanitarian relief programme, 174
hunger crisis, 10
  2002 Hunger Crisis, 234–5
  hungry season, 29, 95, 97, 120, 124,
      171
  outcomes, 11
hydro-electric power stations, 110

'ill-being' definition, 28
income inequality, 23
industrial and trade policy
    adjustment 1988
  macro-economic stabilization, 18
  structural reform, 18
informal cross-border maize trade,
    97
information technology, 110
  Information, Education and
      Communication (IEC), 139–41
  in the coverage of HIV/AIDS issues,
      141
infrastructure failure, and economic
    isolation, 104–17, *see also* energy
    sector; transportation
  cellular phone subscribers, 110
  Public Works Programmes, 117,
      202

regulatory and taxation
  environment, 110–12
telephone subscribers, 110
infrastructure, investment needs in,
  110, 187
Integrated Household Survey, 128
integrity and progress, 218
intercropping, 87, 92, 161, 163
internal transportation, 106–7
International Centre for Research in the
  Semi-Arid Tropics (ICRISAT), 193
International Commitments
  Earth Summit, 227
  Gleneagles Agreement, 157
  Millennium Development Goals, 4,
    8, 12–13, 23, 32–3, 40, 47–8,
    117, 189, 202–3, 206, 215, 218,
    221, 223, 225, 231, 233, 235
  Monterrey Agreement, 223, 227, 232
International community
  donor driven programmes, 95, 101,
    105, 107, 118, 121–7, 133–5,
    168–74, 178, 194, 196, 212–19
  external consultants, 212
  official development assistance, 11,
    206, 225
International health institutions
  Global Fund, 9, 43, 48, 152, 155, 235
  macro economic commission on
    health, 8, 45, 85
  World Health Organization (WHO),
    8–9, 22, 32–4, 37–8, 45
International Maize and Wheat
  Improvement Centre (CIMMYT),
  164
International Monetary Fund (IMF),
  94, 113
  in determining development
    policies, 211
  structural adjustment and
    stabilisation programmes, 18
Ireland, 134, 136n13
Italy, 136n13

James R., 75, 212
Joint Emergency Food Action
  Programme (JEFAP), 172
  objectives, 182n10
Joint Food Crisis Task Force, 171
Jones C., 74

Junior School Certificate of Education
  (JCE), 188

Kamboni, HIV prevalence in, 51
Kamowa O.W., 128
Kanengo, 121
Kaporo, 108
Karonga, 52
Kasina, HIV prevalence in, 51
Kasungu, 136n14
Kelly M.J., 77
Kenya, 197
Krugman P., 94

labour
  affected by HIV/AIDS, 80
  labour intensive agricultural
    exports, 93
  labour reserve economy, 16
  requirement for production
    improvement, 91
lands
  agricultural productivity and land
    policy, 92–4
  land alienation policy, 18
  land encroachment issues, 112
  land policy, 93
  land transfer, 31n5
legal and regulatory environment,
  weaknesses in, 111
legumes, 161–2, 182n1
Lenten Letter, 20
Lesotho, 76
Levy S., 125
Lewis S., 55, 204, 217, 223
liberalisation
  Burley tobacco, 21, 95–6
  market, 15, 96–9
life expectancy, with and without
  AIDS, 66
Lilongwe, 61–2, 67n4, 117n6
  HIV prevalence in, 51
Livingstone, David, 15
Luxembourg, 134

Machinga, 136n14
macro-economics
  indicators, 1994–2003, 26
  management and governance after
    2002, deterioration in, 130–1

macro-economics – *continued*
  management, under President
    Mutharika, 113
  politics and fertiliser subsidies,
    131–5
Magoye soyabean variety, 162
maize
  harvest, fall in, 123
  hybrid, 18
  imports in 2001 and 2002,
    macro-economic consequences,
    125
  imports, 130
  in the southern region, local market
    prices for, 123
  interlinked and complementary
    elements, 167
  maize market liberalisation, 96–7
  Maize Productivity Task Force
    (MPTF), 6, 164–8, 177
  maize seed and fertiliser
    technology, 99
  MH17, 166
  MH18, 166
  prices, 102n10
  production, 7, 95, 163
  production, fertiliser subsidies for,
    98
  starter pack/TIP contribution to,
    120
  weeding and fertiliser use in, 90
malaria disease, 1–2, 28, 34–6, 205,
    see also malaria programme
  annual cost of, 36
  due to rains, 35
  economic cost rise due to, 35
  impact of, 35
  poverty due to, 35
malaria programme
  bed nets, 36
  insecticide-treated nets, 36
  re-treatment campaign, 36
  treatment during pregnancy, 36
Malawi
  burden of ill-health, 28
  colonial economy in, 16, *see also*
    separate entry
  crisis and structural adjustment
    policies in the 1980s, 18–20

debt burden, *see under* debts
development and crisis in, history,
    14–31
diseases prevalent in, *see individual*
    entry
economic performance, 1994 to
    2004, 21–2
ending extreme poverty in, 222–32,
    see also under poverty
    eradication
evolutionary strategy, 6
food crises in, 3, *see also separate*
    entry
gender inequality and domestic
    violence, 29
geographical summary, 14–15
health and disease in, 33–47,
    see also separate entry
health care in, 43–5, *see also*
    separate entry
health services in, 36
historical perspective, 15–20
HIV/AIDS pandemic in, *see separate*
    entry
income figures, 41
at independence, 17–18
industries, 24
international financial institutions
    aid to, 24–5
land policy in, 93
life expectancy, 1, 22
Malawi Congress Party (MCP), 21,
    119
Malawi kwacha, devaluation of, 95
Malawi Kwacha, exchange rate, 114
Malawi today, key challenges in,
    22–6
Malawian diet, 41
manufacturing sector, decline in, 24
multi-party elections, 20
natural resources and people, 1
one-party rule in, 14, *see also*
    separate entry
per capita income, 22, 28, 31n11
position, on the human
    development index, 22
poverty in, *see separate entry*
private sector development,
    constraints to, 25

rural economy, 23
slave trade in, 15
socio-economic situation in 1912,
16
soil fertility, agricultural policy and
famine, 162–9
with and without AIDS, population
projections for, 64
World Bank investment portfolio
in, 18–20
Malawi National AIDS Commission,
50
Malawi Vulnerability Assessment
Committee (MVAC), 133
Malewezi Justin, 7–8, 131, 171, 235
malnutrition/malnourishment, 2, 28,
39–41, 185
in children, 39–41
effects of, 40
and infection, 40
parasitic susceptibility due to, 42
Mangochi, 136n14
manures, 92, 101n3, 161, 166
market
and crop pricing reform, 96–8
market liberalization, lack of, 97
MASAF (the Malawi Social Action
Fund), 106
Maternal and Child Health (MCH)
Clinics, 173
maternal mortality, 37–9
direct causes of, 38
maternal mortality rate (MMR), 37
Mauritius, 112
Mchinji, 108, 157–8n6
HIV prevalence in, 51
media coverage/awareness, of AIDS,
140–1
microbiocides, 156
Migana, 116n3
Millennium Commission (2005), 28,
224
Millennium Commission Project,
232n3
Millennium Development Goals
(MDGs), 23, 206
health targets, 33
malnutrition undermining, 40
realisation, requirements, 218

Ministry of Health (MoH), 38, 128
and Population, 36, 44, 48–9,
135n7, 137, 140, 146–7, 151,
153, 158
Miombo, 88
Mkandawire T., 228, 230
Mkando, 116n3
mobility, 62–3
morbidity, causes of, 35–43
Morris James, 217
mortality
child mortality, 45
emergency obstetric care, 48
increasing mortality rates, 65
infant and under-five mortality, 65
infant mortality rate, 22, 34
maternal mortality, 22, 37–9, 45,
231
and morbidity, major causes, 34
under-five mortality, causes, 39
unsafe abortions, 60
Mother and Child Centres, 127
Movement for Genuine Democratic
Change (Mgode), 131
Mozambique, 21, 63, 76, 163, 195
Mpingangira, Brown, 131, 136n10
Mulanje, 136n14
multi-party democracy, 26–9
emergence in Malawi, 20–2
response to HIV/AIDS, 139
Muluzi, Bakili, 21, 118, 125, 130–1,
139, 167, 229
Mutharika, Bingu, 113, 119, 131
Mzimba, 136n14

Nacala port, 107–10, 115, 195
National Action Group, 111–12
National AIDS Commission, 43, 49,
63, 67n1, 144
5-year plan, 139
National Association of Smallholder
Farmers in Malawi (NASFAM),
102n9
National Committee for HIV/AIDS,
139
National Democratic Alliance
(NDA)131
National Food Crisis Recovery
Programme, 170–1

National Food Reserve Agency (NFRA), 102n8, 122, 135n3
National HIV/AIDS Policy, 153
natural resource endowment, 192
Nchalo sugar plantation, 63
Neno, 136n14
new generation, efforts of, 186
New Partnership for African Development (NEPAD), 104, 190
new technologies to address poverty agenda, 89, 92
Ngalande, Elias, 167
Ngolome, 116n3
NGOs, AIDS undermining the capacity of, 75
nitrogen fixation, 161, 182n1
Nkata Bay, 106, 157–8n6
Nkhotakota, 136n14
  HIV prevalence in, 51
non implementation syndrome, 207
Non-Governmental Organisation (NGOs), 125
Norwegian Government, to rescue food crisis, 133
Ntcheu, 136n14
  HIV prevalence in, 51
Nutritional Rehabilitation Units, 127
Nyasaland African Congress (NAC), 16–17
Nyasaland, 16
Nyerere, Julius, 229

obstetric care, 46
one-party rule, 17, 20, 190
  transporting during, 105
Organisation for Economic Cooperation and Development (OECD), 222
orphans, 145
  due to AIDS, 76

paprika, 24
parasitic infections, 42
Parastatals, 21, 97, 102n5, 201n6
Parliament, 119, 127, 131, 133, 172, 174, 202, 206, 210–11, 214, 233
peasant cash cropping, 16
People Living with HIV/AIDS (PLWHAs), 140

People's Progressive Movement (PPM), 131
Phalombe, 136n14
Phiri A., 173
pigeonpea, 162
plantations, 16
pneumonia, 28
Political Parties (Malawi), 20
  Alliance for Democracy, 21, 131
  Democratic Progressive Party, 119, 131, 218
  Malawi Congress Party, 21, 119, 131, 136n10
  National Democratic Alliance, 131, 136n10
  United Democratic Front, 21, 118, 131, 136n10
politicians focus, need for, 218
population growth, 30n2
post-drought credit expansion, 98
poverty
  2002 food crisis, 119–25
  by the end of the 1980s, 18
  'insider' perspective on, 118–36
  limiting growth, 122–4, 126–7, 144
  poverty trap, breaking out of, possibilities, 4
  and powerlessness, relationship between, 10
  raising the alarm, 124–5
poverty eradication, 216, 222–32
  debts, 228–30
  Green Evolution approach, 5
  Green Revolution, 5
  linked to HIV infection, 56
  National ownership and leadership fundamental to, 231
  need of the hour, 223–6
  new strategies and interventions, 5
  outcomes, 11
  perspective on, 226–8
  Poverty Reduction and Growth Facility (PRGF), 113
  Poverty Reduction Strategy, 47n6, 146
  reduction and growth strategy, 187
  sexual abuse increased due to, 60
Prevention of Mother to Child Transmission (PMTCT), 151
price control, 19

private sector development
  addressing constraints, 187, 195–8
  and AIDS, 73–4
  constraints to, 25
production environment, in the early
  twenty-first century, 88
prostitution, 129
Public Affairs Committee (PAC), 131,
  136n11, 191, 201n2
public sector jobs, AIDS Impacts on,
  74–5
public works programmes, 194

Quick Wins, 224

radio, in civic education programmes,
  191
rail transport, 106–7
regulatory and taxation environment,
  110–12
relay cropping, 161
Republican Party (RP), 131
Richards P., 78
road transport, 106, 115
  condition, 115
  infrastructure, 104
  maintenance, investment in, 194
Rockefeller Foundation, 7, 120,
  163–4, 182n6, 184, 190
rotation crops, 163
Rumphi, 52
rural areas
  poverty in, 29
  rural-urban migration, 28–9
  transportation in, 105

Sachs J., 4, 7–9, 35, 107–8, 200
Safety nets, 180
'safety nets' programme, 121
Saka, A., 162
Sakhome, 116n3
Salima, 106, 136n14
Santhe, 116n3
Savings Club movement, 167
Schistosomaisis, 42
school age children, HIV in, 57–8
school enrolment reduction, due to
  AIDS, 76
Schultzian hypothesis, 5

Sector Wide Approach (SWAP), 45,
  47n7, 138, 146–8
senior management time, 212
sexual abuse, as HIV high-risk sexual
  behaviour, 60
sexually transmitted infections (STIs),
  34, 42, 54, 142
  and HIV/AIDS, 42–3
  management and treatment, 42
  management, syndromic approach
  to, 46n4
  symptoms of, 44n4
Shah M.K., 57
shipping costs, 108
Shire Valley, 95
Sierra Leone, 22
Six-Year Emergency Training
  Programme, 148
slash-and-burn system, 88
smallholders, 93, 101n2, 119, 164–8
  complementary measures, 167–8
  difficulties faced by, 91
  return to free inputs, 168–9
  smallholder agricultural credit
  system, 21, 98
  smallholder cropping systems,
  improved fertiliser efficiency in,
  161
  Smallholder Farmer Fertiliser
  Revolving Fund of Malawi
  (SFFRFM), 198, 201n6
  smallholder subsector (farming
  customary land), 17–18
  smallholder tobacco producers,
  96
  Starter Pack, 164–7
  transportation problems of, 108
soils
  fertility decline, 29
  fertility, 35, 182n6, 183–4
  moisture, 1–2
  nutrient mining, 90
  organic matter, 102
Solow growth model, 82n4
Southern African Development
  Community (SADC), 23
Soyabean
  Magoye, 162
  Promiscuous, 162

Special Crops Act of 1964, 102n6
Strategic Grain Reserve (SGR), 121–2,
    136n12, 170
Striga spp., 91, 101n1
strip cropping, 161
structural adjustment programme, 95,
    98, 178, 220n4
    in late 1979, 94
structural impediments, 82n3
sugar, 107
Swaziland, 76
Sweden, 134
sweet potatoes, 24
    yields 1994–2002, 124
syphilis, 142

targeted inputs programme (TIP),
    135n1, 168, 180
taxation system, burden of, 111
tea, 31n4, 107
telephone subscribers, 110
Tembo, John, 136n10
tenants, 16, 96
Tenga Tenga, James, 1, 220
Tera, international group, 105
thangata tenancy, 16
Therapeutic Feeding Centres (TFCs),
    127, 173
Thonje, HIV prevalence in, 51
Three by Five' Programme, 152–3
Tiimbenawo, 116n3
tobacco, 24, 31n4, 96, 101n4, 107,
    117n6
Toennissen, G., 89
traction, animal, 87
trade
    containers shortage affecting, 201n4
    factors that affect, 201n4
    transforming trading rules, 198–200
tradition and African smallholder
    cropping stems, 87–92
traditional authorities
    in AIDS prevention, 142
    in development activities, 191
Traditional Birth Attendants (TBAs),
    149
transportation infrastructure, 106–9,
    see also individual entries
    affecting production, 199

external transport costs, 24, 115,
    195
external transportation, 107–9
internal and external costs, 115
internal transportation, 106–7
railways, 107–8, 115
road maintenance, 107, 115, 117,
    194, 202
roads, 105, 115, 194
Tree Planting Week, 192
Tuberculosis, 34, 36–7
    DOTS Programme, 37
    drugs and reagents for, 37
    impact of, 36
    National TB Programme (NTP),
        36
    Tuberculosis Control Programme,
        152, 158n8

Uganda, 197
UN, for emergency agricultural
    assistance, 134
UN Millennium Commission, 3–4
    poverty report, 3
UN Millennium Project Task Force, 4
United Democratic Front (UDF)
    government, 21, 131
    Burley tobacco production, 21
    economic growth rates, 21
    free primary education, 21
United Nations Fund for Population
    Activities (UNPFA), 149
United Nations General Assembly on
    HIV/AIDS, 152
United Nations Humanitarian
    Response Team (UNHRT), 128–9
United Nations Office for the
    Coordination of Humanitarian
    Affairs, 134
United Nations Task Force on
    Women, Girls and HIV/AIDS, 56
United States Agency for
    International Development
    (USAID), 134
Universal Charter of Human Rights,
    206
Universal Declaration of Human
    Rights, 220n3
universal fertiliser subsidy, 132

Universal Starter Pack Programme, 98–9, 120–2, 132, 135n1, 165, 168–9, 179–80
objectives, 166
urban areas
over-population in, 29
unemployment in, 29

vertical programmes, 47n7
villages' access to transport in rural Malawi, 105
voluntary counselling and testing (VCT), 139–40
Vulnerability Assessment Committee, 127, 134

water transport systems, 106
WFP (World Food Programme), 106
Whiteside A., 7, 61
women
agricultural labour in Africa, 78
difficulties faced by, 91
HIV among young women, 55
HIV-positive women, 50
school girls, HIV in, 57
tertiary education, 189
violence against, 29

World Bank, 18, 94, 123, 197
in determining development policies, 211
Industrial and Trade Policy approved by, 18
specific sector-based loans from, 18
World Food Programme (WFP), 134, 172–3
World Health Organisation (WHO), 9
Commission on Macro-Economics and Health, 33
on health workforce deterioration, 38
world markets, 187

yields, crops
cassava and sweet potatoes, 123–4
Maize, 90
Rice, 5
Wheat, 5, 164
youth clubs, outcomes, 150

Zambia, 76
zero grazing techniques, 101n2
Zimbabwe, 76, 93, 126
Zomba, 136n14

Printed in the United States
89591LV00001B/105/A